CRITICAL
INSIGHTS

Crime and Detective Fiction

CRITICAL INSIGHTS

Crime and Detective Fiction

Editor
Rebecca Martin
Pace University

SALEM PRESS
A Division of EBSCO Publishing
Ipswich, Massachusetts

GREY HOUSE PUBLISHING

Cover Photo: © Ed Bock/Corbis

Editor's text © 2013 by Rebecca Martin

Copyright © 2013, by Salem Press, A Division of EBSCO Publishing, Inc.

Critical Insights: Crime and Detective Fiction, 2013, published by Grey House Publishing, Inc., Amenia, NY, under exclusive license from EBSCO Publishing, Inc.

∞ The paper used in these volumes conforms to the American National Standard for Permanence of Paper for Printed Library Materials, Z39.48-1992 (R1997).

Library of Congress Cataloging-in-Publication Data

Crime and detective fiction / editor, Rebecca Martin, Pace University.
    pages cm. -- (Critical insights)
    Includes bibliographical references and index.
    ISBN 978-1-4298-3822-1 (hardcover)
    1. Detective and mystery stories--History and criticism. 2. Crime in literature.
I. Martin, Rebecca, 1953 April 17-
PN3448.D4C73 2013
809.3'872--dc23
                                                                    2012049049

ebook ISBN: 978-1-4298-3838-2

Contents_____

Critical Contexts

Critical Readings

Resources

About This Volume _____

Rebecca Martin

As Howard Haycraft sensibly points out in *Murder for Pleasure* (1942), his seminal history of detective fiction, stories that are literally "detective" fiction only came into being when professional detectives arrived on the scene in the nineteenth century. As the present volume illustrates, there are a number of ways in which this narrow definition is misleading and overly restrictive for any exploration of the deep history of crime writing. Indeed, this broad genre has played a role in the social construction of values, attracted the attention of readers over centuries, and had a strong, shaping impact on media such as television, film, and the internet in our own time. Why should we not point to the fifth-century BCE play *Oedipus Rex* as a distant precursor to William Hjortsberg's 1978 novel *Falling Angel*? Such connections would seem to enrich both our understanding and enjoyment of literature and our insights into the cultural inheritance of the west, as well as the place of crime writing in a global context. It is hardly the case that the reputation of Sophocles would be besmirched by the association. There is a far longer tradition of writing about crime—including Daniel's role as investigator and arbiter in the biblical court tale of Susannah and the Elders (second century BCE), Chinese court case stories from the sixteenth century, Shakespeare's early seventeenth-century account of Macbeth's bloody crimes and the murderer's undoing—which we can unapologetically read, study, and appreciate, and in which an investigative character carries the societal values and unusual degree of insight that we expect in a detective. This detective figure may be a professional (that is, a private investigator, a police officer, or another representative of law enforcement, such as a medical examiner, attorney, or judge) or may be an amateur who undertakes an investigation out of curiosity or some more compelling motivation. "Crime writing," then, is a broader category than detective fiction, but the focus of this volume is not on the careful delineation of which works fit into or are to be cast out of particular categories. We have chosen, rather, to be inclusive, as a way to examine the richness of the field of crime writing and the many ways in which crime, its depiction, and its investigation cross narrative, national, and other boundaries. This inclusivity results in a diversity of perspectives—in terms of culture, as well as the signif- icance of point of view (whose story is it, after all?) in telling the tale of a crime—that may offer support to our own closely held ideas of good and evil or make us reexamine our assumptions about community, in- dividual rights, and even the structure and purpose of the law itself.

In addition to being inclusive, this collection is integrative. Rather than providing what have now become conventional chapters on gen- der, race, and class as reflected in crime writing, those subjects are in- tegrated, as appropriate, in each of the essays or in ways that are silent. The chapters that open this collection are indicative of this approach. Ruth Anne Thompson's survey of the cultural and historical context in which detective fiction appeared and grew emphasizes the relationship between the rise of different kinds of crime writing and the class-based differences in literacy and taste in industrializing nineteenth-century England and America. In her essay about the reception of detective fiction at different points in the nineteenth and twentieth centuries, Elizabeth Foxwell gives due prominence to authors Anna Katharine Green and Margery Allingham and carefully notes the unmistakable sexism in the reviews that greeted their works, works now recognized as essential contributions to crime writing as we know it today. Fox- well points out that it is difficult to judge the early reactions to their works when so many reviewers filtered their responses to the authors through their surprise or dismay at the authors' sex. In this volume's "critical lens" chapter, which analyzes one work of distinction in the genre, we offer Kerstin Bergman's timely and innovative examination of Stieg Larsson's phenomenal *The Girl with the Dragon Tattoo*, the story of a powerful woman who crosses boundaries of both genders and genres. Norlisha F. Crawford's chapter offers a comparative analy- sis of three writers of detective fiction whose works provide mystery and entertainment, as well as an opportunity to study the evolution of ideas about race and race relations in twentieth-century America.

Several chapters of this volume examine practices of crime writing in regions whose names—China, Japan, Latin America, Scandinavia—would seem to safely delineate the topics. What we see, however, beginning with Jeffrey C. Kinkley's chapter on Chinese writing about crime is that nation-state boundaries are permeable to varying degrees, with results that are plainly displayed in the crime writing they help construct. Kinkley emphasizes both the continuity and discontinuity of Chinese crime writing. In one sense, the Confucian-inflected law of centuries past is alive and well in contemporary Chinese law enforcement's insistence on criminal confession and on an idea of "social justice" synonymous with social stability, rather than attention to individual rights. On the other hand, Chinese writing from the early twentieth-century to the present day is an almost infallible barometer of the political currents that have swept across the nation, affecting self-expression and, especially, the expression of ideas associated with the West. In fact, how does one talk about "detective fiction" in a society that, for specific cultural reasons, has no term for it? Amanda Seaman, in her chapter on the fiction of Japan and East Asia, sees not only much cross-cultural borrowing, including assimilation of Western literary traditions, but also the growth of very distinctive cultures and practices in Taiwan and Korea. As Seaman notes, the latter have both had a complicated and fraught relationship with Japan, one in which China is also implicated. The popularity of Japanese detective novels in translation in China brings these two essays together in a way that reveals an ongoing cultural exchange between two very different countries. The crime writing and detective fiction coming from Latin America has seen an explosive growth since the 1980s and a similar set of distinctions arising from the histories—of colonialism, of dictatorship, of oppression, and of racial and ethnic inequality—specific to each Latin American nation. As Natalia Jacovkis reports in her chapter in this volume, "the conventions of the genre will serve its practitioners to critically map contemporary society and/or to question official, hegemonic discourses about the national past," including the question of whether "the whole system is corrupt and the state is the biggest criminal of all." In Sara Kärrholm's chapter on Scandinavian crime writing, the problem is first one of defining what is meant by "Scandinavian." The reasons for that are, in themselves, a brief education in history, culture, and cultural influences. It is, she says, hard to discuss a "specifically Scandinavian tradition" when each of the nations involved has its own national identity and culture. In fact, two of the nations—Iceland and Finland—are not, strictly speaking, "Scandinavian," but the five northern European countries, including Norway, Sweden, and Denmark, have in common a somewhat similar development as social welfare states in the post–World War II period. And in a development that could hardly be more different from the crime writing of China, Scandinavian writing, like that of Latin America, is usually informed by social critique. In Scandinavia, it is the failed welfare state, society itself, from which criminal behavior springs, while in Latin America, the writing shows that the rule of law is swept away by political and social failure, whether the society is a dictatorship or a neoliberal democracy.

Joseph Paul Moser's chapter on connections between hard-boiled literature and film noir brings an element of social critique to exploration of detective fiction and noir fiction in the period of the 1930s to 1950s and their cross-genre concern with pre– and post–World War II American masculinity. The familiarity of the modern reader and viewer with the traditions of writing and film covered by the terms "hard-boiled" and "noir" is often made up of a confusion or conflation of writing and visual images. This chapter traces the thematic concerns and tensions that bind literature and film together during this period so crucial to our contemporary understanding of the depiction of crime and criminality in the two media. Susan Elizabeth Sweeney's chapter on "metaphysical" detection demonstrates that in the same period, detective fiction—both golden age and hard-boiled—made the conventions and artfulness of detection so familiar and unmistakable that it opened up the genre to a self-consciousness in which crime writers could begin to give readers metanarratives on crime, detection, and the impossibility of finding and knowing the truth or sorting through multiple truths. Detective fiction is about knowing and thus ripe for subversion in the postmodern era that acknowledges the impossibility of knowing. Different ways of knowing, or acknowledging that knowing is not possible in the conventional Enlightenment sense, are crucial in the practice of detection in the many novels that feature Native American detectives. As we see in Rhonda Harris Taylor's chapter on Native American detective fiction, definitions and boundaries come into play in this area as well. Any consideration of this subgenre of detective fiction must begin by defining who is Native American and by addressing the question of non-Native Americans who write about Native Americans from outside their lived experience.

Given the focus of this collection on detective fiction and crime writing as a global, if not globalized, practice, Malcah Effron's concluding chapter, on the contemporary Anglophone publishing industry and the publication of translated texts, is crucial to considering the future of crime writing and its audience. Effron succeeds in turning the question away from the exhausted issue of American ethnocentrism, to which the success of several translated authors including Henning Mankell and Stieg Larsson has brought a pause, if not a close, to look in detail at the more interesting question of what kinds of books do succeed in translation and what can be learned from their success. The books that do succeed on the scale of Larsson's Millennium trilogy are likely both to offer the comfort of generic familiarity that attracts readers of crime fiction and to serve as the impetus to greater creativity, particularly in the area of social critique, by Anglophone, and especially American, authors. In this regard, it is significant that four full years after *The Girl with the Dragon Tattoo* burst on the US market, a volume in Larsson's trilogy remained in the top twenty-five titles on the *New York Times*' Paperback Trade Fiction list and a crime book by relative newcomer Jussi Adler-Olsen, *The Keeper of Lost Causes*, appeared in the twentieth position on that same list. *The Keeper of Lost Causes* was originally published in Danish as *Kvinden i buret* and has been met with great acclaim on the US market. This *Critical Insights* volume looks both backward in time and forward to provide a rich context for understanding texts of the past and the works that will move this consistently appealing genre into the future.

On Crime and Detective Fiction: Perversities and Pleasures of the Texts

Rebecca Martin

"Detective story writers are often asked why we devote our talents to working in a mere popular convention. One answer is that there may be more to our use of the convention than meets the eye. . . . the literary detective has provided writers since Poe with a disguise, a kind of welder's mask enabling us to handle dangerously hot material."

Ross Macdonald, "Writing the Galton Case," *Self-Portrait*

"When in doubt have a man come through a door with a gun in his hand."

Raymond Chandler, Introduction, *Trouble Is My Business*

If longevity and a widespread pattern of cultural diffusion are measures of significance and success, then we need look no further for evidence of the importance of writing about crime and the work of detection. As Jeffrey C. Kinkley points out in his chapter of this volume, traditional Chinese crime writing dates as far back as the thirteenth century CE, and the subject of much of that literature, Bao Zheng, also called Lord Bao, was a real magistrate who lived in the eleventh century. It could be argued, and has been by many, that crime writing dates still further back in time to as early as the fifth century BCE when Sophocles' *Oedipus the King* was performed in Athens or the period around the second century BCE when the prophet Daniel investigates and adjudicates the case of Susanna and the Elders in the biblical Book of Daniel. Or perhaps we must look to "The Story of the Three Apples," one of the oldest stories, possibly dating as early as the ninth century CE, in the gathering of Persian, Syrian, and Egyptian tales known collectively as *One Thousand and One Nights*. Recently, a strong case has been made by John Scaggs for the sixteenth- and seventeenth-century Elizabethan and Jacobean revenge tragedy, including Shakespeare's *Hamlet* (ca. 1601), as thematically and structurally the closest match for the "movement from ignorance to knowledge" required in narratives of crimes (12). Since the history of detective fiction is not the subject here, most readers will find a satisfactory starting point with Edgar Allan Poe as the first writer of modern detective fiction in the group of stories that includes "The Murders in the Rue Morgue" (1841), "The Mystery of Marie Rogêt» (1845), and «The Purloined Letter» (1845), all featuring C. Auguste Dupin, a talented amateur detective. Our quick tour from China through the Middle East and into England and America reinforces the idea that, as genres or broader discursive practices go, writing about crime and its detection has had a wide geographical range, a place in numerous cultures both Eastern and Western, and has survived, prospered, and spread for hundreds of years. Why?

This chapter will explore the reasons for crime writing's popularity and persistence offered by scholars, critics, and readers in the last two or three hundred years, including the speculations of those who have expressed their disgust that a subject deemed low, sensational, or regressive should be found so appealing by readers. Morally tinged criticism of "sensation" as an attraction in fiction has been laid against the novel since the eighteenth century, attributing moral impurity to those texts that held their readers by offering shocks and depicting extreme emotional states. This bias against spectacular scenes and the emotions they raise traces all the way back to Aristotle. The English gothic novels of the late eighteenth century and Victorian sensation fiction, both precursors of modern mystery and crime writing, had to balance the telling of forward-rushing stories full of chills and shocks and violent behavior with the need to offer closure that would reassure readers (and critics) and return the world to its proper order. We will see that many twentieth-century critics offered answers to the question of "Why detective fiction?" by accepting the eighteenth- and nineteenth-century terms of the argument that required literature to have moral value or risk being denigrated as mere entertainment and a waste of time. In our contemporary culture, this question about morality is no longer asked so directly; however, crime writing, at least some types of crime writing such as true crime, are still suspected of signaling moral failure and prurience in their readers. One way to get deeper into this issue, if not all the way to its resolution, is to investigate what readers say they get from their experience of reading crime fiction. Exploration of these subjects will lead to a consideration of the reader's role in consuming texts about crime, that is, what draws readers in and keeps them reading about subjects and scenes that are often gruesome or, at the very least, morbid. To keep these readers reading, there must be pleasure derived from the act, but in what—if not prurience or bad taste—does this pleasure reside?

For Chinese readers of the Yuan (1260–1368), Ming (1368–1644), and Qing (1644–1911) dynasties, the pleasures of texts about crime lay in their depiction of "ingenuity, intrigue, a quest for justice against all odds—sometimes, retribution or vengeance—and eerie, strange phenomena, including the supernatural," according to Jeffrey C. Kinkley. Readers then, as now, were drawn in by mystery and curiosity, though the mystery was not a "whodunit" since the perpetrator was known from the outset, but rather how the investigating magistrate would uncover and interpret clues about the crime and whether the guilty party would be punished appropriately. The tales contain descriptions of tortures used to obtain confessions, and authors did not shrink from detailed descriptions of wounds or partially decomposed corpses. The stories offered reassurances to readers that crime would be punished, even when it involved the powerful, and that somewhere in the vast Chinese system, there were clever, honest men who would see to it that justice was done. Described in this way, those readers of several centuries ago must seem little different from later readers and indeed our contemporaries. Eighteenth-century English readers were drawn to stories about highwaymen, such as Jonathan Wild, who was profiled by Daniel Defoe in 1725 and featured in a satirical novel by Henry Fielding in 1743; about "reformed" prostitutes, such as the titular character in Defoe's *Moll Flanders* (1722); and about all manner of malefactors profiled in the *Newgate Calendar*. Middle- and upper-class readers had access through such tales to parts of society that were not normally accessible to them and about which they were curious. Seamy but adventure-filled stories about the misbehavior of the criminal class worked to reinforce the middle-class values that were in ascendance at the time; the tales would always end in repentance and, just as in Chinese stories, appropriate punishment, whether it be transportation to the American colonies or death on the gallows.

The repentance of a life of crime or transgressive acts by the lively and often appealing characters who frequent certain eighteenth-century English novels raises a powerful concern that did not enter into Chinese judgments about crime texts: literature as purveyor of moral values. This argument about whether and how crime should be depicted in writing is most prominent in the Anglo-American cultures and is very much entwined with questions about the value of imaginative literature, even imagination itself, that were voiced in eighteenth-century England. This dispute about the novel questioned whether there was any value in fiction itself, because fiction, after all, is not true. While there might be some value in novels that tried to portray real life, the frequently voiced suspicion was that novels that portrayed adventure and romance (in its literary sense of unusual events involving extraordinary persons) would mislead naive readers, particularly female readers, and might be morally damaging. The point is a significant one here, because the novels that were most open to the charge of providing dangerous distractions were the so-called gothic romances, a genre of novels that combine mysteries from the past, family secrets, bloody crimes, dark villains, and exotic locales. Women might be distracted from their proper devotion to their family duties and drawn in by fantastic narratives that "encourage foolish idealism and unjustified paranoia," giving them false ideas about the nature of reality in eighteenth-century England (Pearson 199).[1] These were novels of strong emotions and startling scenes of fear and suffering. Though most of these narratives concluded with the restoration of order and the marriage of the right partners, the secrets revealed through the heroine's efforts were often sinister and disturbing. It is questionable whether marriage on a sunny day could effectively close the doubts about family patriarchs, and indeed patriarchy, and the nature of evil itself that the works raised. The dangerous passions and inappropriate expectations supposedly raised by gothic romances were blamed for leading their female readers into moral error, if not into actual revolution. Eighteenth-century readers, both men and women, admitted to being drawn in by the passions and suspense of the reading experience offered by gothic novels, with accounts of volumes being torn from hand to hand and readers staying up all night, eyes glued to pages. This ambiguous genre's plots and concerns about tears in the fabric of family and abuse of patriarchal power led quite directly to Victorian sensation fiction, in which we find some of the earliest depictions of the professional police detective (Wilkie Collins's Sergeant Cuff in *The Moonstone*, 1868, for one). And along a slightly different line, it also made way for Edgar Allan Poe's depiction of the physical and emotional violence behind the doors of Paris apartments and palaces and the work of that talented amateur detective, M. Dupin. The sensation novel transplanted crime from the exotic, foreign locales of gothic fiction into the heart of the middle-class family in rapidly industrializing nineteenth-century English society. What were the superstitious excesses of the feudal past in the gothic became the insanity, bigamy, murder, or other malfeasance that may lie at the heart of the Victorian family. In its turn, the sensation novel found itself under criticism for provoking "excitement" and inspiring "morbid" interests:

And as excitement, even when harmless in kind, cannot be continually produced without becoming morbid in degree, works of this class manifest themselves as belonging, some more, some less, but all to some extent, to the morbid phenomena of literature—indications of a wide-spread corruption, of which they are in part both the effect and the cause; called into existence to supply the cravings of a diseased appetite, and contributing themselves to foster the disease, and to stimulate the want which they supply. (Mansel 482–83)

The very fact that sensation novels (the name damns the thing) are intent on stimulating the emotions and exciting the imagination is argued to be congruent with disease and moral decay. In his argument, H. L. Mansel complains of the incidents and characters of the novels, as well as low tastes and social status of the readers, the mindlessly repetitious productions of the authors, and the shameful degeneracy of the publishers who publish the books.

As is now apparent, any respectable person, especially a respectable author, picking up a crime novel even at the start of the twentieth century might feel that his or her reading tastes required some defense. Let us backtrack briefly to look at some of the qualities of the early predecessors of modern crime writing that we can now piece together from the criticisms and attempt to view them in a less censorious light. The early writing is plot driven, not character driven. Many readers are riveted by these exciting plots, which feature unusual events, mysterious characters, and the systematic shocks, revelations, and suppressions of information that create a suspenseful narrative and keep a high degree of tension alive in the reader. The narratives are sometimes referred to, in slightly disapproving terms, as "atavistic," as in this comment from contemporary detective novelist P. D. James: "Today the detective story, like many other crime novels, combines an age-old fascination with mysterious death and violence with a concern for less atavistic emotions and the circumstances which give rise to them" ("Moral Dimension"). At the heart of readers' fascination with crime writing, undeniably, is the atavistic impulse to look with open curiosity at death's secrets, not turn away from violence, and give oneself over to powerful storytelling.[2] The stories of Poe and Arthur Conan Doyle, the novels of Raymond Chandler, P. D. James, Henning Mankell, Keigo Higashino, and the works of so many others who write about crime—from true crime to the most metafictional fictions—identify and adopt themes, human situations, patterns of belief, and behavior that are fundamental to our engagements with other human beings and have been for hundreds of years. As this collection surely will show, these topics and concerns cross cultures and generations, even as the way authors deal with them may be culturally conditioned. Cross-purposes between parents and children, coveting what one's neighbor has, the inability truly to know others' minds and motives, and even the questions of how we know anything and what our place is in the world are fundamental to the consideration of the role of crime in society and to detective fiction and crime writing.

Not surprisingly, when writers discuss reasons for their enjoyment of detective fiction, they point to the satisfactions of the Aristotelian plot with its clear beginning, middle, and end, as British detective novelist and scholar Dorothy L. Sayers does in her famous 1936 essay "Aristotle on Detective Fiction," where she notes that what Aristotle really "desired was a good detective story; and it was not his fault, poor man, that he lived some twenty centuries too early" to enjoy contemporary detective fiction (25). Good detective fiction, in these terms, is defined by a well-constructed plot, realistic characters, the functioning of probability in all of its action, and the occasional delivery of appropriately timed "gruesome" shocks ("Aristotle" 25). Sayers points, as well, to the "detective-story proper" as "ancient in origin" and linked in form and function to Greek tragedy ("Omnibus" 53).

The poet W. H. Auden, in his 1948 essay "The Guilty Vicarage," ascribes to the detective fiction he guiltily enjoys the "magical function" of working out "the dialectic of innocence and guilt" (15, 16) in Christian terms: "The fantasy, then, which the detective story addict indulges is the fantasy of being restored to the Garden of Eden, to a state of innocence, where he may know love as love and not as the law" (24). To the detective, Auden attributes the function of the epic hero, such as Roland or Lancelot. He links the detective's quest to vanquish evil and reestablish good to the Holy Grail quest (18) and to the hero who shoulders the guilt of Christians and allows the reader to dissociate from transgression or, more appropriate to Auden's argument, sin. G. K. Chesterton, the English writer and religious and political thinker, in his 1901 "Defence of Detective Stories" connects detective fiction to the medieval epic romance and knights errant, as does Sayers, who likens the detective to Lancelot ("Omnibus" 56). Auden ends his inquiry in this curious way, completing his beautiful statement about "love" and "the law": "The driving force behind this daydream is the feeling of guilt, the cause of which is unknown to the dreamer. The fantasy of escape is the same, whether one explains the guilt in Christian, Freudian, or any other terms. One's way of trying to face the reality, on the other hand, will, of course, depend very much on one's creed" (24). What Auden opens up in his conclusion is the possibility that since modern works are apt to depict many kinds of guilt (and the modern world offers so many), one need not connect to detective fiction in narrowly Christian terms to write, read, and understand the detective story.

While these arguments succeed in raising the status of detective fiction by associating the best such writing with elevated forms such as classical tragedy and the medieval epic, violence is done to the reality of the form. Auden, for example, finds it necessary to define detective fiction in a way that excludes Raymond Chandler. Chandler's style, according to Auden, shows that he is more interested in art than in writing "escape literature" (19). Both Sayers and Auden were explicit that detective fiction could not reach to the level of "art," though, particularly in Auden's case, that opinion is based more on his association of shame and guilt with his craving for the reading and the intensity of the reading experience rather than the style or ideas found in the writing ("Guilty Vicarage" 15). In other words, anything he enjoyed that much could not be good. And in the case of Sayers, the "rigid technique" that she allows detective fiction makes it impossible for the writing to "attain the loftiest level of literary achievement" ("Omnibus" 76, 77). As soon as the detective is humanized, the suffering and humanity of the victim explored, or the workings of the murderer's mind revealed, then the rigid formula has been defied and, whatever the writing is, it is not detective fiction according to Sayers. She says, "Though [the detective story] deals with the most desperate effects of rage, jealousy, and revenge, it rarely touches the heights and depths of human passion" ("Omnibus" 77). At the same time that Sayers and Auden try to elevate the reading and writing they enjoy, they seem to fear going too far in their claims, with both finally insisting that detective fiction, once it approaches the edges of true art, cannot be detective fiction.

Writing in the 1970s, detective novelist Ross Macdonald moved the discussion of the value and appeal of detective fiction forward while keeping one foot in the richest part of previous discussions. Macdonald joins Sayers and Auden in agreeing that "the detective novel is extraordinarily varied and remarkable, but it isn't a great novelistic form, at least not yet" (Interview 95), but in celebrating the variety of the form, he opens up the discussion of value and appeal to encompass a range of fiction that allows for wider, less rigidly confined discussion. As do both Sayers and Auden, he points to the moral value of detective fiction but sees in the fiction a place to extol "mercy" as a higher moral value than "justice" (94). He allows, too, that fiction about crime is informed by classical literature, including the dramatic and literary traditions of Greece and Rome—themselves based on older myths that try to explain and give meaning to life, as well as by such myths and legends as Sleeping Beauty, which most readers know from folktales written down later but are based in the deep past. He touches upon Freudian theory, too, as a new writing of myth. In her interview with Macdonald in the 1980s, Diana Cooper-Clark pinpoints the difference between the morality of Macdonald's detective and those of earlier periods: "[You have written] that everyone walks a moral tightrope everyday [sic]. You have said that Freud 'deepened our moral vision and rendered it forever ambivalent.' Because values aren't there in society, as they were in traditional societies, we have to make ourselves up as we go along" (93). The role of the "mythological" in Macdonald's work and criticism is to ground the acts of modernity in the deep past, hinting at their continuity with the past and showing that "we discover ourselves again by reaching into the past" (86). That past provides a basis, even if it is ultimately unreal, for living in the present. Macdonald explains about myth that "the same stories keep telling themselves and they seem to solve some of our psychic problems or lead to their solution" (90). He goes far beyond the apologetics of Sayers and Auden in claiming that detective fiction "serves as a model for life and action" (*Self-Portrait* 18). That he can go that far, though, in his claims for detective fiction is reliant upon his far more capacious view of what a detective novel is and does: "Detective novels differ from some other kinds of novel, in having to have a rather hard structure built in logical coherence. But the structure will fail to satisfy the mind, writer's or reader's, unless the logic of imagination, tempered by feelings and rooted in the unconscious, is tied to it, often subverting it" (57). This is the same rigid structure to which Sayers refers, but in Macdonald's view, the structure is merely a necessary basis for what can be a richly woven narrative based in imagination, feeling, and the unconscious, through which it will touch readers' desire for a story that has unity and reality and in which they sense a connection to their deepest—one could say, atavistic—thoughts and emotions.

One feature that may account for much of the popularity of crime writing and its enjoyment by readers is the coincidence of the investigator's work with the work of the reader. I refer not to the reader's identification with the character and values of the detective, but to the parallelism of the reader's activity of reading with the narrative depiction of the investigation and interpretation of clues. The investigator's acts of detection are attempts to reconstruct the crime, to make of the individual clues and signs a story that makes rational sense. Peter Hühn has pointed out that there are actually multiple stories being told simultaneously in detective fiction, especially classical detective fiction. He notes, «The plot of the classical detective novel comprises two basically separate stories—the story of the *crime* (which consists of action) and the story of the *investigation* (which is concerned with knowledge). In their narrative presentation, however, the two stories are intertwined" (Hühn 452; italics in orig.). The reader reads both stories in a complicated process of forward movement as the investigation is conducted and backward reflection as evidence is weighed, ordered, and interpreted, creating a new narrative, a narrative of the crime in all of its particulars including motivation. The act of reading itself is an onward moving search for and interpretation of clues, of which each word is a complex sign.

Stories of readers waiting anxiously for new books in their favorite detective novel series (or the latest true crime book), or staying up until the wee hours of the night to relieve their suspense about «whodunit,» point to readers' experience as perhaps being based more in the reading process itself, rather than in their connection with ideas and values. While writing about crime has many manifestations and subgenres, much crime story reading is genre reading. Whether it be the pattern of true crime narratives, the English cozies, or the twenty-second iteration of the investigations of Sue Grafton's private eye, Kinsey Millhone, readers return again and again for the comfort of repetition—for those slight variations in a well-known pattern and with the assurance of an outcome that satisfy by bringing together the threads of the plot, supplying a rationale for the crime, revealing the solution to the act of violence at the center of the narrative, and punishing the perpetrator. The author supplies an ending, though readers of genre fiction have an ambiguous attitude toward the endings of the novels. The pursuit of genre reading, in fact, is a denial of the value or ultimate satisfaction of endings, because what reader does not wait in some pleasurable anxiety for the next entry in the series? Endings, yes. Closure, not necessarily. In enjoying five novels written in a series featuring a particular investigator, what has the reader done but experienced five endings that are felt as temporary episodes of stoppage prior to the next iteration in the series?[3] Repetition as an important structuring device in written narrative, and in oral storytelling before it, has long been understood as a device with multiple functions. It is a mnemonic device, offering ancient bards, modern songwriters, poets, and their listeners a rhythmic structure that connects words to memory and facilitates the oral repetition of parts in their proper order. Psychologically, the work of repetition operates with both a forward movement—the pleasure of repetition that is seen most clearly in children—and an underlying tension focused on the release of ending that is as much physiological as it is psychological, and probably far less intellectual than either.

Sayers referred to detective writing as "the art of framing lies" and speculated on what attracted readers to reading material of which the tacitly acknowledged object is to mislead and "to induce" the reader initially to believe "anything and everything but truth" ("Aristotle" 31). She is neither the first nor the last to puzzle over what attracts readers to such reading. "How," asks a more recent critic, Lisa Zunshine, "can we explain this perverse craving? After all, what is so 'pleasurable' about remaining in the dark for a long time about something sinister and threatening that you really, desperately, passionately want to know *now*?" (121; italics in orig.). As one of the modern literary researchers working with the theory of mind, which is based on contemporary scientific observations and speculations about how our minds gather details about our environment and use them to make sense of our world, Zunshine approaches detective fiction from a cognitive evolutionary psychology perspective. Since the reading of detective fiction does imply a certain amount of perversity in its readers, Zunshine offers some ideas about what makes these readers different from those who do not enjoy detective fiction. Readers who enjoy detective fiction are those who can best

> store information under advisement and, then, once the truth-value of this information is decided, to think back to the beginning of the story and to readjust our understanding of a whole series of occurrences. . . . a story whose premise is that 'everybody could be lying' is a narrative minefield,

and turning it into an enjoyable reading experience may require a particular set of formal adjustments. (132)

She then goes on to analyze exactly what "adjustments" in narrative form successful authors make and to speculate about how readers exercise their ability to see into others' minds and gain pleasure in the process. So much pleasure, in fact, is gained from these perverse exercises that readers seek them out again and again. The theory advanced by Zunshine is just one way in which readers are still grappling with the question raised by Sayers, one that she answered saying that the author must "fram[e] lies in the right way. . . . the right method is to tell the *truth* in such a way that the *intelligent* reader is seduced into telling the lie for himself" ("Aristotle" 31; italics in orig.). There is little evidence that readers of detective fiction and crime writing are more intelligent than other readers, but it is possible that the minds of those particular readers are ones that show a specific kind of development or adaptation that ensures they will both enjoy being lied to and seeing through the lies. And they will seek that enjoyment time after time.

Considering the genre through cognitive evolutionary psychology is just one of myriad new ways in which readers are engaging with detective writing. Other examples include the greater interactivity that it is available to readers who pursue an interest in detective fiction online. We are a long way from the fondly acknowledged pleasures of board games such as Clue, with fans of detection now able to participate in online role-playing games (RPGs), interacting with others to investigate crimes, or to take on a wide range of roles in other software-based games that allow participants to control the action and outcome of the investigation. In one particularly unique situation, though it is not likely to remain unique for long, the 2011 online game L. A. Noire inspired a collection of noir stories by notable authors in the genre, such as Joyce Carol Oates, Lawrence Block, and Megan Abbott. The book, in turn, has been bought by both gamers who came to it via the game and by readers who were not aware of the fact that it was inspired by a game. The *New York Times* review cites this game's "deft, mature hand that lends all the police-procedural gameplay an emotional heft rarely felt in video games" and its reliance on "basic storytelling elements like narrative, character, setting and plot" (Schiesel). The internet offers a new world of access, attraction, and innovation that will ensure fictions of detection and crime will continue to be enjoyed in forms that build on old traditions but take new forms that perhaps cannot even be imagined now.

II.

In *The Maltese Falcon*, Sam Spade offers up a story to femme fatale Brigid O'Shaughnessy, the story of a man named Flitcraft. Flitcraft is a normal man leading a well-regulated life who one day comes close to experiencing a fatal accident—a falling beam from a construction project crashes to earth near him while he is walking along minding his own business. So shaken is he by this chance experience that he leaves his old life and reestablishes his life elsewhere. The irony is that he eventually develops a life that is a precise copy of his old one. Flitcraft's explanation for his disappearance, Spade says, is that "he felt like somebody had taken the lid off life and let him look at the works" (Hammett 63). He discovers the shocking truth: that chance, rather than order, is the force behind life in the world. But old habits of thought and life take over, and once he has "adjusted himself to beams falling, and then no more of them [fall], and he adjust[s] himself to them not falling" (64). While the story appears to have little effect on his listener, Spade in this little tale reveals to readers what has become a signature story of noir detective writing: beams do fall and chance can take us at any moment, but the human mind is most comfortable believing that routines and care will keep us out of trouble. It is possible that this is a lie, but it is an appealing one that allows us to live.

I will end with a slightly different story from writer Ross Macdonald. Macdonald tells the story of his five-year-old grandson who repeatedly threw a towel over his head and announced he was a "monster" and then removed the towel and revealed himself to be a well-known boy. Macdonald sees in these activities the work of the writer of detective fiction: "Disguise is the imaginative device which permits the work to be both private and public, to half-divulge the writer's crucial secrets while deepening the whole community's sense of its own mysterious life" (*Self-Portrait* 48). While the point that, in context, was most significant to Macdonald was the one he was making about the private life of the artist and its relationship to his or her writing, we can draw another meaning from it, one about the role and value of writing about crime. No matter the form it takes, whether disguised as fiction, pseudofiction, or honest fact, this is what crime writing reveals and is perhaps its most valuable function: It reveals to us powerful secrets that we might not discover by any other means; it reveals to us "the whole community's sense of its own mysterious life."

Notes

1. Many eighteenth-century novels warned of these dangers but often in a vein that was half serious, half humorous. See, for instance, Charlotte Lennox's 1752 novel, *The Female Quixote*, whose heroine, Arabella, takes her behavioral cues from Cervantes's seventeenth-century chivalric romance *Don Quixote*. Today, the best known of these novels is Jane Austen's gentle, amusing gothic romance parody, *Northanger Abbey*, published in 1817 but probably written around 1799. Modern readers often will interpret these novels as guides to female behavior that both caution young women to avoid fanciful behavior but that also support a certain amount of female personal freedom that was unusual at the time.

2. Readers interested in exploring this subject further would do well to begin with *The Storytelling Animal: How Stories Make Us Human* (2012), Jonathan Gottschall's recent book that makes use of new discoveries drawn from neuroscience, psychology, and evolutionary biology. It is a good companion to the work of Lisa Zunshine and, like it, is written for the lay reader.

3. This effect has been studied in several genres, all of which illuminate the relationship between readers and their texts in detective fiction reading. Janice A. Radway's study of a community of women who read romance fiction, *Reading the Romance: Women, Patriarchy, and Popular Literature* (1984), is still very valuable. Laura Browder's article "Dystopian Romance: True Crime and the Female Reader" (2006) looks at many of the same questions from the perspective of a different genre. A more broad-ranging consideration is provided by Robert A. Rushing's *Resisting Arrest: Detective Fiction and Popular Culture* (2007),

which looks at repetition, enjoyment, and deferred satisfaction in the reader/ film viewer's experience through the lens of psychoanalytic theory. Readers also might usefully consult "Some Readers Reading," chapter 7 of R. Gordon Kelly's *Mystery Fiction and Modern Life* (1998).

Works Cited

Auden, W. H. "The Guilty Vicarage." Winks 15–24. Print.

Chandler, Raymond. *Trouble Is My Business*. New York: Random, 1988. Print.

Chesterton, G. K. "A Defence of Detective Stories." *The Defendant*. 2nd ed. London: Johnson, 1902. 118–23. Print.

Clute, Shannon, and Richard Edwards. "Episode 51: *L.A. Noire.*" *Out of the Past: Investigating Film Noir*. Clute and Edwards, 16 Aug. 2011. Web. 18 Oct. 2012.

Hammett, Dashiell. *The Maltese Falcon*. 1930. New York: Vintage, 1992. Print.

Hühn, Peter. "The Detective as Reader: Narrativity and Reading Concepts in Detective Fiction." *Modern Fiction Studies* 33.3 (1987): 451–66. Print.

James, P. D. Interview. "The Art of Fiction No. 141." By Shusha Guppy. *Paris Review* 135 (1995): N. pag. Web. 18 Oct. 2012.

___. "The Moral Dimension of the Crime Novel." *Literature Matters* Spring 2006: N. pag. *British Council*. Web. 18 Oct. 2012.

Macdonald, Ross. Interview. *Designs of Darkness: Interviews with Detective Novelists*. By Diana Cooper-Clark. Bowling Green: Bowling Green U Popular P, 1983. 82–100. Print.

___. *Self-Portrait: Ceaselessly into the Past*. Santa Barbara: Capra, 1981. Print.

Mansel, H. L. "Sensation Novels." *Quarterly Review* 113.226 (1863): 482–514. Print.

Martin, Rebecca E. "'I Should Like To Spend My Whole Life in Reading It': Repetition and the Pleasure of the Gothic." *Journal of Narrative Technique* 28.1 (1998): 75–90. Print.

Pearson, Jacqueline. *Women's Reading in Britain 1750–1835: A Dangerous Recreation*. Cambridge: Cambridge UP, 1999. Print.

Sayers, Dorothy L. "Aristotle on Detective Fiction." Winks 25–34. Print.

___."The Omnibus of Crime." Winks 53–83. Print.

Scaggs, John. *Crime Fiction*. New York: Routledge, 2005. Print.

Schiesel, Seth. "1947 Mystery That Matters Now." Rev. of *L.A. Noire*, by Rockstar Games. *New York Times*. New York Times, 16 May 2011. Web. 18 Oct. 2012.

Winks, Robin W., ed. *Detective Fiction: A Collection of Critical Essays*. Rev. ed. Woodstock: Countryman, 1988. Print.

Zunshine, Lisa. *Why We Read Fiction: Theory of Mind and the Novel*. Columbus: Ohio State UP, 2006. Print.

CRITICAL
CONTEXTS

From Mean Streets to the Imagined World: The Development of Detective Fiction _____

Ruth Anne Thompson and Jean Fitzgerald

The literary genre of crime fiction, which also embraces true crime stories, has a 250-year history, dozens of subgenres, and thousands of examples; the essays presented here focus on selected aspects of its global development over the centuries, laying out the general sequence of that development along with some of the better-known examples in each stage. Critics differ about the categories, the characteristics, and the relation of stories to the culture of the times, but whatever their perception, they agree that crime stories have made their way into respectability after a beginning that identified them as low class and marginal.

The age of Enlightenment sparked monumental changes in Western civilization with the focus on human reason and science reflected not only in political, but also in economic and cultural institutions, and especially in the literature of the times, both highbrow and lowbrow. As the nineteenth century dawned, the growth of manufacturing drew people from a rural to an urban existence, where they suffered abysmal working conditions, low wages, overcrowding in slums, and disease, all of which led to new levels of crime. Governments dealt with the consequences of these changes in society in a variety of ways. Labor abuses led to legal reforms, two of which were the limits on working hours of women and children, and educational reform decreeing at least a minimal education up to the age of twelve. Jeremy Bentham's focus on utilitarianism, "the greatest good for the greatest number," gradually improved the conditions so graphically pictured in novels like Charles Dickens's *Oliver Twist* (1838). The changes helped increase the literacy rate and widened the market for cheap publications.

One outgrowth of the cultural upheaval was the increasing number of stories of crime and criminals. These were not new, tracing back to the biblical Cain and Abel story, Greek myth, revenge plays of the sixteenth and seventeenth centuries, and Shakespearean tragedies, as well as the extensive body of Asian material, as described by Amanda Seaman and Jeffrey C. Kinkley in this volume. However, much of the pre–eighteenth-century materials were puzzles, rather than crime stories as the genre is broadly defined today (Scaggs 8). Aberrations in human behavior have had an enduring appeal, and the psychology of the lawbreaker has proved universally fascinating over the centuries. Appearing early in the eighteenth century, Daniel Defoe's *The Fortunes and Misfortunes of the Famous Moll Flanders* (1722) and Henry Fielding's *The Life and Death of Jonathan Wild, the Great* (1743) are purportedly true crime narratives of the lives of actual criminals. True crime stories tend to be "journalistic and literary accounts of exceptional human ghastliness," although the truth in many is clearly in question as "these books freely re-create scenes witnessed by only the dead and the mad" (Ross 70). Critics generally agree that the genre called "crime fiction," with its numerous subgenres of cozy, historical, locked room, thriller, and spy novel has its immediate roots in the gothic novel of the eighteenth century. Occupied as the gothic is with the task of uncovering secrets, identifying motives for heinous acts, and restoring justice in human affairs, it prefigures the detection literature that followed. Stories of mysterious family secrets and threatening strangers present the kinds of puzzles and sensational thrills that drew in readers as crime fiction still does today. The gothic novel, then, is "a site of conflict between pre-Enlightenment and post-Enlightenment ideas" (Scaggs 15). Horace Walpole's *Castle of Otranto* (1764), with its brooding and threatening atmosphere, is one of the first gothic novels, along with Ann Radcliffe's *The Mysteries of Udolpho* (1794), later parodied by Jane Austen in *Northanger Abbey* (1818).

While the gothic novel was available to the more literate middle class from the 1760s through the 1820s, there was a market among the lower classes for sensational crime stories featuring criminals like the eighteenth-century highwayman Dick Turpin. The latter's highly romanticized adventures appeared in many iterations, including the Newgate novel *Rookwood* (1834) by William Harrison Ainsworth.

In England, the population, which had almost doubled from the eighteenth to the nineteenth century (Stearns 330), shifted from farms to cities to find factory work. The social control of criminal behavior under the harsh penal laws of the eighteenth century, later called the Bloody Code, had decreed the death penalty or transportation for over two hundred crimes. The code focused generally on the protection of property and restitution of it to the victims, rather than on the formal pursuit of malefactors. Magistrates, usually the local squires, were responsible for law enforcement, assisted by the watch, the local constable, and paid thieftakers; the squires were depicted in novels like Henry Fielding's *Tom Jones* (1749) as ignorant and biased. The law often provided little protection (Bell 7, 9), however, and victims of theft hired private enforcers to regain their property. Because the thieftakers were just as likely to be criminals themselves, they took advantage of unsuspecting clients.

By the early nineteenth century, as a result of the demand for reform, the Bloody Code had reduced the number of crimes for which hanging was mandated to five. Newgate Prison and public hangings on Tyburn Hill had for years drawn crowds seeking sensational spectacles, which sometimes generated as much sympathy as blame for the criminals. Stories of crime and criminals had circulated among the lower, barely literate population in broadsides, ballads, and chapbooks. *The Newgate Calendar*, also known as the *Malefactor's Bloody Register*, first appeared in 1774 as a collection of news items about crimes (Ó Danachair 12). It was intended as a deterrent to crime, and many homes, even among the middle class, regularly kept copies of it. One version shows a mother pointing out to her young son a body hanging on a gibbet with the accompanying advice:

> The anxious Mother with a Parents Care,
> Presents our Labours to her future Heir
> 'The Wise, the Brave, the temperate and the Just,
> Who love their neighbour, and in God who trust

Safe through the Dang'rous paths of Life may Steer,
Nor dread those Evils we exhibit Here.' (10)

Publication ended in the mid-nineteenth century because of conflict over whether this succeeded as warning or fed the appetite for sensationalism, but not before giving rise in the 1820s, '30s, and '40s to the Newgate novel, which capitalized on the same information in dramatized and exaggerated form. In 1868, public executions were discontinued, and by 1902, Newgate Prison had been razed and Tyburn Tree, the infamous gallows at Tyburn Hill, may have been incorporated into the area that today is Hyde Park.

Protests against the Newgate novels appeared in middle-class periodical press throughout the 1830s because of their "moral ambivalence and unwholesome fascination with crime" (Pykett 26). Edward Bulwer-Lytton's *Paul Clifford* (1830) was one of the first of the genre with its atmosphere of brooding threat, which emphasizes its ties to the gothic novel. It is the story, familiar in many subsequent crime stories, of a man who leads a double life as a gentleman and as a criminal; it begins with the famous line "It was a dark and stormy night." Dickens's *Oliver Twist* is a typical Newgate novel in its depiction of the criminal life of characters like Bill Sykes and Fagan.

Closely allied to the Newgate novel was the sensation novel, prominent in the 1860s and '70s. It titillated readers with stories of bigamy, adultery, seduction, and murder occurring even in middle-class homes. Its popularity was fed by "the tendency of both the expanding penny press and middle-class newspapers to include more crime reporting" (Pykett 32). The worsening conditions in the crowded cities and the newspaper coverage kept the focus on the issue of crime and increased the public's appetite for sensation fiction. The novels were serialized in periodicals and newspapers, and lending libraries made them available to the middle class. The penny dreadful provided the same kind of material to the poorer classes. Wilkie Collins's three-volume sensation novel *The Woman in White* (1860) introduced the amateur detective figure of Walter Hartright and used the technique of multiple perspectives, as Agatha Christie later did in *Murder on the Orient Express* (1934). Collins's *The Moonstone* (1868), with the character of Scotland Yard's Sergeant Cuff, is considered "the first detective novel written in English" (Scaggs 23). *Lady Audley's Secret* (1862) by Mary Elizabeth Braddon was one of many sensation novels she authored under her own name and under several pseudonyms. The works of both of these authors have been reproduced on stage and in film; Collins's work was even adapted for television in 2000 and staged as a musical in London's West End in 2004 and on Broadway in 2005. In America, Edgar Allan Poe published what critics call the first detective short story in which the crime is solved by the ratiocination of a brilliant observer of clues. "The Murders in the Rue Morgue" (1841), set in France, introduces C. Auguste Dupin, whose powers of reasoning were later in the century echoed in Arthur Conan Doyle's Sherlock Holmes as well as hosts of others. Poe's story has "certain Gothic trappings with the rationalism of a post-Enlightenment age of science" (Scaggs 19).

Detection on the Continent

France was another European country that manifested a significant development in crime literature. As Sita A. Schütt puts it, "France, then, whose revolutions, coups and insurrections were bred by a dizzying succession of political regimes was a country notorious for its policing" (60). Émile Gaboriau created the character of Monsieur Lecoq in *L'Affaire Lerouge* (1866), based on real-life thief turned police officer Eugène François Vidocq (1775–1857); Vidocq's memoir, *Les vrais mémoires de Vidocq* (The true memories of Vidocq), which Poe had read, mixed fiction and fact. Vidocq was appointed the first director of the Sûreté Nationale in 1811 and founded the first modern detective agency: Le Bureau des renseignements universels dans l'intérêt du commerce (the office of universal information for commerce). Victor Hugo based the characters of thief Jean Valjean and Inspector Javert in *Les Misérables* on Vidocq ("Vie").

Gaston Leroux in *The Mystery of the Yellow Chamber* (1908) and Georges Simenon with his eighty-four Jules Maigret novels in the twentieth century continued this development of crime fiction on the Continent. Maigret is a contemporary character "grimly aware of social reality [who] refuses to vilify those who have 'wronged' society" (Schütt 74).

Police Departments and Detective Agencies

The development of detective agencies paralleled and, in some cases, preceded that of police departments. The Bow Street Runners, founded in 1749 by the author and magistrate Henry Fielding, worked on commission out of the magistrates' office on Bow Street in London; they were thieftakers who were themselves often "on the take," like Jonathan Wild. Robert Peel's "peelers," or "bobbies," came into existence in 1822, and the Runners were disbanded in 1839. In America, Allan Pinkerton opened his detective agency, Pinkerton's National Detective Agency, in Chicago in 1850 (Scaggs 17), which remains in operation.

The need for more formal law enforcement led to the growing numbers of police forces in Europe and America: Robert Peel's Metropolitan Police in London in 1829, the Boston Police Department in 1838, and the New York Municipal Police (called the Day and Night Police) in 1845. These organizations developed a more scientific approach to policing, especially recognizing, as Peel did, the need for record keeping. The invention of photography in 1839 led to the publication of rogues' galleries of criminals, such as Philip Farley's *Criminals of America; or, Tales of the lives of thieves, Enabling everyone to be his own detective. With portraits making a complete rogues' gallery* in 1876 (Panek 8). Before the adoption of identification through fingerprinting in the mid-1890s (48), there was an interest in the use of phrenology to discover criminal types through configurations of the human skull.

The development of scientific tools in police work included forensics, ballistics, and DNA testing, which radically improved evidence gathering, along with databases such as the FBI's Violent Criminal Apprehension program (ViCAP) and its Integrated Automated Fingerprint Identification System (IAFIS). Cell phones, surveillance cameras, and a host of other innovations have altered the process of crime detection, which today relies as much on technology as on traditional processes of deduction.

Police officers were generally drawn from the lower classes and often received little respect from the public. In New York, the police owed their jobs to the political machine of Tammany Hall, which commonly demanded bribes for appointments to the police department (Panek 45). Until the development of the police procedural in the twentieth century, police in crime fiction also tended to be the inadequate, bungling, or corrupt figures who served as effective foils for the brilliance of the amateur detective protagonist. One of the best known of these is, of course, the character of Inspector Lestrade, who needs the analytical skills of Sherlock Holmes to solve crimes.

The most famous of all detectives, Sherlock Holmes, appeared in the first of four novels by Arthur Conan Doyle, *A Study in Scarlet* (1887). As a master of ratiocination, Holmes, whose exploits appear in over fifty short stories, exhibits mastery of logical deduction. So important is the role of reasoning, claims Howard Haycraft, that "the one completely unforgivable sin in the detective story is the substitution, at any point, of accident, chance, or coincident for logical deduction" (258). Holmes has a direct descendent in Philo Vance, created by S. S. Van Dine (Willard Huntington Wright) in "intricate, learning-heavy New York puzzles [that] dominated the US market" (Knight 83). Doyle's short stories especially influenced the form of American crime stories, which previously had been largely full-length novels serialized in the press (Panek 58). As the premier exemplar of the amateur detective, Holmes has appeared and reappeared in print, film, and television on both sides of the Atlantic. The American actor William Gillette played the character on stage more than a thousand times, introducing Holmes's trademark deerstalker cap and curved pipe. He also starred in a silent motion picture version in 1916 and on radio in 1930 (Moody 228; Panek 105).

But just as in the past, there were also characters who were both criminals and crime solvers; the mirror image of Holmes appeared in the character of A. J. Raffles in *The Amateur Cracksman* (1899) by E. W. Hornung, Doyle's brother-in-law. Raffles is a thief who "varied his burglarious career with detection" (Haycraft 81) and has the same talent for disguise as Holmes. Raffles too has his own Dr. Watson in the person of his old school chum Harry "Bunny" Manders. This detective/criminal character appears repeatedly in crime fiction, underscoring the sometimes-blurred connection between crime and detection, and presenting the criminal as the one most familiar with the process of both performing and exposing the criminal acts. The subgenre, called "rogue fiction," introduces hosts of thieves, swindlers, and murderers, and echoes the reality of the violence outside the pages of crime fiction—from the brutalities of the nineteenth-century labor riots to Jack the Ripper's infamous unsolved murder of six women in 1888 and to the horrors of World War I.

The Golden Age

The period between the two World Wars saw a flourishing of crime fiction so pervasive and widespread it was dubbed the genre's golden age. E. C. Bentley's *Trent's Last Case* (1913; *The Woman in Black* in the United States) introduced a new style of detective fiction in a more contemporary vein, with an "urbane naturalism" (Haycraft 115). The period also introduced the Queens of Crime: Agatha Christie, Dorothy Sayers, Margery Allingham, and New Zealander Ngaio Marsh, which some see leading to the feminization of crime fiction (Horsley 38). Although women had always contributed to the genre, female writers came into prominence with the debuts of Hercule Poirot in Christie's *The Mysterious Affair at Styles* (1920); Sayers's Lord Peter Wimsey in *Whose Body?* (1923); Albert Campion in Allingham's *The Crime at Black Dudley* (1929); and Marsh's Roderick Alleyn in *A Man Lay Dead* (1934). Sometimes referred to as the American Agatha Christie, Mary Roberts Rinehart introduced a light tone in *The Circular Staircase* (1908) with the narrator Rachael Innes, who "never loses her pluck" (Panek 78). Women were usually not, except for Christie's Miss Marple, the detective characters, although as Maureen Reddy points out in her discussion of women detectives, there were many more than some contemporary criticism acknowledged (191). She makes the argument that the usual description of crime fiction "as a movement from man to man, beginning with Edgar Allan Poe, then Arthur Conan Doyle, followed by Dashiell Hammett and so on" is "a distorted and partial history" (Reddy 191), which ignores the substantial body of material by and about women. Settings in many novels in this period tended to be, although not exclusively, in confined areas as in the country house, depicting "small-scale, intimate crimes at the heart of modern middle- and upper-class homes" (Priestman 4). There were also socially enclosed stories in which "lower classes, especially professional criminals, play a very minor role" (Knight 78).

In America, *The Roman Hat Mystery* (1929), by the cousins Frederic Dannay and Manfred B. Lee, introduced the fictional detective Ellery Queen and initiated a series of successful clue-puzzle detective stories that emphasized puzzles and fair play (Scaggs 28). The 1920s also saw the crossword puzzle craze, which "fuse[d] play with the illusion of mental exercise and this corresponded to latent tendencies in the detective story" (Panek 107). The fictional detective Ellery Queen had a long and successful career in print, on radio, and in film; from 1941 onward, Dannay and Lee edited Ellery Queen's *Mystery Magazine* (Knight 83). As the twentieth century progressed, the range of characters occupied with detection grew exponentially. G. K. Chesterton's moral universe of the Father Brown stories first appeared in *Storyteller* magazine in 1910 and in five collections between 1911 and 1935. These stories place "more emphasis . . . on divine than human order," and Fr. Brown is depicted as "gifted with the power of noticing what no one else can see . . . a kind of 'transcendental' Sherlock Holmes" (Horsley 34–35).

Hard-Boiled Private Eyes

The period after World War I, as well as giving rise to the golden age crime fiction, saw America change into "a new fast-evolving social and material environment" dominated by the advance of capitalism and new wealth (Porter 96). In the Roaring Twenties, Prohibition fed a rise in organized crime. Al Capone, who smuggled bootleg liquor, ran prostitution rings in Chicago, and was responsible for the St. Valentine's Day Massacre, was a public figure who, like some criminals before him, garnered sympathy by contributing openly to charity. The general flouting of Prohibition and the public awareness of police corruption generated an increase in private detective agencies and helped popularize the private eye in fiction, a figure characterized not by "superhuman intellectual skills but . . . [by] toughness and tenacity" (Horsley 73). The genre was primarily an American phenomenon, encapsulating frontier spirit in much of the popular American literature of the period (Porter 97). Such works, written by authors like Bret Harte and Jack London, glorified the strong and independent loner who is smarter and tougher than the outlaws he encounters. The hard-boiled private eye inhabits the mean streets of the inner cities and relies not on the questionable protection of corrupt or inadequate police, but on his own sense of honor and obligation, with a cynicism about notions of justice and fair play that leads to a kind of moral ambiguity in the stories. Raymond Chandler analyzes the stylistic elements of this radically new fiction in his essay "The Simple Art of Murder" (1944). The hard-boiled private eye is the antithesis of the suave gentleman-investigator who appears in so many of the golden age stories. Four authors—Dashiell Hammett, Raymond Chandler, Ross Macdonald, and James M. Cain—are identified with the beginning of private-eye fiction. Hammett, who had been a Pinkerton agent, was first published in *Black Mask* magazine with his characters, the nameless Continental Op in *Red Harvest* (1929) and Sam Spade in *The Maltese Falcon* (1930). Raymond Chandler followed Hammett with *The Big Sleep* (1939), featuring detective Philip Marlowe, "a big man unperturbed by violence" who is not "alienated from, but aloof from, the world in which he participates" (Panek 146, 147). These stories raised crime fiction to "a new peak of excellence and popularity" as Chandler's "lean, dynamic and unsentimental narratives created a definite American style" (Haycraft 169). Cain's *The Postman Always Rings Twice* (1934)—with a mix of sex and violence that caused it to be banned in Boston—narrates the story from the perspective of the criminal, the drifter Frank Chambers, in a jail cell (Scaggs 109). In *The Doomsters* (1958), Ross Macdonald's detective Lew Archer and other characters are quite different, as they are dominated not by "the pressure of socio-economic circumstance," but rather by a kind of "Freudian cultural determinism" (Horsley 96). The private eye genre at its most violent appears in Mickey Spillane's *I, the Jury* (1947), with its "graphic representation of scenes of mayhem," and Mike Hammer as a "super-macho punisher-hero" who relies on his fists and gun (Porter 111; Horsley 88). Stylistically, the tough street language used by the hard-boiled private eye owed a debt to the realism of twentieth-century American fiction typified in the prose of Ernest Hemingway, naturalists like Stephen Crane, and muckraking journalists like Lincoln Steffens (Porter 96).

Police Procedural
The police procedural of the mid-century contrasts with the hard-boiled private eye stories. These tales revolve around the teamwork of the police, whose use of new technologies of crime detection shifts the emphasis from ratiocination to the determination and dogged footwork it takes to patiently pile up the clues that make the case. In these stories, one of the first of which is Ed McBain's Eighty-Seventh Precinct novel *Cop Hater* (1956), the police play by the rules.

Mid-Century Changes

During the post–World War II period, the civil rights movement caused a major shift in the culture of the time, analogous in dimension to the shift that occurred with the nineteenth-century Industrial Revolution, and opened crime fiction to a new set of perspectives. Feminism gave rise to the creation of female protagonists such as Cordelia Gray in P. D. James's *An Unsuitable Job for a Woman* (1972), Sharon McCone in Marcia Muller's *Edwin of the Iron Shoes* (1977), and Sue Grafton's Kinsey Milhone in *A Is for Alibi* (1982), characters far different from the gentle and genteel Miss Marple. In addition, the recognition of the presence and rights of ethnic and racial minorities led authors like Tony Hillerman to introduce Joe Leaphorn and Jim Chee of the Navajo tribal police in *The Blessing Way* (1970) and Chester Himes to present black New York City policemen Coffin Ed Johnson and Grave Digger Jones in *A Rage in Harlem* (1957). Norlisha F. Crawford's chapter in this volume examines three African American authors of crime fiction. From this point on, protagonists in crime fiction came from jobs and professions of every kind. Historical mysteries showcase wildly diverse figures, such as Lindsey Davis's Falco in ancient Rome, Brother Cadfael in Ellis Peters's twelfth-century Benedictine monastery, and Margaret Frazer's Joliffe, a wandering player in the fifteenth.

Publishing

The publishing industry flourished with a number of factors contributing to its success at fulfilling the growing demand for crime fiction and true crime stories. Stories of crime have proved irresistible to the public from the early chapbooks and single-sheet broadsides through the gothic, Newgate, and sensation novels and short stories that showcased feats of detection by professionals and amateurs alike. The newly literate audience among the working poor demanded cheap reading matter, so in the 1840s in Germany, F. G. Keller's invention of wood pulp paper and the mechanical printing presses enabled the circulation of the wider variety of written material, such as the penny dreadful and dime novels. The identification with these cheap forms stamped crime fiction as lowbrow, and it was not until the golden age between the two World Wars that the genre began to transcend this limitation. From the end of the nineteenth through the mid-twentieth century, publishers also produced hundreds of crime magazines with a readership in the millions. Many authors, particularly in America, were journalists and editors who could fill pages cheaply, and some writers of "serious fiction" also turned out crime fiction under pseudonyms.

The first pulp-fiction magazine is commonly identified as Frank Munsey's *Argosy* magazine (Panek 109). After a number of false starts and financial collapses in New York, the magazine became a monthly in 1896 and, in six years, was producing half a million copies each month. By the peak years of the 1920s and 1930s, Munsey and other publishers sold up to one million copies per issue of magazines like *The Strand*, *Pearson's*, and *Windsor*, which "were designed for men, though they often had sections for the family" (Knight 81). Perhaps the best known of the crime magazines was *Black Mask* (1920–51), founded by H. L. Mencken and George Jean Nathan. It contained realism and violence, and its popularity rested on the fact that in its pages that "the hard-boiled private detective fired his first shot" (Horsley 76). Dashiell Hammett's detectives, the Continental Op and Sam Spade, first appeared there, as did Raymond Chandler's Philip Marlow. *Black Mask* first identified itself on the 1920 cover as "A Magazine of Mystery, Romance, and Adventure" but, by the spring of 1922, had changed its tagline to "A Magazine of Mystery and Detective Stories." The paper shortages during World War II hastened the end of pulp publishing, which after mid-century was replaced largely by paperbacks, comic books, and television. The appeal of the genre, however, remains strong: Quentin Tarantino's successful film, *Pulp Fiction* (whose inspiration was drawn from *Black Mask*) in 1994 re-creates the atmosphere of the private eye's mean streets with telling effectiveness.

Prizes

As the supply and demand for crime fiction continued to grow, organizations of publishers, writers, and fans also grew. In the latter half of the twentieth century, many of the organizations began to hold regular conventions and award prizes in a range of subgenres. This draws attention to some of the thousands of works of crime fiction published worldwide annually, both increasing sales and establishing criteria for success. One of the better known is the Agatha Award, named after Agatha Christie and given by Malice Domestic, to works that embody Christie's style—that is, a limited environment such as the country house or a train (*Murder on the Orient Express*), an amateur detective, and no violence or sex. The Mystery Writers of America's Edgar Award is named in honor of Edgar Allan Poe and given by a vote on the year's mysteries in print, television, and film. Mystery Readers International presents the annual Macavity Award, which takes its name from the mystery cat in T. S. Eliot's *Old Possum's Book of Practical Cats*. More than fifty such awards for crime fiction in all its forms are given worldwide, testimony not only to the universal appeal of the genre but also its economic success.

New Media

Crime fiction in the twentieth century extended into the new media with advances in the technology of movies, television, audiobooks, board games, web-based and video games, and podcasts. From the first Sherlock Holmes silent movie in 1903 to contemporary video games such as The Case of the Cyber Criminal, the appeal of these new forms has proved as strong as the appeal of the criminal stories of the *Newgate Calendar* two-and-a-half centuries ago. The film noir in the Hollywood of the 1930s gave face and voice to the classic hard-boiled private eyes in trench coats and fedoras from the pages of the pulps, novels, and detective magazines after World War I, and to various incarnations of Sherlock Holmes, Miss Marple, Charlie Chan, Philo Vance, and dozens of other popular figures. *The Naked City* (1948) is a classic police procedural film in which a team of detectives cooperates to find a young model's killer. The black-and-white film and the shots of actual locations in New York present police work with a verisimilitude characteristic of the genre. In the 1930s, radio shows like *True Detective Mysteries*, based on stories from *True Detective Magazine*, began to broadcast. Joseph Paul Moser's essay in this work discusses film noir in depth.

Television seized the genre early on, making crime stories into the staple they remain. *Martin Kane* (1949–54) was immensely popular on both radio and television and was the first of what would become a long stream of video private eyes. The *CSI: Crime Scene Investigation* episode "Unfriendly Skies," which aired December 8, 2000, was a reworking of *Murder on the Orient Express*, a closed-room mystery that in this rendition takes place in the first-class section of a commercial plane (Scaggs 53). *Dragnet* (1951–59) brought Sgt. Joe Friday and the police procedural to the small screen, and *The Untouchables* (1959–63) capitalized on the work of real-life federal agent Elliot Ness and the FBI against the organized crime of the 1920s. In the 1970s and 1980s, police procedural shows appeared with characters like Columbo, Kojak, and the female duo of Cagney and Lacey.

Games, both board games and web-based games, have an affinity with crime fiction in that both require the reader/character/player to make choices. The online game L. A. Noire "evolved from a 19th-century literary tradition that involved contests of deduction and linear modes of problem-solving . . . into something darker and more nuanced—something that offered less certain outcomes" (Clute and Edwards). In perhaps the most modern iteration of the game, L. A. Noire is both an interactive online game and a collection of hard-boiled short stories by noted authors invited to reflect on the game, breaching the boundaries between media.

Conclusion

In addition to the literary respectability that authors and critics brought to the genre of crime fiction and true crime stories, the growth of the publishing industry and the increase of literacy in the nineteenth and twentieth century built a lucrative market that became a dominant force in the development of the genre. The stream of crime fiction produced mysteries that have been categorized, subcategorized, adapted to the airwaves, radio, and recordings, and small and large screens of every kind. Good, bad, indifferent, and occasionally stunning, stories of crime and detection have emerged across the globe in diverse cultures, reflecting philosophical, cultural, and political differences while retaining the essential qualities of crime solving. Critics have examined some of the larger implications of the popularity of the genre, with some seeing it "as a form so committed to the restoration of the status quo that it can only be seen as being in thrall to the existing social order," while others emphasize "the alienation of the private eye" and "the moral ambiguity of the resolution" of the crimes (Horsley 10). Professionals and amateur protagonists of every variety face the challenges of collecting clues and of uncovering the how of method and the why of motivation. However justice is defined, the genre of crime fiction wrestles with the concept from every perspective, in cultures and over continents, so that whatever justice the individual and society demands might ultimately be served.

Works Cited

Bell, Ian A. "Eighteenth-Century Crime Writing." Priestman 7–17. Print.
Clute, Shannon, and Richard L. Edwards. "Episode 51: L.A. Noire." *Out of the Past: Investigating Film Noir.* Clute and Edwards, 16 Aug. 2011. Web. 15 Oct. 2012.
Haycraft, Howard. *Murder for Pleasure: The Life and Times of the Detective Story.* New York: Carroll, 1984. Print.
Horsley, Lee. *Twentieth-Century Crime Fiction.* New York: Oxford UP, 2005. Print.
Knight, Stephen. "The Golden Age." Priestman 77–94. Print.
Moody, Nickianne. "Crime in Film and on TV." Priestman 227–44. Print.
Ó Danachair, Donol, ed. "The Newgate Calendar." Vol. 1. *Ex-classics.com.* Ex-classics Project, 2009. PDF file.
Panek, LeRoy Lad. *Probable Cause: Crime Fiction in America.* Bowling Green: Bowling Green State U Popular P, 1990. Print.
Porter, Dennis. "The Private Eye." Priestman 95–113. Print.

Priestman, Martin, ed. *The Cambridge Companion to Crime Fiction.* New York: Cambridge UP, 2003. Print.

Pykett, Lyn. "The Newgate Novel and Sensation Fiction, 1830–1868." Priestman 19–39. Print.

Reddy, Maureen T. "Women Detectives." Priestman 191–207. Print.

Ross, Alex. "The Shock of the True." *New Yorker* 19 Aug. 1996: 70–77. Print.

Scaggs, John. *Crime Fiction.* New York: Routledge, 2005. Print.

Schütt, Sita A. "French Crime Fiction." Priestman 59–76. Print.

Smith, Kevin Burton, ed. "Martin Kane." *Thrilling Detective Web Site.* Kevin Burton Smith, 2012. Web. 18 Oct. 2012.

Stearns, Peter N. *World History: Patterns of Change and Continuity.* New York: Harper, 1987. Print.

"La Vie de Monsiuer Vidocq." *Vidocq Society.* Vidocq Society, 5 July 2012. Web. 18 Oct. 2012.

"Your Sin Will Find You Out": Critical Perceptions of Mystery Fiction

Elizabeth Foxwell

In 1894, British-born novelist Amelia E. Barr wondered if "the game between criminals and detectives . . . may not be a kind of criminal school, for those whose inclinations lead them in that direction" (593–94). This statement reflects a prevalent perception of mystery and detective fiction as mere, possibly subversive, entertainment that lingers today—despite the inclusion of mystery novels in eminent series such as the Library of America, the considerable critical work that has highlighted its literary merits and motifs, and its distinct moral overtones in good usually triumphing over evil. As Dorothy L. Sayers notes, "It is part of their [detective authors'] job to believe and to maintain that Your Sin Will Find You Out. That is why Detective Fiction is, or should be, such a good influence in a degenerate world" (2).

This chapter will examine the reception of mystery fiction by critics and readers, including reaction to Anna Katharine Green's *The Leavenworth Case* (1878), James M. Cain's *Double Indemnity* (1936), Margery Allingham's *The Tiger in the Smoke* (1952), and Nicholas Meyer's *The Seven-Per-Cent Solution* (1974), as the reaction to these works illuminate certain anxieties and aspects of society. Essential critical pieces on the mystery form, such as W. H. Auden's 1948 "The Guilty Vicarage," also will be discussed.

The Appeal—and Dismissal—of Mystery Fiction

There are various theories on the appeal of mystery fiction to readers, as well as explanations for its perception in some quarters as an unmistakably lowbrow form of literature. Tensions also can be seen between advocates of the English and the American detective story.

In 1901, G. K. Chesterton, the creator of the sleuthing Father Brown, wrote that the detective story is "the earliest and only form of popular literature in which is expressed some sense of the poetry of modern life" (119). In 1911, Ronald A. Knox identified elements of Arthur Conan Doyle's Sherlock Holmes stories that were drawn from classic Greek drama, such as Dr. Watson as chorus. In 1913, mystery author Carolyn Wells stated, "It is the people who are interested in answers who care for detective stories. It is the people who care for the solution of a problem who write and read mystery tales" (4–5). In 1919, mystery writer Anna Katharine Green asserted that murder was the most interesting subject for a mystery tale because, for the reader, "you feel that you *must* know what those silent lips would tell if they could only speak" ("Human Beings" 84; emphasis in orig.).

Julian Symons likens the detective to a "witch doctor who is able to smell out the evil that is corrupting society, and pursue it, through what may be a variety of disguises, to its source" and states that what crime fiction offered from 1890 to the 1940s was "a reassuring world in which those who tried to disturb the established order were always discovered and punished" (15, 16). Reinforcing this view more recently, P. D. James, creator of New Scotland Yard's Adam Dalgliesh, writes that the detective story "confirms our hope that, despite some evidence to the contrary, we live in a beneficent and moral universe in which problems can be solved by rational means and peace and order restored from communal or personal disruption and chaos" (174).

Jacques Barzun posits that because some tales of detection involve material clues, these are cast as mere "mechanical puzzles," which are disliked by readers only interested in "mysteries of the soul"; says Barzun, readers "conclude that detective fiction, being of the order of riddles, can have no connection with literature" (145). Richard Raskin discusses detective fiction's role in undercutting or reinforcing social myths and teaching critical thinking skills. He also deems that detective fiction appeals psychologically to the reader for three major reasons: *ludic*, which involves an aspect of play for the reader; *wish-fulfillment*, which involves the reader in a vicarious experience of adventure or identification with protagonist and/or victim; and *tension-reducing*, which involves the cathartic release of "guilt or anxiety" for the reader (71). Guilt is the major theme in W. H. Auden's "The Guilty Vicarage," as he states that "the interest in the study of a murderer is the observation, by the innocent many, of the sufferings of the guilty one. The interest in the detective story is the dialectic of innocence and guilt" (16). The detective story reader, says Auden, desires to return to the Garden of Eden in a "fantasy of escape" (24).

Raymond Chandler believed that escape occurred in "*all* reading for pleasure"; he held "no particular brief for the detective story as the ideal escape" ("Simple Art" 14; emphasis in orig.). Although the Chicago-born Chandler spent his early years in England, he displayed irritation with the "arid formula" of English detective stories and with the critical perception of US mystery writers as "the Junior Varsity" ("Simple Art" 14, 11). In "The Simple Art of Murder," Chandler casts the English detective story tradition as unrealistic and the American as realistic, whereas his classic expression of "down these mean streets a man must go who is not himself mean" (20) displays a decided romanticism and constructs the detective as the sole arbitrator of justice— one that also exists in the English tradition. Robert B. Parker, who created just such a lone knight with his private eye Spenser, discussed a dimension that sets the US detective apart from the English detective, describing in his dissertation the connections between the frontiersman of the American West and the urban American PI as exemplified by Dashiell Hammett's Continental Op, Raymond Chandler's Philip Marlowe, and Ross Macdonald's Lew Archer. In recognizing these connections, Parker also may have revealed a reason for the appeal of works with such detectives, given their play on facets of American myth and identity.

One of the most notorious dismissals of mystery fiction is Edmund Wilson's "Who Cares Who Killed Roger Ackroyd?" (1945), written as part of a series of articles for the *New Yorker*. In it, Wilson refers to the uproar after the publication of his first article criticizing mystery fiction and then proceeds to dismiss nearly all the authors subsequently recommended by readers; these include British writers Margery

Allingham and Dorothy L. Sayers and New Zealander Ngaio Marsh. Qualified respect is paid to certain works of John Dickson Carr and Raymond Chandler (both Americans). The mystery genre, states Wilson, is "a field which is mostly on a sub-literary level" (259), although he had previously offered some diluted praise for James M. Cain in his 1940 essay "The Boys in the Back Room" (19–22).

There have been those who have sounded the death knell for mystery fiction. Somerset Maugham believed that imitators lacking the skills of Hammett and Chandler "killed the genre" with detectives "so outrageous that they have become preposterous" (121). Science fiction writer John Wyndham predicted that sci-fi would replace detective fiction because "the number of people bored with routine detective stories has been increasing" (1). More than fifty years after these dire predictions, the genre still flourishes because, according to Robin Winks, it "continues to mirror society, not only in its concern, its moral awareness, and its language. It helps tell us who and where we are, as individuals" (Introduction 9).

The Leavenworth Case: An American Pioneer

Although Anna Katharine Green often is credited erroneously with creating the first American detective novel[1] with her first book, *The Leavenworth Case* (1878), she faced sexism and mixed reviews in the immediate aftermath of the novel's publication.[1] Praise tended to arrive later, as her publisher acknowledged in a December 1905 ad in the *Bookman*: "The book that becomes a classic rarely attracts great popular attention when first published. It begins its life quietly and modestly, and steadily wins its way into the favor of the intelligent public by merit. . . . Such is the history of *The Wide, Wide World, Uncle Tom's Cabin, The Leavenworth Case*" (71). *The Leavenworth Case* seems to have been affected by its status as a first novel—that is, in reviewers identifying weaknesses in composition ("a clever but inexperienced hand," according to the *New York Herald*) and in periodicals declining to review it. There is no *New York Times* review of the book, and it is listed only under "publications received" in the *North American Review* and "books received" in *Lippincott's Magazine*. Its status as a work of detective fiction and the fact that its author was a thirty-two-year-old woman—albeit one of the country's earliest female college graduates—also must be considered in determining its likelihood to be reviewed and, when reviewed, to receive a fair evaluation.

An aspiring poet and the daughter of a lawyer, Green was inspired to write her first novel by the work of French mystery writer Émile Gaboriau, seeking an antidote to boredom after earning her degree [Hatch 160; Maida 21–22; Woodward 168–69]. She constructed a murder of millionaire Horatio Leavenworth behind his locked library door, with suspicion swirling around his servants, his nieces Mary and Eleanore, and his secretary, James Harwell. Detective Ebenezer Gryce investigates.

Some did recognize the skill of the writer. Wilkie Collins—to whom Green was often compared in *Leavenworth* reviews and whose technique in *The Woman in White* is echoed in Green's novel (W. Collins 455)—wrote George Haven Putnam, Green's publisher, with his reaction to the book. Stated Collins, "Her powers of invention are so remarkable—she has so much imagination and so much belief (a most important qualification for our art) in what she writes, that I have nothing to report of myself, so far, but most sincere admiration" (qtd. in Putnam 52). After noting a few deficiencies, the reviewer in *The Literary World* singled out the book's "ingenious planning and patient execution, indicative of genuine talent" (28). "Told with a force and power that indicate great dramatic talent in the writer," summed up the *St. Louis Post-Dispatch* (2).

A preoccupation with the author's gender is evident in some reviews of *The Leavenworth Case*. Although mentioning *Leavenworth*'s "effective plot," the *Daily Alta California* opined, "It is a remarkable book to come from the pen of a woman" ("New Publications" 1). "That a lady should have displayed such knowledge of the methods of law as is manifest in this exciting story, is a pleasant surprise," stated the *New*

Orleans Times-Picayune (11). The book, noted the *Saturday Review*, is "marked here and there by signs of a lady's imperfect acquaintance even with criminal law, the simplest part of the science most perplexing to her sex" ("American Literature" 126). Wrote the *New York Evening Express*, "It seems almost impossible that so ingeniously written, so powerfully dramatic and ingeniously constructed a novel should have emanated from the pen of a woman—it is mannish, from cover to cover" (1). Stated L. B. Lang in *The Academy*, Green "has proved herself as well able to write an interesting a story of mysterious crime as any man living" (160).

Green did not believe that her mystery works would inspire criminal acts, because she did not "put the emphasis on the *manner* of the act, but on the motives behind it and on the novel and strange situations which come in working out the mystery" ("Human Beings" 86; emphasis in orig.). She confessed to one occasion of unease, when she dispatched one victim via a hatpin and feared that she had "suggested a new way of crime. When I found that murders had actually been committed in that way *before* I wrote the book, I was intensely relieved" (86; emphasis in orig.).

In 1886, a charge of plagiarism was leveled against *The Leavenworth Case* in *The Literary World*, refuted by Green's publisher, G. P. Putnam's Sons, and later by Nickerson. They both concluded that it was merely the author's attempt to increase sales for his or her work. The writer was signed "Stylus," which Nickerson identifies as the anonymous author of the 1877 novel *All for Her*, also known under the titles *St. Jude's Assistant* and *A Cruel Secret* (232 n15). She states that the two books bear little resemblance to each other.

In 1884, the French newspaper *Le Livre* reported that *The Leavenworth Case* was a great success in America, having sold 70,000 copies, although it mistakenly attributed the novel to Wilkie Collins ("Gazette" 333). A Putnam ad in the March 26, 1898, issue of the *Critic* stated that *The Leavenworth Case* had sold 100,000 copies; at the time of Green's death in 1935, the number of copies sold was listed as more than 150,000 ("Anna K. Green Dies"). In 1888, a writer friend of Green—her cousin was Green's sister-in-law—reported that *The Leavenworth Case* had been used at Yale to demonstrate the pitfalls of circumstantial evidence and that Chief Justice Morrison Waite had called the book "the greatest work ever written by a woman" in 1882 (Hatch 161). It was adapted as a play in 1891, which later starred Green's husband, Charles Rohlfs (Maida 25–26), and as films in 1923 and 1936. The book appears on the Haycraft Queen Cornerstones list of essential mystery works (R. Collins, "Haycraft Queen"). S. S. Van Dine, creator of detective Philo Vance, sums up its legacy this way:

> It did more, perhaps, than any other book to familiarize the English-speaking public with a genre which, at that time, had not yet become definitely recognized as a distinct and unique type of literary entertainment, either in England or in America. And, in thus creating a consciousness of the detective novel as a definite form of literary art, it was of supreme importance. (iv–v)

Double Indemnity: Attraction and Repulsion

In the preface to *Three of a Kind* (1943), James M. Cain wrote that he was "probably the most mis-read, mis-reviewed, and misunderstood novelist now writing. . . . I make no conscious effort to be tough, or hard-boiled, or grim, or any of the things I am usually called" (vii, viii). Cain's aggrieved tone and repudiation of labels can be understood when considering the reaction to *Double Indemnity* and the censorship that resulted in Cain losing a considerable amount of money.

Double Indemnity had its roots in an anecdote told by Cain's journalist colleague Arthur Krock, as well as Cain's past experience in insurance and his father's position in an insurance company (Madden 29). Cain stated that because he needed cash, he wrote it "very slapdash and very quick" (qtd. in Brunette and Peary 125) and told his agent that it was "a piece of tripe" (Skenazy 34). An interesting phenomenon of attraction/repulsion can be seen toward *Double Indemnity*'s narrative of an insurance man colluding with a glamorous blonde to kill her husband and collect the insurance money. Readers reportedly lined up at newsstands as the periodical *Liberty* published each new installment in early 1936 when Cain was forty-three (Hoopes 276); *Double Indemnity* was published as part of the book *Three of a Kind* in 1943. As Arthur Frederic Otis wrote in a review in the *Chicago Daily Tribune*, "You won't like it, but you can't leave it" (E16). *Time* magazine called Cain "one of the world's most vivid tellers of dingy stories" and characterized *Double Indemnity* as "carnal and criminal" ("Dingy Storyteller"; "New Pictures"). John Hutchens in the *New York Times* called Cain "a first-rate storyteller" (BR 7). Raymond Chandler—who adapted Cain's novella for the screen and was polite in a 1944 letter to Cain, especially about his dialogue—had previously called Cain "every kind of writer I detest, a faux naif" in a 1942 letter to Blanche Knopf (*Selected Letters* 28, 23).[2] He likened Cain's writing to a "brothel with a smell of cheap scent in the front parlor and a bucket of slops at the back door" (23). Journalist Martha Gellhorn took issue with Cain's "godawful endings" (119), and professor-writer Albert Murray, in a letter to Ralph Ellison, called Cain's work "crap."

The *Times Literary Supplement* did not review *Double Indemnity* after its British release in 1945. In the same year, *Double Indemnity* was issued in an Armed Services edition for US service personnel. In 2005, West Point professor Elizabeth Samet noted regarding mailing books to a soldier named Andrew in Iraq, "I have also sent James M. Cain's *Double Indemnity*. . . . Cain turns out to be as big a hit with Andrew's platoon, which evidently has a taste for the hardboiled, as he had been with my father in the Second World War." Writing after the reissue of *Double Indemnity* in 1969, fellow mystery author Ross Macdonald viewed the novella as "a rather large action boiled down to a concentration approaching that of dramatic poetry" (BR49). Leonard Cassuto sees direct links in Cain's work to the domestic themes of nineteenth-century sentimental fiction (89).

Film adaptation also demonstrated the attraction/repulsion dichotomy. When Cain's agent shopped the novella to Hollywood in 1935, the Hays Office censored it, citing its "illicit and adulterous sex relationship," "low tone," and "sordid flavor" (Phillips 54). Interestingly, it also stated that *Double Indemnity* could be used as a "blueprint for murder" (54)—another occasion of the fear of mystery fiction inspiring criminal activity. Although Billy Wilder succeeded in obtaining Hays Office approval in 1943, Cain first deemed the delay had lost him ten thousand dollars and later revised his estimate to hundreds of thousands (Cain, "Postman Rings Thrice"; Brunette and Peary 127). Actor Brian Donlevy, offered the role of insurance agent-turned-murderer Walter Neff, turned it down as "too distasteful" ("Screen News" 8). Singer Kate Smith, best known for her rendition of "God Bless America," urged moviegoers to stay away from the film because of its "scabrous view of American life," but the opposite seems to have occurred (Wuntch D3), and the film is considered important in the development of film noir.

Unease also may surround *Double Indemnity*'s literal femme fatale, Phyllis, who lures Walter from the straight and narrow to murder and his own death. As Elisabeth Bronfen notes in the context of the film, Phyllis "chooses destruction at every turn" (104); the text is more explicit about her obsession with death (see Cain, *Three of a Kind* 326). Thus, *Double Indemnity*, which is told from Walter's point of view, can be read as a cautionary tale against the power of women to lead men into ruin.

The Tiger in the Smoke: An Author Shifts Gears

In a 1941 Columbia University Press poll, British author Margery Allingham was ranked number eight of the top ten favorite mystery writers ("Who Done It" 19). At the time of publication of *The Tiger in the Smoke* in 1952, she was forty-eight years old and had published over twenty books, most featuring sleuth Albert Campion. She described her technique in general as "a surprise every tenth page and a shock every twentieth" ("Margery Allingham" 5). But in *Tiger*'s examination of good and evil and a hunt in the London fog (the "smoke") for the serial killer with the evocative name of Jack Havoc, Allingham was attempting to write a different sort of novel than one presenting a single murder and subsequent investigation. The results were mixed in a critical sense, although Allingham biographer Julia Jones noted that the author did well with revenue from book royalties and serialization (291). *Tiger* was a selection of the Doubleday Book Club in 1952 ("Book Club Selections" 258) and appeared in *John Bull* in early 1952 as well as in the *Boston Globe* from February to May 1953.

Some reactions reflect dissatisfaction with Allingham breaking away from her customary whodunit to write a crime novel. In the *New York Times*, Anthony Boucher called the book "an ambitious and often wonderful failure . . . which fell apart both as fiction and as detection," although he acknowledged that it had her "finest writing and characterization to date" (BR17). *Times Literary Supplement* reviewer Maurice Lane Richardson likened the novel to "an unevenly baked cake in which there are too many different kinds of fruit" (497). Noted thriller author Graham Greene viewed *Tiger* as "absurd," "unreal," and "an irritation" (55), whereas Ralph Partridge thought Allingham lacked "the masculine cut and thrust of the old master [Edgar Wallace]" (218). Later, Luana Ellis judged it "oddly disappointing" (130), and writer Nicolas Freeling, who displayed a prejudice against Allingham's type of mystery, called it "deplorable trash" (130).

Others recognized the strengths of the book, however. Alice Hackett in *Publishers Weekly* lauded its "good characterization, good suspense, thrills, and mystery" (435). The *Boston Globe*'s Avis DeVoto thought it "the best Allingham yet" (A29), and Ainslie Baker in *Australian Women's Weekly* considered it "creepy, ingenious" (2). *Kirkus* called it "satisfying", and the Wilmington, Delaware, *Sunday Star* praised it as "not only a fine tale of suspense but also a well-written and well plotted novel" ("Week's Thrillers" 6). In the *New York Times*, poet Phyllis McGinley clearly understood Allingham's aims when she stated, "This is a different genre. It is all suspense, all chase, in the John Buchan tradition. But it is good, very good" (BR26).

Fellow mystery writer and critic H. R. F. Keating later deemed *Tiger* "one of the peaks of crime fiction" and "a story so powerful, so onwardly rushing, that it can carry . . . the weightiest of considerations, good and evil" (103), and *Possession*'s A. S. Byatt called it simply a "masterpiece." In 1956, *Tiger* was adapted for a film starring Donald Sinden and Bernard Miles, although Allingham's Campion did not appear in this version. Director Roy Ward Baker regarded it as "only a half success," attributing problems to an inadequate cast; he had wanted Jack Hawkins or Stanley Baker (qtd. in Dixon 152–33). It was adapted for BBC Radio in November 1963 and February 1984 ("Saturday Sound" 12; Dear 35).

The Seven-Per-Cent Solution: Holmes on the Couch

Although Sherlock Holmes parodies date to 1893 (Watt and Green 1), not long after the first Holmes work, *A Study in Scarlet*, was published in 1887, *The Seven-Per-Cent Solution* (1974) by the twenty-eight-year-old Nicholas Meyer stands out. Through a case involving the threat of war and the treatment of Holmes's cocaine habit by psychoanalysis founder Sigmund Freud, Meyer offered a modern exploration of psychology and addiction within a traditional frame of Doyle-style storytelling.

Meyer's novel hit the *New York Times* best-seller list within weeks of its release and remained on the list for forty weeks ("Best Seller List"; Meyer, *View* 50). It received the Gold Dagger Award from the Crime Writers' Association, and its 1976 film adaptation earned an Oscar nomination for Meyer's script. Overall, its reviews reflected warm approval. "An engrossing story," said Justin Kaplan in the *Boston Globe* (A107). "Immensely entertaining," summed up Philip French in his *Times Literary Supplement* review (184). "What a splendid book this is, and what grand fun," stated L. J. Davis of the *Chicago Tribune* (F3). "Stylish and, at times, quite compelling," deemed Henry McNulty for the *Hartford Courant* (8F). "Meyer carries off the Holmes-Freud adventure with great ingenuity and élan," wrote Jean M. White for the *Washington Post* (BW4). "Delightful reading for anyone—a must for Holmes devotees," stated Edmund Fuller in the *Wall Street Journal* (28). A *Publisher's Weekly* article on the "Baker Street Boom," coupled with a *New York Times* article that identified Meyer's book as part of a "Sherlock Holmes Craze" (Shenker 44), suggest that Meyer's novel may have arrived at the right moment for public receptivity. The *Baltimore Sun* sounded one sour note in the review by R. E. McDaniel, who called it "a bland brew" (D7).

Meyer's construction of the book provides clues to its positive reception. For one, it displays a thorough knowledge of and respect for the Holmes canon. For example, Meyer is billed as the editor of a long-lost manuscript, with Watson, the traditional narrator of Holmes's cases, listed as the author. It thus assumes, as is typical in the Doyle universe, that Holmes and Watson were real people. Chapter titles such as "A Study in Hysteria" mirror such Doyle titles as *A Study in Scarlet*. Appearances by well-known supporting players, such as Holmes's brother Mycroft and the hound Toby, as well as a climactic scene atop a train provide familiar echoes of Doyle's work. The narrative is situated during the gap between Doyle's "The Final Problem" (in which Holmes was believed to have perished at the hands of his nemesis, Moriarty, at Reichenbach Falls) and "The Adventure of the Empty House" (in which Holmes returns and states that he has been performing in Europe as a violinist since Reichenbach). A further reinforcement of the time frame is Holmes's encounter with Rudolf Rassendyll, the hero of Anthony Hope's *The Prisoner of Zenda*. For the Doyle devotee, Meyer provides plausible answers for Holmes's "missing" months as well as his fixation on Moriarty.

Meyer had been inspired to write the book through a conversation with his psychoanalyst father that likened his profession to detection (*View* 41). The author felt so strongly about his approach that he left his publisher, Harcourt, for Dutton after Harcourt's editor stated that

Meyer's book only had to have "the *illusion*" of a period novel and performed significant edits with which the author disagreed (*View* 46; emphasis in orig.). Although Meyer was a new novelist, his sense of his work's viability seems to have been on target, given the public reaction.

Conclusion

The works analyzed here reveal anxieties over mystery and detective fiction inspiring criminal activity, opposing views over the roles of the sexes, discomfort with an author deviating from a tried-and-true formula, and tension between those who view the genre as a legitimate form of literature and those who regard it as lowbrow. On a more positive note, it also is clear that a modern discussion of psychology and substance abuse could find a receptive audience through the use of a beloved character and the familiar entertainment medium of mystery storytelling.

Robin Winks notes that Georges Simenon's Commissaire Maigret "is honored with a statue in Delfzijl, Holland, and Holmes with a pub on Northumberland Avenue, London, while I am unaware of any statue of Captain Ahab" (Introduction 2). His argument can be extended to the present day with the installation of a statue of Andrea Camilleri's Inspector Salvo Montalbano in the author's Sicilian hometown, Porto Empedocle, which is identified with Montalbano's fictional residence of Vigàta (Rinaldi 6, 146). Individuals can read the plaque in San Francisco that indicates where Dashiell Hammett's Brigid O'Shaughnessy gunned down Miles Archer; they can tour the Oxford haunts of Colin Dexter's Inspector Morse; and they still write to Sherlock Holmes, not to any character of Herman Melville's creation. Winks views this phenomenon as "a comment on cultures and the role literature plays within them, however, and not a comment on the literature itself" (Introduction 2). But it seems telling that it is mystery fiction, not another form of literature, that inspires this devotion—a reverence for and recognition of the seekers of truth and justice.

Notes

1. The actual first American detective novel was *The Dead Letter: An American Romance* by Seeley Regester (pseudonym of Metta Fuller Victor, 1866).
2. Chandler's negativity toward Cain needs closer examination here. In a letter to James Sandoe, Chandler stated that Knopf (also Cain's publisher) was fond of comparing his work to Cain's, presumably in the hope that the luster of Cain's best-selling power would rub off on Chandler's books and that he did not care for the practice (*Selected Letters* 26). In a letter to Blanche Knopf, Chandler refers to himself as "rid[ing] around on [the reputations of] Hammett and James Cain, like an organ grinder's monkey" (*Selected Letters* 23). A resentment of Cain's success could be a possibility. Cain, in turn, was not a fan of Chandler's or Hammett's books and disliked comparisons of his work to his contemporaries' in the hard-boiled subgenre (Brunette and Peary 114).

Works Cited

Allingham, Margery. *The Tiger in the Smoke*. 1952. New York: Carroll, 2000. Print.
"American Literature." *Saturday Review of Politics, Literature, Science, and Art* 25 Jan. 1879: 126. Print.
"Anna K. Green Dies; Noted Author, 88." *New York Times* 12 Apr. 1935: 23. Print.
Auden, W. H. "The Guilty Vicarage." Winks, *Detective Fiction* 15–24.
Baker, Ainslie. "Fadeout in Fog for Famous Sleuth of Fiction." *Australian Women's Weekly* 8 Oct. 1952: 2. Print.
Barr, Amelia E. "The Modern Novel." *North American Review* 159.456 (1894): 592–600. Print.
Barzun, Jacques. "Detection and the Literary Art." Winks, *Detective Fiction* 144–53.
"Best Seller List: General." *New York Times* 15 Sept. 1974: 507. Print.
"Book Club Selections." *Publishers Weekly* 19 July 1952: 258. Print.
"Books: Dingy Storyteller." *Time* 24 May 1943: N. pag.. Time Inc., 2012. Web. 29 Oct. 2012.
"Books Received." *Lippincott's Magazine* Feb. 1879: 264. Print.
Boucher, Anthony. "Criminals at Large." *New York Times* 10 Apr. 1955: BR17. Print.
Bronfen, Elisabeth. "Female Fatale: Negotiations of Tragic Desire." *New Literary History* 35.1 (2004): 103–16. Print.
Brunette, Peter, and Gerald Peary. "James M. Cain: Tough Guy." *Backstory: Interviews with Screenwriters of Hollywood's Golden Age*. Ed. Patrick McGilligan. Berkeley: U of California P, 1986. 110–32. Print.
Byatt, A. S. "Why I Love Margery Allingham." *Telegraph* [London]. Telegraph Media Group, 8 Dec. 2007. Web. 29 Oct. 2012.
Cain, James M. "Postman Rings Thrice." *New York Times* 21 Apr. 1946: 51. Print.
___. *Three of a Kind* [Career in C Major, The Embezzler, Double Indemnity]. 1943. New York: Knopf, 1944. Print.
"The Case of the Baker Street Boom." *Publishers Weekly* 8 July 1974: 56. Print.

Cassuto, Leonard. *Hard-Boiled Sentimentality: The Secret History of American Crime Stories*. New York: Columbia UP, 2009. Print.
Chandler, Raymond. Letter to Blanche Knopf. 22 Oct. 1942. Chandler, *Selected Letters* 21–23.
___. Letter to James M. Cain. 20 Mar. 1944. Chandler, *Selected Letters* 27–28.
___. Letter to James Sandoe. 26 Jan. 1944. Chandler, *Selected Letters* 26–27.
Selected Letters of Raymond Chandler. Ed. Frank MacShane. New York: Columbia UP, 1981. Print.
___. "The Simple Art of Murder: An Essay." 1944. *The Simple Art of Murder.* New York: Ballantine, 1980. 1–21. Print.
Chesterton, G. K. "A Defence of Detective Stories." 1901. *The Defendant*. New York: Dodd, 1902. 118–23. Print.
Collins, Rod. "Haycraft Queen Cornerstones: Complete Checklist." *Classic Crime Fiction*. Rod Collins, n.d. Web. 29 Oct. 2012.
Collins, Wilkie. Letter to G. H. Putnam. 1883. *The Public Face of Wilkie Collins: Letters 1874–1883*. Ed. William Baker, et al. London: Pickering, 2005. 453–55. Print.
Davis, L. J. "Finally, the Real Holmes Story: A Cracking Good Adventure." *Chicago Tribune* 18 Aug. 1974: F3. Print.
Dear, Peter, ed. "Today's Television and Radio Programmes." *Times* 25 Feb. 1984: 35. Print.
DeVoto, Avis. "Thrills and Chills Dept." *Boston Globe* 3 Aug. 1952: A12. Print.
Dixon, Wheeler Winston, ed. *Collected Interviews: Voices from Twentieth-Century Cinema*. Carbondale: Southern Illinois UP, 2001. Print.
Ellis, Luana. "Audio Reviews." *Library Journal* 15 May 1991: 130. Print.
Freeling, Nicolas. *Criminal Convictions: Errant Essays on Perpetrators of Literary License*. Boston: Godine, 1994. Print.
French, Philip. "Conanical." *Times Literary Supplement* 21 Feb. 1975: 184. Print.
Fuller, Edmund. "Getting the Dope on Sherlock Holmes." *Wall Street Journal* 10 Sept. 1974: 28. Print.
G. P. Putnam's Sons. Advertisement. *Bookman* Dec. 1905: 71. Print.
___. Advertisement. *Critic* 26 Mar. 1898: 223. Print.
___. Letter. 10 May 1886. *Literary World* 29 May 1886: 185. Print.
"Gazette bibliographique." *Le Livre* 10 May 1884: 329–52. Print.
Gellhorn, Martha. Letter to Max Perkins. 17 Oct. 1941. *Selected Letters of Martha Gellhorn*. Ed. Caroline Moorehead. New York: Holt, 2007. 117–19. Print.
Green, Anna Katharine. *The Leavenworth Case*. 1878. New York: Penguin, 2010. Print.
___. "Why Human Beings Are Interested in Crime." *American Magazine* Feb. 1919: 39+. Print.
Greene, Graham. *In Search of a Character: Two African Journals*. New York: Penguin, 1994. Print.
Hackett, Alice. "PW Buyers' Forecast—August 20–25." *Publishers Weekly* 26 July 1952: 435. Print.
Hatch, Mary R. P. "The Author of 'The Leavenworth Case.'" *Writer* July 1888: 159–62. Print.

Hoopes, Roy. *Cain: The Biography of James M. Cain.* 1982. Carbondale: Southern Illinois UP, 1987. Print.

Hutchens, John. "A Cain Three-Decker." *New York Times* 18 Apr. 1943: BR7. Print.

"In Other Cities." *New York Dramatic Mirror* 26 Sept. 1891: 9. Print.

James, P. D. *Talking about Detective Fiction.* New York: Random, 2011. Print.

Jones, Julia. *The Adventures of Margery Allingham.* Pleshey: Golden Duck, 2009. Print.

Kaplan, Justin. "Watson Gets His Revenge." *Boston Globe* 25 Aug. 1974: A107. Print.

Keating, H. R. F. *Crime & Mystery: The 100 Best Books.* New York: Carroll, 1996. Print.

Knox, Ronald A. "Studies in the Literature of Sherlock Holmes." 1911. *Diogenes Club.* Diogenes Club, 1999. Web. 15 Oct. 2012.

Lang, L. B. "New Novels." *Academy* 22 Feb. 1879: 160–61. Print.

Rev. of *The Leavenworth Case,* by Anna Katharine Green. *New Orleans Times-Picayune* 19 Jan. 1879: 1. Print.

Rev. of *The Leavenworth Case,* by Anna Katharine Green. *New York Evening Express* 10 Dec. 1878: 1. Print.

Rev. of *The Leavenworth Case,* by Anna Katharine Green. *New York Herald* 30 Dec. 1878: 6. Print.

Rev. of *The Leavenworth Case,* by Anna Katharine Green. *St. Louis Post-Dispatch* 14 Dec. 1878: 2. Print.

Macdonald, Ross. "Cain x 3." Rev. of *Cain x 3: The Postman Always Rings Twice, Mildred Pierce, Double Indemnity. New York Times* 2 Mar. 1969: BR1+. Print.

Madden, David. *Cain's Craft.* Metuchen: Scarecrow, 1985. Print.

Maida, Patricia D. *Mother of Detective Fiction: The Life & Works of Anna Katharine Green.* Bowling Green: Bowling Green State U Popular P, 1989. Print.

"Margery Allingham . . . Wrote Her First Murder Story at Six." *Evening Times* [London] 6 Oct. 1965: 5. Print.

Maugham, W. Somerset. "The Decline and Fall of the Detective Story." *The Vagrant Mood: Six Essays.* London: Heinemann, 1952. 91–122. Print.

McDaniel, R. E. "Schlock Holmes, Esq." *Baltimore Sun* 15 Sept. 1974: D7. Print.

McGinley, Phyllis. "A Report on Criminals at Large." *New York Times* 7 Sept. 1952: BR26. Print.

McNulty, Henry. "Pipe Dream?" *Hartford Courant* 18 Aug. 1974: 8F. Print.

Meyer, Nicholas. *The Seven-Per-Cent Solution: Being a Reprint from the Reminiscences of John H. Watson, M.D.* New York: Dutton, 1974. Print.

___. *The View from the Bridge: Memories of Star Trek and a Life in Hollywood.* New York: Viking, 2009. Print.

Murray, Albert. Letter to Ralph Ellison. Spr. 1953. *Trading Twelves: The Selected Letters of Ralph Ellison and Albert Murray.* Ed. Albert Murray and John F. Callahan. New York: Vintage, 2001. Print.

"The New Pictures." *Time* 10 July 1944: N. pag. Time Inc., 2012. Web. 29 Oct. 2012.

"New Publications." *Daily Alta California* [San Francisco] 23 Dec. 1878: 1. Print.

Nickerson, Catherine Ross. *The Web of Iniquity: Early Detective Fiction by American Women.* Durham: Duke UP, 1998. Print.

Otis, Arthur Frederic. "James M. Cain Rings the Bell Three Times." *Chicago Daily Tribune* 25 Apr. 1943: E16. Print.

Parker, Robert Brown. "The Violent Hero, Wilderness Heritage, and Urban Reality: A Study of the Private Eye in the Novels of Dashiell Hammett, Raymond Chandler, and Ross Macdonald." Diss. Boston U, 1970. Print.

Partridge, Ralph. Rev. of *The Tiger in the Smoke*, by Margery Allingham. *New Statesman and Nation* 23 Aug. 1952: 218. Print.

Phillips, Gene D. *Some like It Wilder: The Life and Controversial Films of Billy Wilder*. Lexington: UP of Kentucky, 2010. Print.

"Publications Received." *North American Review* Jan. 1879: 111–12. Print.

Putnam, George Haven. "Wilkie Collins on *The Leavenworth Case*." *Critic* 28 Jan. 1893: 52. Print.

Raskin, Richard. "The Pleasure and Politics of Detective Fiction." *Clues: A Journal of Detection* 13.2 (1992): 71–113. Print.

"Recent Fiction." *Literary World*. 18 Jan. 1879: 28. Print.

Rev. of *The Tiger in the Smoke*, by Margery Allingham. *Kirkus Reviews* 21 Aug. 1952: N. pag.. Kirkus Reviews, 17 Mar. 2012. Web. 29 Oct. 2012.

Richardson, Maurice Lane. "On the Run." *Times Literary Supplement* 1 Aug. 1952: 497. Print.

Rinaldi, Lucia. *Andrea Camilleri: A Companion to the Mystery Fiction*. Ed. Elizabeth Foxwell. Vol. 3 of *McFarland Companions to Mystery Fiction*. Jefferson: McFarland, 2012. Print.

Samet, Elizabeth D. "War Stories: What West Point Graduates Are Reading in Iraq." *American Scholar* 22 June 2005: 118–23. Print.

"Saturday Sound." *Times* [London] 9 Nov. 1963: 12. Print.

Sayers, Dorothy L. Introduction. *Third Omnibus of Crime*. Ed. Sayers. New York: Coward, 1942. 1–7. Print.

"Screen News Here and in Hollywood." *New York Times* 31 July 1943: 8. Print.

Shenker, Israel. "Sherlock Holmes Craze Is Far from Elementary." *New York Times* 12 Nov. 1974: 44. Print.

Skenazy, Paul. *James M. Cain*. New York: Continuum, 1989. Print.

Symons, Julian. *Bloody Murder: From the Detective Story to the Crime Novel—A History*. London: Faber, 1974. Print.

"Theatrical Gossip." *Washington Post* 11 Oct. 1895: 7. Print.

Van Dine, S. S. Introduction. *The Leavenworth Case*, by Anna Katharine Green. New York: Modern Age, 1937. iv–v. Print.

Watt, Peter Ridgway, and Joseph Green. Introduction. *The Alternative Sherlock Holmes: Pastiches, Parodies, and Copies*. Burlington: Ashgate, 2003. 1–2. Print.

"Week's Thrillers: *The Tiger in the Smoke*." Rev. of *The Tiger in the Smoke*, by Margery Allingham. *Sunday Star* [Wilmington, DE] 28 Sept. 1952: 6. Print.

Wells, Carolyn. *The Technique of the Mystery Story*. Springfield: Home Correspondence School, 1913. Print.

White, Jean M. "Adventures of Sigmund and Sherlock." *Washington Post* 15 Sept. 1974: BW4. Print.

"'Who Done It': Fiction Lures Literary Folk; Voracious Readers of Mysteries Tell

Their Likes and Hates." *New York Times* 18 Apr. 1941: 19. Print.

Wilson, Edmund. *Classics and Commercials: A Literary Chronicle of the Forties.* 1950. New York: Macmillan, 1999. Print.

Winks, Robin W., ed. *Detective Fiction: A Collection of Critical Essays.* Englewood Cliffs: Prentice, 1980. Print.

___. Introduction. Winks, *Detective Fiction* 1–14.

Woodward, Kathleen. "Anna Katharine Green." *Bookman* Oct. 1929: 168–70. Print.

Wuntch, Philip. "A Titan of Cinema: Billy Wilder Balanced Cynicism with Compassion." *Toledo* [Ohio] *Blade* 1 Apr. 2002: D3+. Print.

Wyndham, John. "Roar of Rockets!" *John O'London's Weekly* 2 Apr. 1954: 1–2. Print.

From "The Case of the Pressed Flowers" to the Serial Killer's Torture Chamber: The Use and Function of Crime Fiction Subgenres in Stieg Larsson's *The Girl with the Dragon Tattoo*_____

Kerstin Bergman

The Girl with the Dragon Tattoo (2008; *Män som hatar kvinnor*, 2005), by the Swedish crime writer Stieg Larsson, has not only been one of the world's best-selling novels of recent years, but also instrumental in paving the way for the international breakthrough of Swedish crime fiction. However, the dust jacket of the original Swedish cover of the novel alludes to at least five different crime fiction subgenres, thus creating uncertainty as to how *The Girl with the Dragon Tattoo* should be categorized and perhaps also be read.[1]

In the beginning of *Dragon Tattoo*, journalist Mikael Blomkvist is convicted of aggravated libel against capitalist Hans-Erik Wennerström, after which he takes time out from his work at *Millennium* magazine. He is then hired by the industrialist Henrik Vanger to write a family chronicle and to investigate what happened to his teenage niece Harriet Vanger, who in the 1960s disappeared from Hedeby Island, where the family lives.[2] When Blomkvist realizes there is a serial killer at work, the unconventional hacker Lisbeth Salander, freelancing as an investigator for a private security firm, is hired to assist in his research. Salander, who is under guardianship by the state, simultaneously finds herself in conflict with her new, abusive legal guardian, Nils Bjurman. Eventually Blomkvist and Salander solve the mystery of Harriet and identify and confront the serial killer. They then gather evidence of the crimes committed by Wennerström, and in the end, Blomkvist is vindicated.

Many critics have also noted Larsson's juggling of different crime genres and his novel's numerous and explicit intertextual references to other works in crime fiction history. Furthermore, *Dragon Tattoo* has contributed to inspiring increased genre variation, especially in

Swedish crime fiction, by breaking the dominance of the police procedural subgenre, which has been central to the Swedish tradition
since Maj Sjöwall and Per Wahlöö's influential Martin Beck series
(1965–75). The aim of this essay is to examine the use and function of different crime genre elements in *Dragon Tattoo*. By making a genre-focused and close reading of the novel—thus examining detective characters, modes of detection, crimes and criminals,
settings, and other genre characteristics—implicit and explicit genre
patterns and features will be highlighted.[3] The result of this analysis
will show *how* Larsson plays with the genre and what consequences
this has for his novel as a whole. An underlying thesis of the essay
is that Larsson's diverse genre applications have contributed to the
international success of the novel.

Paratextual Genre Signals[4]

Already on the dust jacket of the first Swedish edition of *Dragon Tattoo*, it is made clear that this crime novel encompasses several different
crime fiction subgenres. The photo on the front—a close-up of a girl's
face with her eyes taped shut (simultaneously fulfilling the function of
a cover girl)—that is immediately suggestive of a psychological thriller
and so entices fans of this genre to purchase the novel. Meanwhile, the
text on the front cover of the jacket is reminiscent of a magazine cover:
"Millennium" (the trilogy title) is positioned like a magazine title in
big letters at the top of the page; the book's ISBN number is similarly
located at the very top, as if substituting a magazine issue number; and
the novel's title and the rest of the cover information serve as tempt-
ing "teasers" for the content of the specific magazine issue. Moreover,
the little snippets of text under the various headlines also resemble in-
gresses to newspaper articles. In sum, the design of the front cover is
indicative of a crime thriller with investigative journalist detectives as
its main protagonists.

The back cover of the dust jacket displays a photograph of an
idyllic scene complete with seafront, summer cottages, and glittering

water. As the image has been tinted in a dull bluish and sepia tone, however, there is a sense of something sinister boding over the landscape. This sense of foreboding is further emphasized by a quote from Salander: "Everyone has secrets . . . It's just a matter of finding what they are" (*Dragon Tattoo* 41). The back cover thus complements the front in positing the novel in the thriller genre. The front flap meanwhile lists the novel's most important characters and, in so doing, evokes the classic whodunit genre, where such lists are common praxis.[5]

On the back flap, Larsson is presented as a journalist and an expert on neo-Nazi movements and other antidemocratic organizations. The author presentation thus also anchors the novel in a "real" Swedish context and introduces the genre of journalistic nonfiction crime writing. This genre is further evoked in one of the teasers on the front cover, where it is states that "46% of the women in Sweden have been subjected to violence by a man," as well as by the aforementioned magazine-like features.

Additionally, the "headlines" on the front cover of the dust jacket can be linked to the different "cases" of the novel—for example, "Journalist Convicted" (Wennerström), "The Case of the Pressed Flowers" (Harriet), "The Vanger Industries—A Deteriorating Family" (Harriet; the serial killer). Finally, the novel's Swedish title, *Män som hatar kvinnor* (Men who hate women), encompasses all the cases and thus sums up the main theme of the novel.

By examining the paratextual elements of the dust jacket, the reader becomes aware of at least five different crime subgenres within which to place the novel: the psychological thriller, the whodunit, the journalist detective novel, the children's crime novel, and the true crime story. This indicates that the publisher intended to market the book as a multigenre crime novel, something that had previously not been common in Swedish crime fiction.[6] To what extent the genres indicated by the paratexts are employed in the novel will be examined here.

Explicit Genre References

Larsson connects his story to the crime genre in many different ways. Most explicit is perhaps the mentioning of other crime writers throughout the novel. Henrik, for example, compares the Harriet case to something by Dorothy Sayers (78), thus evoking the whodunit. From a library, Blomkvist picks up "two mysteries by Elizabeth George" (115), another author with strong affinities to the whodunit genre (Scaggs 53–54). Later on he reads a hard-boiled mystery by Sue Grafton, whereupon the narrative immediately jumps straight to Salander, who, in true hard-boiled crime hero fashion, is taking revenge on the rapist Bjurman, reclaiming her power and agency (202, 203). Another hard-boiled author Blomkvist reads is Sara Paretsky, at which point (as if Paretsky's hard-boiled woman hero has suddenly inserted herself into Larsson's novel) Salander enters the room and confidently seduces Blomkvist (314–15). In the first two cases, the crime fiction references contribute to associating the Harriet investigation with the whodunit genre, while the last two introduce imminent events.

Furthermore, Blomkvist reads Val McDermid's *The Mermaids Singing* (1995). Mentioned on three separate occasions (279, 281, 288), this is the most referenced crime novel in *Dragon Tattoo. The Mermaids Singing* is a combination of police procedural and psychological thriller, with a story that partly mirrors the serial killer story of *Dragon Tattoo*, but where it is men, not women, who are abducted, tortured, and murdered. The placement of the McDermid references thus mark the transition in Larsson's novel from whodunit mystery to serial killer thriller. The last time McDermid's novel is mentioned, Blomkvist finishes it and concludes that "[its denouement] was grisly" (288). This presages Blomkvist and Salander's impending showdown with the serial killer.

Elsewhere in the novel, Blomkvist finds in a cottage on Hedeby Island several children's detective stories: "half a dozen Kitty books, some Famous Five novels by Enid Blyton, and a Twin Mystery by Sivar Ahlrud—*The Metro Mystery* [*Tunnelbanemysteriet*, 1954]" (232).

Hedeby Island is not only the closed-off setting of the whodunit and the den of the serial killer. With "cubbyholes, wells, vegetable cellars, outhouses, and attics" (123), it could have been taken from a Nancy Drew mystery or a Blyton novel—or of course from one of Astrid Lindgren's Kalle Blomkvist stories. The repeated references to children's detective stories add a streak of humor and stand in stark contrast to the ghastly and far from child-friendly events of Larsson's novel (the serial killer storyline, the rapes of Harriet and Salander). Thus, these intertextual references make the events not only seem even more despicable, but also contribute to lightening up what is in essence a shocking story. Simultaneously, these references also function as a reader's guide to the Harriet mystery, indicating that perhaps she was not killed after all—children rarely are in children's detective stories—even though everybody at this point in the novel believes she was. The references also contribute to creating a sense of childhood adventure that adds to the page-turning quality of the novel.

A very different kind of crime reference occurs when Henrik's niece, Cecilia Vanger, reads Swedish journalist Gellert Tamas's *The Laser Man* (2002), a true crime book about John Ausonius, the attempted Swedish serial killer in the early 1990s.[7] Ausonius primarily shot men with immigrant backgrounds, which prompts Cecilia to think of her father, Harald Vanger, and his Nazi sympathies (204). Swedish reality and society are thus evoked as parallels to the events of the novel. This highlights the novel's social criticism by bringing it closer to the reality of the (Swedish) reader. At the time, Cecilia (and the detective protagonists) does not suspect that there is a serial killer in the family, but her thoughts still foreshadow later developments.

Detectives and Modes of Detection

Akin to most journalist detectives in crime fiction, Blomkvist is said to have once aspired to be a crime reporter—before he became established as a "political and financial reporter" (42). Notwithstanding, it is Blomkvist's journalistic skills that are in demand when Henrik asks him to "question all the old conclusions [of the original Harriet investigation] exactly *the way an investigative reporter would*" (95; emphasis added). Blomkvist also stresses in a conversation with Henrik that he is "not a private detective" (110), cautioning his new employer not to be too optimistic about the result of the investigation. Despite Blomkvist's reluctance, he and Salander both resemble hard-boiled private detectives not only in many of their investigative techniques, but also in the sense that they are guided by strict, personal moral codes (273–74; Scaggs 62–64). In Blomkvist's case, his moral code is intimately intertwined with his role as an investigative journalist, as his ambition is to reveal crimes and injustices, but sometimes his moral code is also in conflict with his professional role. For example, at the end of *Dragon Tattoo*, he finds himself unable to publish the Vanger family chronicle that he spent almost a year researching and writing. He believes it would be a lie to publish it without exposing the two serial killers in the family; in any case, publishing it would destroy "Harriet's life all over again" (461). Therefore, he cannot publish the story, even though this goes directly against his professional ethics. To Henrik, he says, "Congratulations. You've managed to corrupt me," but Henrik argues, "You had to choose between your role as a journalist and your role as a human being. I could never have bought your silence" (461, 462). Being a human being in this sense stands at the center of both Blomkvist's and Salander's moral codes. This is also closely tied to the hard-boiled heroes, as well as many police heroes, not least from the Swedish tradition, who often side with the weaker party out of so-called human concern (Bergman, "Well-Adjusted Cops" 40–41).

Blomkvist is repeatedly referred to as Kalle Blomkvist throughout the novel.[8] Following on from the dust jacket, the Kalle reference is further introduced in the first chapter with it being explained how the nickname was first coined. By chance, and in a way that could have been taken straight out of a Lindgren detective novel, the reader is made aware of how Blomkvist had once solved a bank robbery, which had prompted the tabloids to come up with the headline "*Kalle*

Blomkvist solves the case" (12; italics added). The first morning on Hedeby Island, Blomkvist also thinks jokingly of his situation in similar headline terms—"*Kalle Blomkvist—on a research trip in the back of beyond"* (114; italics in orig.)—as if he found himself on a juvenile detective adventure. The Lindgren reference highlights Blomkvist's boyish qualities and how he, although being intelligent and skilled, might sometimes need someone more experienced to take care of him when things get serious.

In a similar parallel, explicit references to Astrid Lindgren's child-hero Pippi Longstocking are found in the novel (42). Pippi is known to be one of the most independent heroes of children's literature, and likewise, Salander is a very independent crime fiction hero. Her primary literary forerunners are found among the heroes of the hard-boiled tradition. This type of hero is generally "a loner, an alienated individual who exists outside or beyond the socio-economic order of family, friends, work, and home," and "answers to nobody but him- or herself" (Scaggs 59, 60). The smart, hard-boiled PI figure also "resorts to physical violence and coercion to achieve his [or her] goals," and "is conspicuously hostile to the forces of law and order, but yet, nominally, at any rate . . . shares their aim to restore and maintain social order" (61). This is an apt description of Salander, who is completely self-reliant, has a brilliant mind, uses violence and extortion to survive and get what she wants, and tries to evade the grasp of any kind of authority, but still aims to mete out justice—or at least revenge—on behalf of victimized women.

If Blomkvist and Salander can primarily be regarded as the investigative journalist and the hard-boiled detective, respectively, their modes of investigation are considerably more diverse in terms of genre affiliation. The investigation into Harriet's disappearance is characterized by logical reasoning (ex. 80), something that is typical of crime fiction in general, but of the classic detective fiction and golden age whodunit in particular (Scaggs 37, 40). Additionally, the thorough accounting for everyone's whereabouts at the time of Harriet's disappearance (ex. 78–79) strongly resembles how investigations are conducted in the whodunit genre, where timing is often crucial for establishing what really happened (Scaggs 51).

While perhaps contrary to logical reasoning and meticulous examination, intuition constitutes another common mode of detection in crime fiction. Thus, in spite of the scientific tradition dominating crime fiction (Scaggs 41), gut feelings, hunches, and instincts are all staple "tools" used by crime fiction detectives to guide them toward the solution. Larsson, for his part, lets his readers know that "over the years Blomkvist had learned to trust his instincts" (224). Blomkvist's instincts come across almost like a moral compass, preventing him from making mistakes, while also steering him toward the answer to the mysteries. Furthermore, he and Salander often propose solutions that in an intuitive way foreshadow the solution: for example, when they cannot make the timeline of the murders fit, Salander suggests that perhaps the serial killer is "two people. One older, one younger" (317). Simultaneously, this provides the attentive reader with a clue to the solution. As the final confrontation draws closer, Salander also experiences "a premonition of some approaching disaster" (324), which creates a sense of uneasiness on the part of the reader, who knows something bad is about to happen.

As an open, unsolved case from the past, the case of Harriet also evokes the modern police procedural, where this type of "cold case" is common. An essential feature of the cold case story is an interview with the officer who originally handled the case. Blomkvist conducts this interview with Gustaf Morell, the officer in question, who explains that every officer has an unsolved case that forever haunts him, and he compares his obsession the "puzzle about Harriet" with an older colleague's preoccupation with the "case of Rebecka," a particularly grisly murder of a young girl in 1949 (156). The gruesome details of Rebecka Iacobsson's murder bring to mind the elaborate murders found in serial killer thrillers (ex. Scaggs 116–17), and the parallel between the detectives' respective obsession with the cases foreshadows later discoveries of a link between them.

Swedish crime fiction in the early twenty-first century has been dominated by psychological explanations that link the behavior of criminals to experiences in their childhood. Blomkvist, for one, repeatedly attempts to uncover this type of psychological explanation as he aims to understand the people he investigates. Salander, however, rejects such theories, countering that everyone is free to make their own choices, something she and Blomkvist even argue about (373–74). Nevertheless, the psychological model is to some extent still applicable in *Dragon Tattoo*, as many of Larsson's villains have had bad childhoods, invoking expected stereotypes. The issue is somewhat complicated by a number of characters who are good in spite of having experienced childhood abuse (Salander most prominent among them). This notwithstanding, Larsson, through the character of Salander, takes a critical stance toward what has been an almost uniform praxis in Swedish contemporary crime fiction.

The way Salander (and Blomkvist) often break the law in order to conduct their investigations is particularly common to the hard-boiled genre, where the personal "moral code" of the detective is generally prioritized over the law (Scaggs 62–64).[9] Clear inspiration from the hard-boiled genre can also be traced in how they handle the aftermath of the final confrontation with the killer, by covering up what has happened instead of notifying the police. In so doing, Blomkvist goes against his instincts both as a journalist and as a citizen; on the other hand, it comes naturally to Salander, who lacks confidence in the law enforcement authorities. In this context, she is portrayed as the independent, hard-boiled hero, while Blomkvist comes across as weaker, instead letting Salander handle everything (364–72). Blomkvist and Salander thus complement each other, harnessing methods and modes of investigation from several different crime genres. For example, Blomkvist displays greater social skills, while Salander possesses stronger technical and physical abilities. However, as the cases are intertwined, so are the contributions of Blomkvist and Salander: they are equally logical, systematic, intuitive, and contribute to the progress of the investigations.

Politics, Settings, and Other Genre Elements

Since the 1960s, Swedish crime fiction has been strongly imbued with a sense of social and political criticism. This is a tradition that Larsson clearly ascribes to, and the critique brought forward in *Dragon Tattoo* particularly concerns the systematic oppression of and violence against women, the injustices of the speculative financial market, and the failings of financial journalism in bringing the latter to account. Among the most disturbing examples of the oppression of women is the way Salander is abused by Bjurman. Here, Larsson employs a rather journalistic manner of presenting facts about Swedish society as he explains the system of trustees and guardianship, which in the novel affects Salander's legal status. While explained in a neutral tone, it is nevertheless described how Salander's first guardian, Holger Palmgren, used his common sense to interpret the rules in her favor (179–80), while Bjurman used them to satisfy his personal sadistic desires (ex. 176–78). Larsson thus shows that it is not the rules in themselves that are wrong per se, but rather the way in which they can be misused for sinister purposes.

An underlying presence throughout the novel is the Wennerström case. It is only when the cases of Harriet and the serial killer(s) are solved that the case is brought to the forefront of the novel again. The Wennerström story is a key element in the criticism of corruption in the financial market in particular and of big capitalism in general. The capitalist villain is also a common figure in the hard-boiled genre, as well as in many modern spy and finance thrillers (Scaggs 109, 120). Swedish financial journalism is lambasted through Blomkvist's explicit criticisms, as when he describes how many journalists idolize rather than scrutinize the big players of the financial market (53, 83–84). Critiques of the media and the Wennerström case—in combination with the strong feminist criticism of the abuse of women that runs through the novel—thus contribute to placing Larsson's novel firmly in the tradition of crime fiction with a political agenda.

The class perspective implicit in Larsson's social critique is also present in the depiction of the Harriet case. Obvious parallels can be discerned between the wealthy and secretive Vanger family and the upper-class families of the British whodunit tradition. Indeed, the family in which each member has a motive for murder and many family members are enemies is a staple in the genre (Scaggs 48–49). As Henrik explains, a Vanger family chronicle would "make Shakespeare's tragedies read like light family entertainment" (70). Cecilia adds that such a tale would be "in the spirit of the Addams family" (228), and it is within this family milieu of violence, tragedy, and horror that the villain can be found.[10] Rich and conflict-ridden families are a prominent feature also in the American hard-boiled tradition, where it is common for the villain to belong to a corrupted and greedy upper class (Scaggs 109). Thus, in *Dragon Tattoo*, the Vanger family and the many intrigues surrounding it bring together both the whodunit and the thriller.

It is not only the many Vanger family members but also their dwellings that feature in the novel. In crime fiction, architecture is commonly used to indicate the moral status of its inhabitants. Old, traditional wood and stone buildings are frequently used to illustrate goodness, while modern steel and glass structures tend to represent evil. On Blomkvist's arrival to Hedeby Island, most of the houses are described as "solid stone structures from the early twentieth-century," except for one: "The last house was of a different type, a modern, architect-designed home built of white brick with black window frames" (110). The modern house belongs to Harriet's brother, Martin Vanger. When he later invites Blomkvist to dinner, the house is said to be "furnished in black, white, and chrome" with "expensive designer pieces" (149). Blomkvist notes, "It was also impersonal. The artwork on the walls was reproductions and posters, of the sort found in IKEA. The bookshelves . . . housed a Swedish encyclopedia and some coffee table books" (149). The coldness of architecture and décor is matched by a cultural emptiness in terms of art and literature. This is only balanced by a well-equipped kitchen and a large collection of jazz records, revealing the owner's interest in cooking and music. In crime fiction, many detectives have a preference for food, cooking, and music—often classical or jazz. This is often considered a modern substitute for the (upper) class markers of the British whodunit genre (Scaggs 91–92). However, music and cooking are also favored by many crime fiction villains, Thomas Harris's serial killer Hannibal Lecter being a well-known example. In combination with the architecture and the lack of interest in the humanistic fields of literature and art, the preference for music and cooking suggests that Martin might belong in the category of villains.

A strong focus on setting is often pointed out as characteristic of Swedish crime fiction (Lundin 8–9), and in particular, depictions of the elements of nature are both detailed and commonplace in most Swedish crime novels—something that can be traced to the heritage of the Swedish literary tradition. One aspect of this is the frequent use of weather descriptions to illustrate the mood of the detective and the status of the investigation. Larsson, for his part, uses the weather to show how problems escalate. Talking to Dirch Frode, Henrik's lawyer, Blomkvist looks "at the sky, where rain clouds had begun to gather," and Frode says, "'Looks like a storm is brewing . . . If the winds get too strong, I'll have to back you up'" (297). Frode's words make the transition from external weather to metaphor explicit. The conversation also signals the transition from cozy whodunit to serial killer thriller, and a few minutes after Frode leaves, Martin stops by and threatens Blomkvist (280–81).

The genre shift is also mirrored in other elements of the story. One morning Blomkvist and Salander find the mutilated corpse of the cat, Tjorven, on their doorstep (315)—a clear warning not to pursue the investigation further.[11] Killing cats (or other pets) as an attempt to scare the detective off is a fairly common motif in crime fiction. By using elements of the genre in this way, Larsson doffs his cap to more experienced readers of crime fiction, enabling them to put *Dragon Tattoo* in the context of a large number of other crime novels. The incident of the dead cat also introduces the common thriller element of time pressure: the event gives Blomkvist "an ominous feeling, as if he were about to run out of time" (319). This is one of many signals of the transition from whodunit to thriller, indicating an increase in tempo and danger as the final showdown draws near. Soon Blomkvist is running through the woods hunted by a shooter (326–27), just like the heroes in numerous action thrillers. Once back to safety, Salander states, "This may have started out as a historical mystery but . . . [now] we can be sure we're on somebody's trail" (331). Even the characters of the novel are therefore aware that their fictional world is switching genre.

One of the most characteristic story elements of the psychological thriller is the protagonist who, against all common sense, enters dark and dangerous places. In *Dragon Tattoo*, it is Blomkvist who visits the probable serial killer's house late at night, unarmed and without telling Salander or anyone else where he is going or even who he suspects. He knows it is a stupid thing to do, telling himself, "*Don't be a damn fool,*" yet "he could not resist the temptation" (345; italics in orig.). Consequently, and somewhat predictably, he is captured by the serial killer and held prisoner in his basement (346)—another common motif from psychological and serial killer thrillers. Additionally, like in so many thrillers, the murderer recapitulates and brags about his crimes to the imprisoned Blomkvist (353–55, 358–60). Yet in the manner of the whodunit, where it is generally the detective who in the end reveals all, Larsson lets Harriet and Blomkvist explain the missing pieces of her case to each other (386–92).

While Blomkvist makes the discovery leading to the present killer, Salander simultaneously uncovers the identity of the earlier serial killer. Larsson alternates between their perspectives and locations, thus causing the reader to worry about what is going to happen before the detectives do. The double perspective increases the suspense by dragging out the scene in the murderer's basement, making the reader wonder whether Salander will find Blomkvist before it is too late. This uncertainty of whether the hero will survive is common to the thriller genre (Scaggs 107). Luckily, Blomkvist is partnered with a hard-boiled action hero, and Salander arrives at the last moment to save his life (360–62), only minutes later to partake in a dramatic motorcycle car chase (362–63), thus further underscoring her role as an action hero.

Genre Diversity—A Road to Success?

After examining the form and content of Larsson's text, two of the five crime genres as evidenced by the Swedish dust jacket cover of *Dragon Tattoo* stand out as dominant. The novel can be principally labeled as a fusion of complex intellectual clue puzzle with all the elements of a classic whodunit and ghastly psychological serial killer thriller that includes the most horrifying elements of the genre: kidnapping, torture, incest, rape, and murder. Additionally, the novel encompasses elements from children's detective fiction, police procedurals (in particular from the Swedish tradition characterized by social criticism), and action thrillers. The main genre shift in the novel is that from the whodunit clue puzzle, associated with the Harriet case, to the psychological thriller of the serial killer case. The transition is gradual, but with the turning point marked by several genre indicators, such as threats made against the detectives, the metaphoric use of the approaching storm, and the increase in tempo illustrated by Blomkvist's sense of running out of time. Furthermore, the evolution from intellectual clue puzzle to thriller gradually increases the suspense, thus contributing to the page-turning qualities of the novel.

When it comes to detective characters and modes of detection, much of Larsson's inspiration is derived from the hard-boiled genre. This can likely be ascribed to his choice of non–police officers in the investigative roles, in combination with the thriller genre's dangers and demands for action. The serial killer thriller often features police detectives or assigns the role of main protagonist to one of the victims.

Larsson's detectives are not police officers, and although branded *potential* victims, their (and in particular, Salander's) hard-boiled qualities see them emerge victorious from the final showdown with the serial killer. This outcome is also foretold already when Salander reverses the power position in relation to Bjurman, a character who mirrors the sadistic nature and misogynistic attitude of the novel's serial killer(s).

Crime fiction is arguably the most popular fiction genre today, as indicated by best-seller lists all over the world. The genre's success is often credited to the suspense elements in combination with, in most cases, a straightforward language, a realistic depiction of contemporary society, and the readers' desire to explore their fears in a safe context. Even so, the success of Larsson's *Dragon Tattoo* has eclipsed that of many other best-selling crime fiction novels, in Sweden as well as internationally. The most common explanation for this is that Salander is an uncommon and compelling crime fiction hero and, at least in explaining its international success, that there is a general curiosity among readers abroad about the modern Swedish welfare state. This is a simplification, however. The fact that the novel transcends traditional crime fiction reading circles—and so has embraced a larger readership—has played a crucial part in the novel's overwhelming success. I would suggest that Larsson's experimenting with crime fiction subgenres has contributed to its broad appeal. To experienced crime fiction readers, the mix of genres provides a sense of satisfaction, as their extensive genre knowledge is confirmed through their recognition of the elements and practices of different subgenres, as well as the implicit and explicit references to familiar crime writers and novels. Moreover, the combination of genres makes the novel attractive to discerning crime fiction readers with their many specific genre preferences: to readers who would for example normally favor just suspenseful thrillers or to those who solely read challenging clue puzzles. To a less experienced crime fiction reader, someone who perhaps normally finds crime fiction too formulaic, the utter complexity of Larsson's novel—a result of his genre play—makes the novel stand out and appear compelling compared with more genre-typical novels. Additionally, Larsson not only plays with the crime genre, but makes many explicit and implicit references to other popular fiction. Most obvious is perhaps Salander's affinities with the powerful women heroes of the action film genre, but there are also elements of fantasy, horror, and romance in *Dragon Tattoo*, thus making it a novel that potentially caters to an even wider range of readers. Larsson obviously had fun writing his novel, using his wide genre knowledge and turning *Dragon Tattoo* into an unusual genre hybrid, and readers the world over are obviously appreciating his efforts.

Notes

1. For the sake of brevity, the novel will subsequently be referred to as *Dragon Tattoo*. When discussing the dust jacket, it is the first Swedish edition, *Män som hatar kvinnor*, that is used. Quotes from the dust jacket are my own translation unless otherwise stated. For all other purposes, the first US edition, *Dragon Tattoo*, will be referenced.

2. The numerous members of the Vanger family will, after first being introduced by their full name, subsequently be referred to only by their first name, while remaining characters will be identified by their surname.

3. There are many good studies on crime fiction subgenres, but in order to keep the list of works cited here concise, predominantly referenced is John Scaggs's *Crime Fiction* (2005).

4. According to Gérard Genette, "paratext" refers to the elements surrounding the actual text, that is, elements of the book cover, title, headlines, and so on, that help direct the reader's reception of the text.

5. Other paratextual elements are a diagram of a family tree in *Dragon Tattoo* (7) and two maps in *Män som hatar kvinnor* (103, 139). The family tree in the American edition is not found in the Swedish edition, while the maps of the island present in the Swedish original are omitted in the American version. Maps are an "almost obligatory presence" in the classic whodunit (Scaggs 51). Other reading aides in the form of images, lists, and clues are found throughout the novel (*Dragon Tattoo* 171, 246, 252–53, and 297). Graphical presentation of the clues gives the reader a chance to interpret them and solve the intellectual puzzle before the characters do, thus giving the readers the impression they are part of the investigative process. This narrative trick is characteristic of the whodunit genre (see Scaggs 37–38).

6. From the published email exchange between Larsson and his Norstedts editor, Eva Gedin, it is clear that the Larsson was interested in having a say over the

cover's appearance, but probably never got to do so before he died (Larsson and Gedin 37–39, 44, 47, and 50). The final cover chosen—credited to Norma Communication—is most likely to have been the publisher's in-house creation, whereby Gedin in particular played an important part in the decision making.

7. Between the summer of 1991 and early 1992, Ausonius shot eleven people with the intention of killing them. One person died as a result, while the others were severely injured but survived.

8. Another Lindgren reference is that the cat staying with Blomkvist on Hedeby Island is called Tjorven (*Dragon Tattoo* 158), the unusual nickname of an inquisitive girl in Lindgren's popular 1960s *Seacrow Island* franchise of television series, novels, and films. Blomkvist also finds Lindgren's *The Children of Noisy Village* (1962; *Bullerby Boken*, 1961), *Kalle Blomkvist och Rasmus* (1953; *Bill Bergen and the White Rose Rescue*, 1965), and *Pippi Longstocking* (1954; *Pippi Langstrump*, 1945) in an island cottage (232).

9. In the police novel, for example, such transgressions tend to be fewer due to the nature of the profession (Bergman, "Lisbeth Salander" 139).

10. The Addams family refers to the horror-loving family featured in the American television comedy series and films from the 1960s to the 1990s.

11. The Lindgren-inspired name of the mutilated cat indicates that the child-friendly aspects of the story are over as events escalate. See also note 8.

Works Cited

Bergman, Kerstin. "Lisbeth Salander and Her Swedish Crime Fiction 'Sisters.'" *Men Who Hate Women and Women Who Kick Their Asses*. Ed. Donna King and Carrie Lee Smith. Nashville: Vanderbilt UP, 2012. 135–44. Print.

___. "The Well-Adjusted Cops of the New Millennium: Neo-Romantic Tendencies in the Swedish police Procedural." *Scandinavian Crime Fiction*. Ed. Andrew Nestingen and Paula Arvas. Cardiff: U of Wales P, 2011. 34–45. Print.

Genette, Gérard. *Paratexts: Thresholds of Interpretation*. Trans. Jane E. Lewin. Cambridge: Cambridge UP, 1997. Print.

Larsson, Stieg. *The Girl with the Dragon Tattoo*. Trans. Reg Keeland. New York: Knopf, 2008. Print.

___. *Män som hatar kvinnor*. Stockholm: Norstedts, 2005. Print.

Larsson, Stieg, and Eva Gedin. "The Larsson–Norstedts E-mail Exchange." Trans. Laurie Thompson. *Afterword: Stieg Larsson, Four Essays and an Exchange of E-mails*. London: MacLehose, 2010. 23–51. Print.

Lundin, Bo. *The Swedish Crime Story: Svenska Deckare*. Trans. Anna Lena Ringarp, Ralph A. Wilson, and Bo Lundin. Bromma: Jury, 1981. Print.

Plain, Gill. *Twentieth-Century Crime Fiction: Gender, Sexuality and the Body*. Edinburgh: Edinburgh UP, 2001. Print.

Scaggs, John. *Crime Fiction*. New York: Routledge, 2005. Print.

A Comparative Assessment: Rudolph Fisher's *The Conjure Man Dies,* Chester Himes's *Blind Man with a Pistol,* and Ishmael Reed's *Mumbo Jumbo*_____

Norlisha F. Crawford

Rudolph Fisher and Chester Himes are, in a sense, literary ancestors to Ishmael Reed. Among their respective bodies of work, the best examples for tracing those connections—and where they part—are found in looking at their shared use of detective fiction. In the hard-boiled detective fiction genre, Fisher wrote *The Conjure Man Dies* (1932) and Himes wrote nine novels, including *Blind Man with a Pistol* (1969), while Reed brought elements of the genre to the creation of his novel *Mumbo Jumbo* (1972). Stephen Soitos says when African Americans write in the genre they employ traditional black literary tropes because the authors are "always conscious of racism and social injustice" (32) when creating their stories. Looking at Fisher's, Himes's, and Reed's fiction, one finds, among other shared attributes, parody, the blues ethos, and a deep respect for African American cultural forms as ways to combat racism and intraracial conflicts. Each author represents within his fictional settings the complexities of shifting, sometimes divisive, perspectives among African Americans, as they gained stronger social, political, and economic footholds within the US cultural mainstream. Each author uses the genre's rhetorical convention of searching for answers to "whodunit" as a way to probe the injustices of Jim Crow segregation, giving witness to the complications of building lives under constrictions that are diametrically opposed to the tenets of US democratic freedom. But as time passed and the ebullient feelings fostered by the Harlem Renaissance period faded, Himes's and Reed's works expressed the more ambivalent attitudes of the mid-twentieth century about racial progress. By upending the established expectations of a very popular literary form that promises not only answers but the restoration of balanced societal order, both authors signaled their profound questioning of a variety of approaches that were being argued as best for solving the real-life crimes of socioeconomic and political inequality that African Americans continued to face.

When Fisher's novel was published, the fecund artistic period that became known as the Harlem Renaissance had come and gone. The 1920s had provided a full decade of postwar prosperity and deep skepticism. In Harlem during that period, some of the money brought into the community's economy was from whites who flocked there in search of exotic adventure and pleasure among the neighborhood's inhabitants of color. The excitement was there, as blacks—homegrown, among them many migrants from around the country, as well as multiethnic and foreign-born—produced some of the nation's best indigenous fusion music forms, jazz and the blues, along with new singing styles, dance, literature and poetry, theater, paintings, photography, sculpture, and intellectual publications including essays, magazines, and newspapers. Wealthy whites' patronage of the arts and individual artists provided some in the black middle class with firmer financial footing, for a while. One of them, poet Langston Hughes, reports presciently in his seminal 1926 essay, "The Negro Artist and the Racial Mountain," that it was from within the black working classes that jazz and the blues arose, along with a new confident attitude, fueled by a more pronounced sense of racial identity, political bearing, and cultural pride. All of which would become an historical basis for the later black arts movement of the 1960s.

But a discernible pall of cynicism also served as a backdrop for the 1920s. World War I had been one of the most destructive conflicts in the modern age. The evolutionary development of more effective killing tools, in particular, the machine gun, had left Americans feeling vulnerable—physically, spiritually, and psychologically—even as money flowed into the coffers of many who had profited from the violent conflict. And some of that money flowed, like a river tributary, into Harlem. Then the economic depression hit. With the crash of 1929, the money, if not Harlem's creative spirit, came to a screeching halt. Fisher's *Mystery Tale of Dark Harlem*, as *The Conjure Man Dies* is subtitled, featuring four detectives on two teams, reflects all of those competing and intertwined historical and cultural elements from the insider perspectives of Harlem's residents.

In detective fiction, individual communities and their cultural values are placed under scrutiny, revealing, as Reed says, "the mysteries, the secrets, of competing civilizations" (qtd. in Soitos 183). In *The Conjure Man Dies*, the contested "civilizations" are the constructed configurations in the US national imagination about peoples of African ancestry, as individual citizens and as racial and ethnic groups, by comparison to individual citizens and ethnicities of white and European ancestry. Beginning with its title, Fisher's novel challenges the notion that racial and ethnic differences undermine what Americans can share: a national identity. The "dark" of Harlem referenced in the subtitle is wordplay, setting the reader up for a reversal of the stereotype that associates malevolence with the absence of whiteness. Referencing instead the predominant racial identity of the characters, the darkness of Harlem is immediately shown as a signifier for vivacity, community cohesion, and complexities. The opening paragraph states:

> Encountering the bright-lighted gaiety of Harlem's Seventh Avenue, the frigid midwinter night seemed to relent a little. She had given Battery Park a chill stare and she would undoubtedly freeze the Bronx. But here in this mid-realm of rhythm and laughter she seemed to grow warmer and friendlier, observing, perhaps, that those who dwelt here were mysteriously dark like herself. (3)

Darkness is introduced as comfortingly familiar, promising good times and a respite from the cold. A metaphorical association with night itself, as a time of sensuousness, keen self-awareness, and feminine power is created by Fisher. It is a place where nature, as if a discerning goddess, can sometimes show favor.

Reading about the lives of Harlem's citizens, one finds that their desires, their faults, their day-to-day experiences with each other are the standard human mix of simple, complex, and most often, combinations of the two. They are people doing the things Americans of all stripes do to achieve stability. They are seeking opportunities to gain steady sources of income, comforting homes, the respect of their peers, loving families and friends, and romantic partnerships. The novel implicitly asks why that set of desires would not be the domain of any racial group. It is fitting, then, that Frimbo, an African by birth, is at the heart of the mystery. He is black and an impressive man, unabashedly a skilled practitioner of the ancient rituals of his native clan, dignified in his carriage and composed in his demeanor. Detective Perry Dart asks how could Frimbo not "produce effect" on anyone who met him (Fisher 305). Of royal lineage, Frimbo had become a respected Harlem community member as a trained scientist-turned-psychic (although Dr. John Archer derisively describes him as a "fortune teller" at the outset) by the time of his apparent murder. The detectives who become involved to determine who killed Frimbo probe into the lives of a diverse group of characters, all of whom suggest the variety of characteristics and issues to be found within the black American community of 1920s Harlem. The investigating teams consist of a medical doctor and a police detective and of two working-class friends, one of whom is a private detective. The four are African American males, but markers of difference between them, including class strata, temperaments, approaches to values and culture, and even skin tones add shades of individuality to the four characters. There are few female characters included in the novel, but at least one is prominent in the plot and key to the mystery's resolution. Language styles, music, religious practices, and belief systems are intertwined with interests professional and standardized, formal and personal, giving the arc of the characterizations even more roundedness and specificity.

The first to become involved with investigation of the case is Dr. Archer. He is brought in because his home and practice are housed in a brownstone directly across the street from the apparent murder site. When Frimbo's body is discovered in his office by another man,

Bubber Brown, the doctor is asked to come and examine "the supine figure" (Fisher 7). While Archer is doing so, a third principal in the story, Jinx Jenkins, is introduced by Brown as the person who found Frimbo in his current state. Fisher carefully details the physical build, demeanor, and skin color of each character. Archer is "a tall, slender, light-skinned man of obviously habitual composure" (5). His language is arch—formal, dispassionate. Jenkins is a "tall, lank, angular figure," a young man of "similarly light complexion except for a profusion of dark brown freckles, and of a curiously scowling countenance that glowered from either ill humor or apprehension" (5, 6). Jenkins says little, but when he does, like young Mr. Brown, he speaks in a vernacular English. Asked if he had seen Frimbo fall or strike his head when he was consulting with him, Jenkins answers: "No, suh, doc. . . . He didn't do nothin' the whole time I was in there. Nothin' but talk. He tol' me who I was and what I wanted befo' I could open my mouth. Well, I said that I knowed that much already and that I come to find out sump'm I didn't know. Then he went on talkin', tellin' me plenty" (9). There is a hint of humor, but it is specifically parody because Jenkins also is giving a self-confident and critical assessment of Frimbo's skills. There is a nod to prevailing racialized caricatures of blacks, but Jenkins's testimony is also straightforward and convincingly delivered. Brown is "short, round, black" and "excited," by contrast, managing in a stammering voice to begin his appeal to Archer for help with, "Is—is you him?" (5). Bubber Brown's speech is nonstandard but also colloquial (that is, familiar, jocular, and self-assured), as he spends time exchanging information at the scene of the crime and over the course of the novel. Fisher delineates the characters' likely social class and individual temperaments by their language forms, but he takes care to show all of the characters as competent and self-possessing, thereby deflating racialized stereotypes of simplemindedness and class estrangements.

Jinx Jenkins had come to Frimbo to discuss his current state of unemployment and ways to change that course for his future. He

---

believes, based on his cultural values, that Frimbo has the skills to advise him. In the end, Jenkins's consultation with Frimbo holds the key to resolving the mystery of who killed Frimbo and why. Jenkins is "convincing," carefully detailed, and "definite" (Fisher 77) in the police interview conducted after he is charged with the murder. Although a full investigation occurs before Jenkins is shown to be not guilty, the credibility he establishes with the primary detective by the initial testimony is what ultimately contributes to Jenkins's acquittal. Similarly, Brown's expertise in ferreting out information based on insider community knowledge is crucial to finding clues to the answers. Because Jenkins is implicated early as the likely perpetrator of the murder, Brown is driven by loyalty and friendship to get involved with the investigation. In the first place, however, it is because Brown understands the market value of both his access to particular kinds of community information and his ability to get people to relax with and reveal information to him that he is already a private investigator when Frimbo's apparent murder is discovered. Driven by his desire to work for himself, Bubber Brown had chosen to become an independent business owner, with Jenkins working as his assistant. The business card Brown gives to Dart identifies Brown as "Detective," with a Fifth Avenue office address and a specialty in locating "cheaters and backbiters" (48). He has chosen a viable market in Harlem because he says, "Folks'll pay to catch cheaters when they won't pay for other things" (49). Consistently, while Fisher may call into play contemporary stereotypes of the early twentieth century—as he initially does in the "dark Harlem" of the title—he also presents another completely opposed and nonjudgmental possibility for readers to gain understanding about the rational choices made by his black characters. In other words, he asks readers to step out of the trap of prejudice and culturally ingrained notions to see that the characters are simply representatives of human qualities that anyone might relate to, despite any individual differences. By extension, he suggests seeing actual black human beings in those ways, too.

Perry Dart enters the story as the official police detective who is assigned the case; he is an example of Fisher's approach to challenging racialized and color stereotypes. Dart was among the first of "ten Negro members of Harlem's police force to be promoted from the rank of patrolman" (Fisher 14). As such, he enters the scene with the authority that is conferred by his professional standing and commanded by his demeanor. He is dark skinned, comparing favorably to the dark night itself; his brain is "bright, alert, practical." Dart is described as

a Manhattanite by birth, [who] had come up through the public schools, distinguished himself in athletics . . . and having himself grown up with the black colony, knew Harlem from the lowest dive to loftiest temple. He [is] rather small of stature, with unusually thin, fine features, which falsely accentuated the slightness of his slender but wiry body. (14)

From the start of the investigation, it is clear that Dart and Archer are professional equals. Despite having a more relaxed style than Archer, Dart conducts the inquiries in Standard English and is direct. It also is clear from the moment he enters the story that Dart is going to be the heroic figure in the novel. While Archer clearly possesses professional knowledge and employs precise formal speech, echoing the voice of the narrative frame, he lacks the overall savvy that Dart displays within the fictional community's context. When Archer begins to rethink the efficacy of his own conduct when initially inspecting the dead body, Dart interrupts, saying, "Never mind. There's no law against your moving him or examining him, even if you had suspected murder— as long as you weren't trying to hide anything. People think there's some such law, but there isn't" (19–20). Dart establishes himself as the leader on the scene, even when dealing with another expert. He is the novel's source for authority; he is decisive, focused, and at ease as he conducts business in his area of expertise.

Fisher is showing what his contemporary Langston Hughes identifies as the renaissance of self-awareness that grew in the 1920s among

African American artists, but his words have wider-ranging implications for the spirit of the period:

> We younger Negro artists who create now intend to express our individual dark-skinned selves without fear or shame. If white people are pleased we are glad. If they are not, it doesn't matter. We know we are beautiful. And ugly too. The tom-tom cries and the tom-tom laughs. If colored people are pleased we are glad. If they are not, their displeasure doesn't matter either. We build our temples for tomorrow, strong as we know how, and we stand on top of the mountain, free within ourselves. (694)

The perspectives and sensibilities that one finds in Chester Himes's Harlem novels are shared with Hughes and with Fisher, even with decades separating their respective works' publication. Perry Dart also is the "educated, sensitive African American" that Stephen Soitos describes as the aesthetic basis for Reed's later PaPa LaBas character (185). Dart has the racial sensibilities and strength of character that Himes will lament as missing in the leadership ranks of Afro-America after the violent chaos of the 1960s sets in. Recognizing the richly complex connections within their racial and ethnic group was advantageous for African Americans, even as one also maintained a sense of being a distinct individual, free within one's self. That principle captures Himes's approach to both his personal life and his literary work, to a point.

When Himes's detective fiction novels were published, from 1957 to 1984 (the last one posthumously), the modern civil rights movement was in full swing. And yet, by 1965, unabated police brutality against urban African Americans was at such a fever pitch that, in response, uprisings for justice from within black communities began erupting literally with fiery (and often deadly) force all around the country, and they continued to erupt for the next years. Adding fuel to the flames, US military involvement with the internal conflict in Vietnam had just begun the preceding year. By 1965, Malcolm X was dead. The Black

Panther Party was devolving already into a shadow of its original organizational self, as its ranks were decimated by police and FBI murders of its members as well as internal rifts. By 1968, Martin Luther King Jr. was dead. Writing from self-imposed exile in France, Himes offered a dire warning to his compatriots back in the United States. The civil rights movement's momentous political and legal gains in the United States were in jeopardy because a violent sense of recklessness pervaded and a leadership vacuum had developed in black America.

In the ninth novel in the Harlem series, *Blind Man with a Pistol*, Himes gives full rein to his growing sense of skepticism, disappointment, anger, and fear that the strengths of African American creativity, optimism, cultural acuity, life-saving humor, and accumulated historical knowledge would be eclipsed by the sheer lack of coherent, competent, ethical, and insightful leadership, with an eye for the future. In the series prior to this novel, Himes had largely embraced the culture of Harlem as a microcosm reflecting the overall beauty of African American resourcefulness. He admired Fisher and the Harlem Renaissance period, with which Fisher was also associated, saying, "It was one of the greatest movements among black writers that existed up to then" (Williams 49). In the first novels in the series, Himes shows his affection for the fictional Harlem, connecting with Fisher's presentation. Things changed, however, with *Blind Man with a Pistol*. Although still in detective fiction form, Himes says it was "a serious book" because it addressed the "absurdity of racism in black behavior as well as white behavior" (qtd. in Margolies and Fabre 151, 153).

According to Himes, massive violent resistance alone might rule a day—briefly relieving some of the pent-up emotions among African Americans and unmooring justifiably some of the assumptive privileges accorded whiteness—but the war being waged by African Americans who were seeking full citizenship and a just nation would be lost. Himes argued the need for a cadre of shrewd men with a deep understanding of both the ways of white supremacy (so that it could be addressed and dismantled) and the ways African Americans themselves acquiesce to the structures of white supremacy (so that they could be freed from crippling self-abasement). Otherwise, a critical mass of African Americans could be sidetracked by their own individual ignorance or duped and led astray by scam artists, false prophets, or, most dangerous of all, sincere people who were simply not savvy enough about the complexities of the situation to serve well in leadership roles.

In *Blind Man with a Pistol*, Marcus Mackenzie, a young black man, is passionately leading an interracial movement for "brotherly love" in order to solve the race problem. Of his sincerity the novel's narrating voice says, "No one doubted him. The intensity of his emotion left no room for doubt. But one elderly black man, equally serious, standing on the opposite side of the street, expressed his concern and that of others. 'I believe you, son. But how you gonna get it to work?'" (Himes 23). As a man deeply suspicious of ideologies of any type, Himes was not sure how a black man could get beyond the corruptions of US society to rise to the job before being neutralized by or co-opted into the corruptions of mainstream values. On one hand, Mackenzie's desired outcome was a sound rational conclusion for which to aim. The black/white divide had to be frankly assessed with the two groups working together, if changes were to be made for dismantling sociopolitical, economic, and educational barriers, so that equal access to opportunity for all citizens was not just possible but could become the societal norm. Yet how can that seismic change in programming be brought to fruition when whites and blacks have both been so damaged by the circumstances of their historical relationships? That is the fundamental question with which Himes leaves his readers.

Himes was known for "refus[ing] to glorify blacks or categorize them as different from other groups" (Margolies and Fabre 155). In *Blind Man with a Pistol*, Himes stretches credibility to the extreme, showing that his poor and working-class characters' basic instincts are to simply live as well as possible under whatever circumstances they find themselves, conflating community leadership, religious practices, family values, history, and culture into survival modes that are sometimes familiar to readers, but often stunningly nonsensical. Echoing Fisher's carnival presentation in his Harlem, Himes takes his Harlem portrayals further, into the grotesque:

> Ghetto people, as a way of life, kill, steal, lie, cheat and use any and all means (except work, which is most often denied them) to obtain means, right suspected wrongs, nurture their emotions, afford sex fulfillment or perversions, provide self-respect or at least self-pride, to buy excitement, titillation, leisure and even peace of mind. (qtd. in Margolies and Fabre 155)

That description opens the door for understanding a fundamental difference between what Fisher suggests at his novel's close and what Himes suggests with his novel's denouement. Fisher's 1932 novel ends on a lively blues note and the balm of "Jes' ordinary common sense" (316). The ethos of the blues—that one may be down but not out—is a cultural support that provides a sense of fitness in the face of trying circumstances. Common sense also provides for problem resolution. With both in play for the two best friends, Bubber Brown and Jinx Jenkins, readers leave *The Conjure Man Dies* with the novel's tensions allayed. And yet, while their individual problems related to the Frimbo case may have been resolved, none of the deeper wounds of Jim Crow's constrictions are relieved or even acknowledged.

The two detectives' dilemmas at the close of *Blind Man with a Pistol*, by comparison, are starkly unsettling for many readers. Until *Blind Man with a Pistol*, Grave Digger and Coffin Ed, the recurring African American detective team in Himes's Harlem series, had been forceful and unambiguous in their views about the situation in Harlem. They saw the dual layers of (in)justice in Harlem that were powered by Jim Crow traditions and practices as much in evidence as in all other institutional systems within the United States. The detectives tried to bring some balance to the tipping scales by turning a blind eye to certain underground economic activities and acculturated responses chosen to confront the lack of opportunities afforded to other Americans. But by 1969, Himes had become distrustful of the promises for change in the United States. Accordingly, his fictional detective team reaches an impasse about how to move forward with progressive action against the racism that is splintering their community. Will imposing order and continuing to fight to enforce the rules of law bring justice to black Americans? Or, as Marcus Mackenzie and his randy Brotherhood adherents feel, will forming intimate interracial alliances between blacks and whites alleviate racism? Or will violent rebellion, militancy, and black power prove more effective, as argued by General Ham, a prophetic, charismatic, and self-described "plain and simple soldier in this fight for right" (Himes 76)? Ham and his disciples of the Temple of Black Jesus worship a jet-black Jesus who has been lynched by those who would give black people no mercy in the quest to subjugate them. Is Ham right when he suggests, "We got to fight, not race" (highlighting his disdain even for the term "race leader") (76)? Indecision related to those polarized positions unmoors Grave Digger and Coffin Ed as a team and "brothers." Himes's novel closes with a riot, in which warring sides from various opposing groups collide in the streets. The two detectives, unable to restore order, report to their white lieutenant that they have lost all control and "that makes no sense" (191), highlighting the lack of resolve Himes feels.

Three years after the publication of *Blind Man with a Pistol*, when the country was even more fully into the heyday of the modern civil rights movement, Reed's *Mumbo Jumbo* was published. The black arts movement that fostered in part Reed's literary evolution had flowered in the 1960s, with clearly drawn roots from the earlier Harlem Renaissance period of the 1920s, the setting for *Mumbo Jumbo*. According to Himes biographer Robert E. Skinner, "shades of Digger and Ed" can be seen in Reed's PaPa LaBas, whom Skinner describes as its "Hoodoo protagonist" (xx). Further, Skinner argues that *Mumbo Jumbo*'s "experimental nature" links it with "what Himes was trying to accomplish in . . . *Blind Man with a Pistol*" (xx). Indeed, in Reed's PaPa LaBas character, one finds the kind of effective leader who is both in sync with the societal moment and with the particulars of black life, the leadership that in *Blind Man with a Pistol* Himes suggests is needed. The connection is a real sense of black self-worth despite racist New World putdowns; it is a sensibility that, according to Reed, Himes, and Fisher, can be revived if each black person can access the spiritual strengths that come from understanding the African past. When questioned by Archer about why he continued to practice what Archer sees as unscientific rites with male gonads, Frimbo responds, "I perform the rite, which has been a secret in my family for generations, whereby I am able to escape the set pattern of cause and effect. I wish I might share that secret with you . . . who has the intelligence to use it and the balance not to abuse it" (Fisher 268–69). Frimbo, like General Ham and like PaPa LaBas, was not trying to be a perfect person, but he did want to be understood as a culturally learned black man who desired genuinely to lead "the racial flock" to a place of self-confidence and strength.

PaPa LaBas is working in Harlem with a small group of young followers, from their operational headquarters, a brownstone derisively called the Mumbo Jumbo Kathedral by those who oppose the group's teachings about the power of Jes Grew. Jes Grew is the essential element that all black cultures share worldwide, according to believers such as LaBas. Like a deeply buried ancient tree root, with tentacles that spread wherever blacks travel and settle in the African diaspora, one could trace outbreaks of Jes Grew sprouting up, bringing creativity and joy for life. LaBas says one sees Jes Grew's infection in the added zest of an improvised jazz note or in a certain corresponding jerk of the head "when the spirit hits" at church or in the locomotion of the hips when one gets is into "the swing" of a blues lyric.

LaBas reasons that the more profound value of Jes Grew, however, is in its potential for proving the powerful knowledge that black cultures represent. Jes Grew is "capable of wising people up" (Reed 139). With that knowledge, black self-love, self-acceptance, and self-appreciation would grow as well. Otherwise, black cultural practices would be disparaged as merely entertainment, "coon mumbo jumbo" (4). Black people knew better; they were moved genuinely by the creative spirit of Jes Grew, but they are "lusting after relevance" regarding the importance of what they produced (4). Papa LaBas, like Frimbo, thinks African Americans need a trustworthy guide for deciphering meanings of the symbols of relevance from the ancient world. In *Mumbo Jumbo*, a literary text, the Egyptian *Book of Thoth*, is that guide. Unfortunately, it has been stolen and hidden. Luckily, LaBas is a "jacklegged detective of the metaphysical who is on the case" (212). He says he has "licensed myself" to conduct the search (212); he will not be side-tracked, crippled, or corrupted.

A character at the close of *Mumbo Jumbo* says, "Time is a pendulum. Not a river" (Reed 218). Himes's Harlem novels swing forward, deepening the import of Fisher's novel; Reed picks up where Himes leaves off, moving forward by formulating the kind of attuned detective that Himes suggests is needed for finding effective resolutions to problems within black communities. Soitos argues that Reed also returns to Himes in ways that connect the two authors' Harlem-set works structurally and in their shared outlooks about the fallacies of the detective fiction genre itself. All truth-finding abilities related to ending the crime of racism are flawed; none are able to capture finally a resolution for addressing the complexities of the situation:

> *Mumbo Jumbo* is very much an anti-detective novel in that it ambitiously posits a mystery that can be solved only in abstract terms and so fails to satisfy the primary detective convention of *positive resolution* . . . In relation to Himes's last detective novels [*Blind Man* and *Plan B*], this elementary concept of detective fiction [also] was dramatically questioned. (Soitos 183; emphasis added)

Fisher abdicates on that interrogation, choosing instead to end with a feel-good close.

There is a multifaceted journey traveled when reading the crime fiction works of Fisher, Himes, and Reed. Within the genre, each author addresses, to varying degrees, racialized experiences among blacks over time in the United States. Readers are given evidence that there is an ongoing national environment of injustice, but what to do about that situation is not so easy for African Americans to resolve even after decades of looking for answers.

Works Cited

Fisher, Rudolph. *The Conjure Man Dies: A Mystery of Dark Harlem*. 1932. Ann Arbor: U of Michigan P, 1992. Print.

Himes, Chester. *Blind Man with a Pistol*. New York: Morrow, 1969. Print.

Hughes, Langston. "The Negro Artist and the Racial Mountain." *Nation* 23 June 1926: 692–94. *Nation Archive*. Web. 24 Oct. 2012.

Margolies, Edward, and Michel Fabre. *The Several Lives of Chester Himes*. Jackson: UP of Mississippi, 1997. Print.

Reed, Ishmael. *Mumbo Jumbo*. 1972. New York: Scribner, 1996. Print.

Skinner, Robert E. Introduction. *Chester Himes: An Annotated Primary and Secondary Bibliography*. Comp. Michel Fabre, Robert E. Skinner, and Lester Sullivan. Westport: Greenwood, 1992. Print.

Soitos, Stephen F. *The Blues Detective: A Study of African American Detective Fiction*. Amherst: U of Massachusetts P, 1996. Print.

Williams, John A. "My Man Himes: An Interview with Chester Himes." *Conversations with Chester Himes*. Ed. Michel Fabre and Robert E. Skinner. Jackson: UP of Mississippi, 1995. 29–82. Print.

CRITICAL
READINGS

Five Hundred Years of Chinese Crime Fiction _____

Jeffrey C. Kinkley

The antiquity of Chinese crime fiction, its ingenuity, and its observation of multifarious social phenomena give it international appeal. The Chinese have written about crime for two millennia, although hints of generic or formula crime stories from the most ancient times are known only from secondhand descriptions. During the past century, many Chinese people considered large swathes of their old literary culture a burden that they must leave behind to become fully modern and globalized. This has led the Chinese crime story, like many other aspects of Chinese culture and society, to take unexpected turns. Chinese writers' concern with social justice, regardless of changes in their social system, remains the great constant in their works. Unfortunately, English translations are scarce.

Mystery and its resolution by a great detective are staples of the Western crime fiction genre, handed down from such authors as Edgar Allan Poe and Arthur Conan Doyle. Seen from that perspective, traditional Chinese crime fiction typically has an inverted plot. The reader knows from the start who committed the crime and how. Suspense comes from wondering how the detective will figure it out and punish the villain. This formula characterizes most ancient dramas, *cihua* (ballad stories or *chantefables*, which included sung portions), and collected short stories that tell of crimes and injustices solved by China's favorite great judge, Bao Zheng (999–1062; also transliterated as Pao Cheng), or Bao Gong (Lord Bao). The earliest stories and dramas about Lord Bao date back to the Yuan dynasty (1260–1368), but most extant editions of the fiction are from the Ming (1368–1644) and Qing (1644–1911) eras. Judge Bao was an official of such legendary reputation that peasants praised him in folklore and temples enshrined him as a god. His devotion to justice could be invoked in prayer.

In imperial China, the emperor appointed all local magistrates and higher officials. Even a low-level magistrate was judge, jury, prosecutor, tax collector, and local administrator, all in one person. As they knelt and looked up at him in abject terror—possibly awaiting torture, a method of supposedly solving a crime that Judge Bao did not abjure—common Chinese people accused of crimes saw the magistrate primarily as a stern and paternalistic judge. He did not have license to kill, however. China had a long and complex legal code that required the emperor and his Ministry of Punishments to preapprove all capital punishment, and Chinese law reflected Confucian precepts. The law punished the murder of a father by his son more harshly than the murder of a son by his father. It gave more rights to literati than to commoners and more to men than to women. In some of the fiction, traditionally marginal characters such as Buddhist monks are likely perpetrators. In ancient times, as in modern times, a case was truly closed only after the criminal confessed. Wilt Idema, Stephen West, and George Hayden have translated some of the dramas in separate editions. Collections by Leon Comber and by Yin-lien Chin et al. translate, or retell, a few of the Ming dynasty stories. The originals in Chinese contain court documents and were written in literary Chinese, which even then was a dead language that functioned somewhat like Latin in medieval Europe.[1]

Traditional Chinese writing about crime often employs mystery, suspense, and sleuthing, and sometimes a series detective who is consistent from one story or play to the next. However, the main elements are ingenuity, intrigue, a quest for justice against all odds—sometimes retribution or vengeance—and eerie, strange phenomena, including the supernatural. *Gongan* (pronounced "goong-ahn" and meaning "court cases") is the general term for ancient Chinese writing about crime. Gongan rarely depicts a crime without the legal verdict and punishment. Even many detective stories of the modern period follow up after the criminal is identified, to show that he is dealt with by the law. Judge Bao and his colleagues were celebrated not only because they were smart, but also because they were incorruptible; they were willing to accuse the mighty—people who in a corrupt and hierarchical system seemed untouchable. Despite this ancient Chinese fascination with justice and the legal process, one cannot be certain that all gongan stories are about court cases, for the Chinese term has had other applications as well. Chinese stories of crime and detection are, however, told in many genres of nonfiction and fiction, some of which contain multiple cases. Magistrates wrote casebooks telling how cleverly they had solved true crimes, and ancient scholars collected famous cases and grouped them in forensic and even literary order, as in *Tangyin bishi* (or *T'ang-yin-pi-shih*; English: *Parallel Cases under the Pear Tree*). This collection narrates cases in pairs and tells, for instance, of chemistry experiments that can detect poisons. Other literati of imperial times wrote short essays about "strange cases."

Fascinating ingenuity might appear in the crime itself. A murderer might drive a long nail up into the brain through the victim's nostril or apply poison to the corners of the favorite book of a reader who licks his thumb when turning pages. Ingenuity might also figure in the detection, if the judge uses imaginative tests and clever questioning. Intrigue, in the old Judge Bao tales, might involve penetrating a conspiracy of the emperor's relatives or having the judge go out sleuthing in disguise, a titillating scenario given his august and bureaucratic remove from the common people. "The strange" includes odd portents or ghosts and reincarnations of victims who might appear in a magistrate's dream to reveal the true culprit and appeal for justice from beyond the grave. The judge could use a suspect's own superstitious beliefs to expose him, by sending runners to dress up as ghosts, confront the accused along a dark and lonely road, and scare him into an on-the-spot confession.

Whatever the initial hook, and whether or not the plot is suspenseful, the reader experiences catharsis in seeing the criminal confess and justice prevail. Apart from its interest in crime and the justice system, Chinese writing about crime has never been tightly defined as a genre. Until the twentieth century, all fiction was in ill repute in China. The elite literati class saw fiction as inferior history, less edifying than narratives based on fact. Fiction and drama supposedly appealed to base interests of the common people; drama could communicate with the illiterate, and actors were, in effect, a lower caste. The low status of crime stories, trading in cheap tricks such as suspense, motivated Chinese crime story authors—who often remained anonymous—to elevate crime stories by filling them with moral lessons and bureaucratic legal phraseology.[2]

Great epic and episodic novels, such as Luo Guanzhong's fourteenth-century *Romance of the Three Kingdoms*, appeared in China during the last five hundred years, but crime fiction was not so esteemed. Judge Bao remained popular with the common people as a character in operas. In the nineteenth century, so-called gongan tales starring Judge Bao and other great judges, such as Shi and Peng, took the form of epic chivalric or martial arts novels. These can be seen as predecessors of the kung fu (*gongfu*) movies popular with international audiences today. One of China's first lithographed novels was Shi Yukun's *The Seven Heroes and Five Gallants* (1889; also called *Three Stalwarts and Five Gallants*), excerpts of which have been translated by Susan Blader as *Tales of Magistrate Bao and His Valiant Lieutenants*. The full novel features Judge Bao only at the beginning and not so much as a detective but as the leader of a posse of heroic vigilantes who set out to right wrongs using stratagems and martial arts disciplines and weapons. Mystery, detection, revenge, and martial arts have been linked in much Chinese popular fiction, film, television, and video games ever since.

The Dutch diplomat and Sinologist Robert Hans van Gulik (1910–67)[3] translated a Chinese book he called *Celebrated Cases of Judge Dee*, which stars a famous historical judge, Di Renjie (670–700), and has a noninverted mystery plot structure like the Anglo-American classics. The book's subtitle calls it an eighteenth-century work, but literary historians have attributed the work to the late nineteenth century. The story's structure may reflect Western influence, although its historical local color is relatively authentic. Van Gulik went on in the 1950s to compose two dozen historical or period Chinese mystery novels and short stories of his own, with Judge Dee as sleuth. Among them are *The Chinese Maze Murders*, *The Chinese Bell Murders*, and numerous other books subtitled *A Judge Dee Mystery*. These stories are basically of the European golden age type, with whodunit plots, multiple cases, and local Chinese color derived from van Gulik's historical research. Some of the crime and detection devices come from casebooks like the *Parallel Cases* and old Ming dynasty fiction. Early on, van Gulik had his own Chinese mysteries translated into Japanese and Chinese to win an audience in Asia, and ultimately he did—in China, decades later, after both van Gulik and Mao Zedong had passed on. At the end of the twentieth century, China's own mystery fiction aficionados embraced van Gulik as an honorary Chinese author, Gao Luopei.

Mystery fiction's status changed in the twentieth century. Fiction's low reputation finally ended during China's vernacular literary revolution of the late 1910s and 1920s, when the old literary Chinese language was suddenly and decisively replaced by modern Mandarin during a tidal wave of Western and Japanese influences in education, the arts, and public discourse, called the New Culture movement. Translations of Western mystery fiction into the old literary Chinese exploded even prior to that cultural transformation. They amounted to as much as a third of all fiction in print in the first decade of the twentieth century, which was the last decade of the Chinese monarchy.

The very popularity of culturally exotic tales by Eugène Sue, Edgar Allan Poe, Arthur Conan Doyle, and Maurice Leblanc caused Chinese critics to accuse crime fiction of pandering to popular taste for sex and violence. They argued that the translations and their Chinese imitations partook of Western sensationalism. Yet these works also reflected the most vulgar and outdated aspects of the old, nineteenth-century Chinese culture of treaty ports like Shanghai, including its semiclassical Chinese language, which lacked modern grammar, vocabulary, and punctuation. Early whodunits available in Chinese did cater to traditional reading habits instead of revolutionary or modernizing taste. Given their low origins and unclear genre definition, many Chinese mystery stories ever since have mixed "modern Western" themes of scientific detection with "old-fashioned" romantic, martial arts, revenge, and ghost-story themes. Detective stories are often looked down upon for that reason by Chinese intellectuals today.[4]

A turning point arrived in the 1920s and 1930s. The complete adventures of C. Auguste Dupin, Sherlock Holmes, and Arsène Lupin, among others, were retranslated into modern Mandarin, and China's own authors began to write their own Western-style whodunits in that language. Chinese authors used modern vocabulary to tell of murders and thefts in a modern *Chinese* world of handguns, telegraphed clues, anonymous telephone calls, and safecracking. The full panoply of devices from the Western genre, including locked-room mysteries, red herrings, secret codes, railway timetables, shots in the dark, bumbling cops, cat burglars, gentleman thieves, underworld masterminds, and occasionally narration of the story by an assistant detective—a "Watson"—appeared in a native Chinese guise.

The key figure of the transition was a poor and mostly self-taught young man from Shanghai, Cheng Xiaoqing (1893–1976). A teacher who began writing old-style romantic and adventure fiction in treaty-port literary Chinese to sustain himself, Cheng warmed to Doyle when hired to translate Sherlock Holmes stories into the old language; he later superintended the retranslation project that made the complete Holmes adventures available in a very modern, spoken Chinese. He also translated stories about Philo Vance, the Saint, Charlie Chan, and other detective heroes. (Shanghai theatergoers could also see Charlie Chan in films.) Meanwhile, Cheng created China's most famous native series detective, Huo Sang, acknowledged by the author and readers alike to be "the Asian Sherlock Holmes." He has his own loyal Watson, Bao Lang.

Maurice Leblanc's gentleman-thief Arsène Lupin was perhaps China's second-best-loved Western sleuth. In the 1920s, another

Shanghainese, Sun Liaohong, created an equally cunning Chinese trickster called Lu Ping, "the Asian Arsène Lupin." Just as Leblanc inserted "Herlock Sholmes" into some of his Lupin mysteries to let a Frenchman run circles around a vain and excessively logical Brit, so Sun Liaohong put the Asian Holmes—and even the English Holmes and French Lupin—into some of his stories, so that Lu Ping could demonstrate the superiority of China's own intelligence, wisdom, sense of humor, and *joie de vivre*. A Lu Ping mystery is available in English in *Stories for Saturday* (2003).

Many Chinese consider the 1930s and 1940s the golden age of the Chinese detective story. Unlike the Communist culture czars who after the 1949 revolution would ban all their stories, Cheng Xiaoqing and Sun Liaohong did not view their borrowing of Western detective themes as kowtowing to Western cultural imperialism or to Shanghai's swashbuckling capitalist society. They took pride in the cosmopolitanism and modernity of Shanghai and its fictional detectives, which they viewed as historically progressive and international rather than Western. Cheng felt that technically informed detection and deduction made the modern whodunit a font of lessons in science for a modernizing citizenry. Critics such as King-fai Tam, Annabella Weisl, and Timothy Wong stress that Cheng Xiaoqing exemplifies Chinese aspirations to be sophisticated and up to date. Cheng was not a revolutionary like many of China's "serious" writers during China's nationalistic May Fourth period (ca. 1919–42), but the language and plots of his stories support reformist positions on behalf of modern sensibilities, the rights of women and young people, and the exposure of corruption. These were major concerns of China's New Culture movement.[5] Timothy Wong's translations of several of Cheng Xiaoqing's short stories in *Sherlock in Shanghai* capture the flavor of Shanghai as Cheng saw it—from its glittering cafés to its dark underworld—but his main achievement lies in the complex and suspenseful plots, often involving multiple mysteries, that he wove into his longer works, which are not translated.

After the People's Republic of China was founded in 1949 by the Chinese Communist Party led by Chairman Mao Zedong, not only did China's homegrown crime and detective stories, both ancient and modern, go out of print—on the way to being banned—so too did Western crime stories. Basic mass literacy levels soared, but as successive Communist Party-led political campaigns unfolded in the 1950s and 1960s, reading for entertainment and writing that did not criticize capitalism greatly declined. Most of China's ancient and even early twentieth fiction and poetry, both serious and popular, faded from public memory; few read the old literary Chinese language anyway.

Most classics of Western literature, including the adventures of Sherlock Holmes, which were said to propagandize for capitalism and imperialism, also faded from popular memory. Chinese students studied Russian in the 1950s, though it was dangerous for a citizen to be caught reading Tolstoy or even Gorky after the Sino-Soviet rift of the 1960s and particularly during the Cultural Revolution of 1966 to 1969, when China's schools and literary publications ground to a halt. Major crimes like bank robberies, opium use, prostitution, and spectacular heists themselves grew rare as a powerful police and neighborhood watch system took hold in the cities; few farmers, isolated from cities in people's communes, had the time, interest, or household lighting to read nonfiction, much less fiction. In the cities, large fortunes were broken up and so were the old criminal gangs. In the 1950s, imitations of Soviet mystery fiction about rounding up spies from capitalist countries were popular. During a period of political relaxation in the mid-1950s, even Cheng Xiaoqing was assigned to write novels about police detectives ferreting out saboteurs of the Communist revolution. His career as a eulogizer of socialism was short lived.[6]

Stories, even stereotyped ones, celebrating the socialist legal system and its obvious prowess in fighting crime, failed to develop. There may be several reasons for this. Government work, including criminal investigations, was secret. Trials were few and mostly closed. Major offenders were often dealt with in mass accusation rallies aimed at educating and intimidating the public. The prestige of judges greatly declined, due to their low education levels and obvious subordination to the Communist Party officials who appointed them, directed them, and often met with them beforehand to decide a verdict before the trial; the conviction rate was over 99 percent. Much punishment and "justice" was in fact meted out ad hoc by the police, who could send offenders to a penal farm for reeducation-through-labor without a trial. Common people saw the police as thugs fond of beatings and summary street justice. Lawyers disappeared from society after the late 1950s. The very prospect of a trial that gave voice to adversarial versions of the truth, whether in life or in literature, was viewed by the Communist Party as insubordinate and potentially destructive of public order and national unity.[7]

The lid came off after Mao Zedong died in 1976. When Deng Xiaoping gained power over the Communist Party in 1978, he began opening up China to the outside world, reestablishing a market economy, and loosening everyday surveillance over ordinary Chinese as well as restrictions on their habits and livelihood. Citizens traded in their lookalike blue pants and tunics for colorful clothing. Restaurants, stores, and street-side merchants popped up. As the economy prospered, cheap fiction magazines, affordable electric lights, and televisions and refrigerators began to spread to ordinary Chinese households. So did crime. By the 1990s, one could find a private room (and not just a people's park) in which to meet a lover—or a partner in crime. Crime stories began to flourish, along with most of the ancient, modern, and world literature and nonfiction best sellers that had been banned in China for so long. The complete adventures of Sherlock Holmes were reprinted, and finally, in 1986, a large selection of mysteries solved by Huo Sang. (Huo Sang solved crimes in China; Holmes investigated crimes that reflected only on faraway countries.) Agatha Christie's novels were printed in the millions; in time, Simenon, John le Carré, Ian Fleming, Robert Ludlum, and P. D. James saw print. Next came Scott Turow, John Grisham, and Lisa Scottoline; Erle Stanley Gardner and Elmore

Leonard remained little known. Television cop shows like *Hunter* (American) and *Derrick* (German) were popular in the 1980s, and China developed its own police dramas.[8]

China's domestically produced crime fiction revived in the late 1970s, along with Chinese enterprise, consumerism, and the legal system. The Ministry of Justice and the lawyer's profession were reconstituted. In 1979, China got its first criminal code since the Communist Revolution, and there was a short-lived democracy movement from 1978 to 1980. Unauthorized publications appeared on walls in downtown Beijing; fiction exposing crimes and corruption by the high and mighty of the former Maoist regime—under the Gang of Four—grew bold and sometimes deployed mystery and suspense, devices that were contraband under Maoism. Well-plotted stories that told of crimes committed by ordinary Chinese people, instead of class enemies, appeared.

How this could have happened so suddenly is itself a mystery. China's well-educated and well-connected class had private libraries at home, and even during the terror of the Cultural Revolution, Red Guards sometimes looted and took possession of public library holdings to read instead of burn. A few Red Guards passed around hand-copied crime and conspiracy mysteries of their own creation during the years of disorder. Chinese authors fond of suspense and criminal conspiracy proved to be a quick study, able to shift quickly from socialist formulas to less political crime-story formulas. The new post-Mao crime fiction necessarily reflected a different society from that of 1930s Shanghai. Some of the exciting new mysteries were even set in China's poor and bleak rural communities. China had no private investigators, only detectives in its rough-and-tumble police force—Public Security—most of whom were ex-military. Guns were scarce and bullets were scarcer, even for the few policemen and people's militia who had access to arms. However, people kept their savings in cash; there were no checks. As private markets sprang up again between 1978 and 1981, business ethics, already thought by many to be a contradiction in terms, were rather uncertain. A dual price system and a separate currency for funds converted from foreign exchange allowed black markets to flourish.[9]

In the politically unsettled years of the late 1970s, sensational stories with fictional characters accused Communist Party officials—of the "old" Maoist regime—of spectacular crimes. That included theft, often of public goods; murder, motivated by politics, greed, or bureaucratic advancement; and rape, which powerful male Party members in life had perpetrated on many a helpless ex-Red Guard once she was sent down to the countryside. Local tyrannies were generally the target, not Party Central in Beijing. Much anticorruption literature, from the days of Judge Bao until the present, points the finger not at excessive centralization of power, but at local dictatorships that run amok because the upper levels are asleep. The solution proffered is for shrewd and politically pure work teams to come down from Party Central to avenge the survivors of the wronged and punish the feudal fascists. Communist Party censorship squelched writers' accusations against the top leadership, but many readers craved a restoration of order by a just and powerful leader.

The more politically explosive works—featuring criminal conspiracies within the Communist Party itself—are collected in English anthologies with suggestive names like *The Wounded*, *Stubborn Weeds* and Liu Binyan's *People or Monsters?* Wang Yaping's 1978 story "Sacred Duty" is a seminal early work criticizing legal injustice and cruel labor camp conditions, available in *The Wounded*. In the 1980s, prison camp memoirs, both nonfiction and fictionalized, became a subgenre within what the Chinese called "literature about the legal system," which otherwise referred to crime and detective fiction.[10] Zhang Xianliang's nonlinear, modernistic plots about the psychic dissociation experienced by prison victims in his *My Bodhi Tree* and *Getting Used to Dying* can be read in English. As shown by Zhang and other memoirists, the biggest crimes are against humanity.

Politically sensitive works were banned after political crackdowns in 1981 and later years, but a new kind of socialist police procedural survived. Few works are available in English; intriguing collections of stories in the original Chinese appeared in Hong Kong from Cen Ying, who anthologized notable detective stories and crime stories, respectively. Most works came from little-known authors and were printed in popular Chinese magazines of the early 1980s. The detective stories are close to the Doyle and Cheng Xiaoqing formula, except that the great detective is a people's policeman or policewoman—shrewd, observant, self-sacrificing (as in Maoist fiction), and given to telltale quirks and tics when ratiocinating—but not so nonconformist as Holmes, though often just as willing to take legal shortcuts. These stories feature confusing clues in a particular crime venue, multiple suspects, clever bits of deduction, and an unlikely culprit exposed near the end, followed by the detective's own recap of the steps by which he or she solved the crime. Ordinary police procedure such as stakeouts and intensive, as opposed to clever, interrogations seldom figure in the plot, but the corpses tend to be gruesome.

An example is "Mousha fasheng zai Zingqiliu yewan" ("The murder happened late on a Saturday night"), by Wang Hejun, in the Cen Ying detective story collection. One Saturday night, a young worker takes his fiancée out to a movie. His corpse is found the next morning in a lake, with the head cruelly mutilated. A great police detective, Ol' Gao, and his assistants—including an admiring Watson figure who can read his boss's face for clues to what he is thinking—find the knife that gouged out the victim's eyes, some oil laid down to make his path slippery, and other clues. They investigate suspects. One is the sort that political campaigns of the Mao years taught everyone to hate—a boy of "bad class background" who has done prison time and still acts like a hoodlum. He wanted the fiancée for himself. Yet, he was a loyal Communist Youth Leaguer who turned bad only in the Cultural Revolution, when his father was persecuted, so one can also sympathize with him. Indeed, he is not the murderer; that would be too obvious. Another suspect is of the type that rode atop the crest of Maoist political extremism and was never wholly dethroned. This suspect is the arrogant son of a

Communist official. He had the knife. And yet he is not the murderer. Shrewd Ol' Gao, who wears his own political stripes—scars from unjust torture during the Cultural Revolution—figures out that the victim had his eyes gouged out by the official's son. However, after pacing off walking distances with a stopwatch, Gao arrests a little old lady for the murder: the victim's future mother-in-law, who wanted a more promising match for her daughter than a worker. In this type of story, the great police detectives seem free to follow their own leads and directives, as if they were private investigators.

The formula above might be called "the classical whodunit with Chinese (socialist) characteristics." A second formula might take the name of "penal law melodrama" or "contemporary gongan story," with old Judge Bao reincarnated in the uniform of a people's procurator (prosecutor), judge, police officer, or sometimes even a preliminary hearing interrogator. His—sometimes her—job is to pin the crime on the right person while overcoming imperfections in the legal system and bureaucratic pressure from above. (It is hard to know the gender of the authors, although publishers claim that the readership for crime fiction is overwhelmingly male.) Oftentimes the new "people's" Judge Bao figure must tail, accuse, and ultimately prosecute his or her own Communist Party boss, all the while intoning fervent proclamations or pious hopes about the sacredness of rule of law. These works contain much suspense, typically revolving around the question of whether the hero can get the evidence on the culprit and make it stick. As in the original gongan stories, the identities of the culprits are often disclosed early on. Suspense comes from hard-boiled confrontations between good and bad, including good and bad officials. Chase scenes are common.

Chinese detective fiction faced challenges to its creativity amid general prosperity during the 1980s and later decades. Many new laws were enacted and surveillance over private lives and conversations was greatly diminished, apart from camera surveillance of the streets—and later, government hacking of computers and mobile devices. Still, freedom of expression and genuine rule of law faced periodic setbacks. A nationwide "strike hard [against crime]" campaign in 1983 and subsequent years reinstituted mass arrests and summary executions before crowds in stadiums, evoking memories of Maoist political campaigns. Campaigns against spiritual pollution in 1983 and bourgeois liberalization in 1987 chilled political protests and adventuresome criticism of legal institutions and official corruption in reportage and fiction.[11]

Even so, in the freer atmosphere of 1984 to 1985, popular magazines dedicated to fiction and nonfiction about crime cases began to flourish.[12] All magazines were officially published by the government and guided by the Propaganda Department. Some of the most popular police magazines were published by law enforcement organizations. *Zhuomumiao* ("Woodpecker"—a bird that pecks out vermin) came from the ironically titled Masses' Press of the Ministry of Public Security, which ordinarily published police manuals and wanted to earn serious money by selling fiction. The ministry encouraged policemen and policewomen to write up their cases for the reading public and even sponsored workshops to discover new talent. The Ministry of Justice got into the action by releasing a literature monthly about the Chinese legal system. Beijing's local Public Security forces printed their own *Gold Shield* detective magazine. Similar official magazines and racy tabloids, some printed and distributed in the cities unofficially (and illegally) by peasants, sprang up nationwide. Chinese law enforcement saw this as legal system literature that could propagandize for public order and obedience. This also appealed to legal reformers, who saw fiction as an ameliorative tool for a legal system still in the making. The biggest blow came after the massacre and general cultural crackdown that terminated the Tiananmen democracy and protest movement of 1989. Cop shows, some of them foreign, were no longer shown during prime time after that, and all literary and artistic expression suffered setbacks until Deng Xiaoping revived his faltering reforms in 1992.

China's first full-fledged crime and detective novels since the revolution appeared and flourished after the mid-1980s. This included voluminous novels with multiple subplots, myriad characters from all social classes, genre-crossing elements of romance and savagery, the melodrama of seeing good guys escape from impossible predicaments and prevail in the end, and a cliffhanger at the end of each chapter, as in China's traditional novels from outside the crime genre. Ex-cop and prison guard Lü Hai Yan's epic 1985 best seller *Bian yi jing cha* (Plainclothes policeman) was a trendsetter. Lü's police colleagues loved the work because its moral seriousness and social commentary not only elevated cops-and-robbers fiction, but also made their profession seem high-minded and even progressive. The plot stresses the need to decide cases by professional police procedure instead of politics, and its hero is a fine young person who is repeatedly thwarted by old fogies. The public warmed to those sentiments, too, and also to the novel's crisscrossing plots; its implicit criticism of police torture, brutality, and starvation on prison farms; and exposure of the dissolute lives of the sons and daughters of Communist royalty. The work earned the cachet of serious literature because it could be read as a coming-of-age novel (bildungsoman), like the nineteenth-century European epics that for many Chinese represented the cream of world literature, before the West supposedly became sexualized and decadent. Lü's hero suffers two years of hard labor because he destroys photos of righteous protestors he took with his own secret spy camera. Readers knew that the police had such devices, but they were surprised to see them mentioned in print.

Liu Zong Dai's 1988 novel *Gong an hun* (Public security spirits) appeals to interest in ghost stories, romance, and family melodrama. The hero, an orphan who grew up to be an unflinchingly just cop, has a caring and protecting surrogate father—his police chief—and an evil "sibling," a bad cop. The hero cop, referred to by the public with the nickname of legendary ghost-catcher Zhong Kui, is tasked with tracking down reports of mischief made by ghosts. He discovers a night counterfeiting ring and solves two murders committed in the cover-up.

Other fiction writers attempted to enter the psychology of cops, criminals, and ex-convicts, though not always penetratingly. Wang

Xiaoying's mammoth 1988 novel *Ni wei shui bianhu* (Whom do you defend?) provides a feminist look at women lawyers, whom she knew by experience to be discriminated against both by gender and profession; lawyers for defendants at odds with Chinese officialdom are still sometimes charged with abetting their clients' alleged crimes. Besides dealing with dust-ups with state bureaucrats who dislike celebrity attorneys—the heroines' legal services office is one of China's first—the women lawyers must do some detection of their own before deciding whom they really *should* defend. After all, accused liars and wife-abusers seek their services. Meanwhile, the lawyers must cleave to or fend off husbands, old boyfriends, and exes—themselves middle-aged professionals who went to law school with other women in the 1950s, training to become judges, lawyers, or prosecutors. Politics virtually ended the need for those specialties at the end of the 1950s. Regaining their former careers, pride, and moxie before Communist Party-appointed judges is part of the women lawyers' collective midlife crisis. It also represents their foundering, newly reborn profession.

Playing for Thrills is a 1989 novel atypical of China's mystery crime fiction but is also a rare work available in English by an author most famous for nongeneric fiction: onetime bad-boy novelist Wang Shuo. The novel's antihero narrates in a clipped, hard-boiled style appropriate to his status as a petty urban drifter, gambler, and con man. He must quickly find out if he did in fact murder a man a decade earlier, as the police say. That requires some reconstruction of his memory. *Playing for Thrills* has been compared to the film *Memento* (2000), partly thanks to Wang Shuo's fractured, nonlinear narrative and his paranoid, postmodern questioning of identity, the line between waking and dreaming, and reality itself. The lack of an existential or moral compass fits a hustler who must investigate his own past. It also suits his angst-ridden generation and its urban lowlifes, whose airs of superiority in fiction would be off putting were they not so good at dissecting an entire society that had fallen into a spiritual cesspool. Wang Shuo has been compared not only to Raymond Chandler but also to

Jack Kerouac and Kurt Vonnegut. Like most Chinese who write more generically about crime, Wang Shuo focuses on society as the larger culprit, and he dissects it with humor.

With China in an unprecedented age of urban commercial prosperity, and Communist Party control still supreme but in the shadows, crime fiction no longer seems at the cutting edge of art, entertainment, or social criticism. Blockbusters on the silver screen come from Hollywood or are Sino-international coproductions featuring martial arts and period atmosphere. Audience interactive shows have been the rage on television. Young people are absorbed in the internet, video games, and Chinese forms of online and mobile networking. On the other hand, detectives and mystery, and parodies of their genres, have entered China's avant-garde fiction, as in Nobel Prize contender Mo Yan's farcical and satirical 1992 novel *The Republic of Wine*.

Anticorruption fiction became a sensational new crime subgenre in the late 1990s, until another Communist Party clampdown in 2002. In life, giant, insolvent, state-owned factories were being closed down and restructured, throwing thousands into unemployment. The typical crime in this fiction is the looting of state enterprise assets and pension funds by local officials and their protectors higher up in the bureaucracy. A heroic and impartial municipal or provincial official goes about sleuthing, tamping down social unrest, and gathering incriminating materials on corrupt officials up to the level of vice governor or deputy provincial Communist Party chief—no higher, decreed by the censors. A work team from Party Central then descends to reward the good official and lock up the bad ones. An odd, but actually realistic, parallel with the old Judge Bao cases is that the avenging heroes with the power to punish crime are civilians in the Party and state bureaucracy, not police professionals.

Detective fiction, sometimes with crossovers to science fiction and postmodern themes, is written in Taiwan, but Japanese social detective novels in Chinese translation have higher status there. Martial arts fiction—notably by Jin Yong and analyzed by John C. Hamm—and film predominate in Hong Kong. Japanese crime fiction has great market share in mainland China, too, though there are also native Chinese authors, many with day jobs in the legal, law enforcement, and/or legal education professions.

A recent phenomenon of globalization is crime fiction set in China and with a Chinese flavor written by Western-educated, expatriate, or even surrogate Chinese authors. Their global influence reflects the power of the West's commercial publishing houses and Western-inspired fantasies of what individual expertise and intuition could accomplish if unleashed in China. The Chen Cao mysteries by Qiu Xiaolong (resident of St. Louis) and the Mei Wang mysteries by Diane Wei Liang (resident of London) were composed by those expatriates in English, their second language. Lisa See's Red Princess mysteries and Catherine Sampson's Chinese mysteries are contributions by an American and a Briton, respectively. They have lived and traveled in China. He Jiahong, a famous law professor in China, has written mysteries in Chinese for his American-trained character Hong Jun to solve; they are popular in French translation.

Like other detective novelists popular in China, these globalized authors excel at observing China's fast-changing society, and they describe it with some temporal and geographical distance. The writers born and raised in China—Qiu, Liang, He—all have doctorates from American universities. They turned to fiction writing as a second career, as did Sampson. He's and Liang's sleuths are true outliers in Chinese society—a lawyer and a female private investigator, respectively. Private eyes and lawyers still operate only on sufferance from the police, who enjoy a monopoly on criminal investigation. Qiu's and See's heroes are similarly independent-minded cops who sometimes find themselves in joint Sino-American crime investigations. This device is also used by Sampson, whose investigators are a Chinese male private eye and a British television producer and single mother. For realism's sake, the privately employed detectives have contacts in Public Security. Liang's Mei Wang character used to work in the ministry. She quit and set up her own firm due to the 1989 Beijing massacre and sexism in the bureaucracy. All these authors revel in local color and love to explain Chinese customs, both traditional and latter-day, such as corrupt practices adapted to China's unique bureaucratic capitalist economy. Such detail is after all a staple of the genre. Inspector Chen Cao, like his creator Qiu Xiaolong, is a poet and a literary critic. While working, he recites poems, both ancient and modern, Chinese and foreign.

As middle-aged writers thinking outside Public Security's "box," these authors are also on a mission to expose official corruption and restore public memory of evils such as the Cultural Revolution and the Tiananmen massacre. The China-born among them may feel nostalgia for the lost innocence and neighborly feelings lacking in China's consumerist urban society today. All their heroes fight for the underdog—the poor, the persecuted, underpaid factory girls, migrant construction workers (China's "undocumented" workers)—and yet, as detectives, they reason and observe in classic whodunit style. These are works of global appeal that contain the latest reincarnations of a very Chinese icon: old Judge Bao.

Notes

1. For further information on the history of Chinese law and criminal punishment, see Bodde and Morris, Sprenkel, Shapiro, and MacCormack. See also Kinkley, *Chinese Justice, the Fiction* 101–69.
2. For more on the development of Chinese fiction, see Knight and Mair.
3. See Herbert for more about van Gulik's life and work.
4. For more on Chinese literary trends in the early twentieth century, see Kinkley, *Chinese Justice, the Fiction* 170–240, and Cheng Xiaoqing.
5. Chow Tse-tsung (Zhou Cezhong)'s *The May Fourth Movement: Intellectual Revolution in Modern China* (1960) and Ellen Widmer and David Der-wei Wang's *From May Fourth to June Fourth: Fiction and Film in Twentieth-Century China* (1993) offer overviews of these two periods, respectively.
6. For more on the Cultural Revolution, see Link, *The Uses of Literature*.
7. For further information on the legal system in modern China, see Bodde and Morris, Sprenkel, Shapiro, and MacCormack.
8. See Link, *Stubborn Weeds*, for more on post-Mao literature in general.

9. For details on the post–Cultural Revolution era and law enforcement, see Kinkley, *After Mao*.
10. Philip F. Williams and Yenna Wu have analyzed such works.
11. For further reading on the 1983 and 1987 crackdowns, see Tanner.
12. See Kinkley, *Chinese Justice, the Fiction* 282–301.

Works Cited

Bodde, Derk, and Clarence Morris. *Law in Imperial China: Exemplified by 190 Ch'ing Dynasty Cases*. Cambridge: Harvard UP, 1967. Print.

Cen Ying, ed. *Zhongguo dalu zhentan xiaoshuo xuan* [*A Selection of Mainland Chinese Detective Stories*]. Hong Kong: Tongjin, 1980. Print.

___. *Zhongguo dalu zui'an xiaoshuo xuan* [*A Selection of Mainland Chinese Crime Stories*]. Hong Kong: Tongjin, 1981. Print.

Cheng Xiaoqing. *Sherlock in Shanghai: Stories of Crime and Detection*. Trans. Timothy C. Wong. Honolulu: U of Hawaii P, 2006. Print.

Chin, Yin-lien C., Yetta S. Center, and Mildred Ross, ed. and trans. *The Stone Lion and Other Chinese Detective Stories: The Wisdom of Lord Bau*. Armonk: Sharpe, 1992. Print.

Chow Tse-tsung (Zhou Cezhong). *The May Fourth Movement: Inellectual Revolution in Modern China*. Cambridge, Harvard UP, 1960. Print.

Comber, Leon, ed. and trans. *The Strange Cases of Magistrate Pao: Chinese Tales of Crime and Detection*. Rutland: Charles Tuttle, 1964. Print.

Gui Wanrong. *T'ang-yin-pi-shih: Parallel Cases from Under the Pear-Tree: A 13th Century Manual of Jurisprudence and Detection*. Trans. Robert Hans van Gulik. Leiden: Brill, 1956. Print.

Gulik, Robert Hans van. *The Chinese Bell Murders*. London: Joseph, 1958. Print.

___. *The Chinese Maze Murders*. The Hague: Hoeve, 1956. Print.

___, trans. *Celebrated Cases of Judge Dee (Dee Goong An)*. New York: Dover, 1976. Print.

Hamm, John Christopher. *Paper Swordsmen: Jin Yong and the Modern Chinese Martial Arts Novel*. Honolulu: U of Hawaii P, 2005. Print.

Hayden, George A. *Crime and Punishment in Medieval Drama: Three Judge Pao Plays*. Cambridge: Harvard UP, 1978. Print.

He Jiahong. *Crimes et délits à la Bourse de Pékin* [*Crimes and Misdemeanors at the Beijing Stock Exchange*]. Trans. Marie-Claude Cantournet-Jacquet and Xiaomin Giafferri-Huang. La Tour-d'Aigues: L'Aube, 2005. Print.

___. *Hanging Devils: Hong Jun Investigates*. Trans. Duncan Hewitt. Camberwell: Penguin, 2012. Print.

___. *L'énigme de la pierre Oeil-de-Dragon* [*The Mystery of the Dragon-Eye Gem*]. Trans. Marie-Claude Cantournet-Jacquet and Xiaomin Giafferri-Huang. La Tour-d'Aigues: L'Aube, 2003. Print.

Herbert, Rosemary. «Van Gulik, Robert H(ans).» *The Oxford Companion to Crime and Mystery Writing*. Ed. Herbert. Oxford: Oxford UP, 1999. 38–39. Print.

Idema, Wilt L. *Judge Bao and the Rule of Law: Eight Ballad-Stories from the Period 1250–1450*. Singapore: World Scientific, 2009. Print.

Kinkley, Jeffrey C., ed. *After Mao: Chinese Literature and Society, 1978–1981*. Cambridge: Council on East Asian Studies, Harvard U, 1985. Print.

___. *Chinese Justice, the Fiction: Law and Literature in Modern China*. Stanford: Stanford UP, 2000. Print.

___. *Corruption and Realism in Late Socialist China: The Return of the Political Novel*. Stanford: Stanford UP, 2007. Print.

Knight, Sabina. *Chinese Literature: A Very Short Introduction*. Oxford: Oxford UP, 2012. Print.

Liang, Diane Wei. *The Eye of Jade: A Novel*. New York: Simon, 2008. Print.

___. *Paper Butterfly*. New York: Simon, 2008. Print.

Link, Perry, ed. *Stubborn Weeds: Popular and Controversial Chinese Literature after the Cultural Revolution*. Bloomington: Indiana UP, 1983. Print.

___. *The Uses of Literature: Life in the Socialist Chinese Literary System*. Princeton: Princeton UP, 2000. Print.

Liu Binyan. *People or Monsters? and Other Stories and Reportage from China after Mao*. Ed. Perry Link. Bloomington: Indiana UP, 1983. Print.

Liu Zong Dai. *Gong an hun* [*Public Security Spirits*]. Beijing: Masses, 1988. Print.

Lu, Hsin-hua, and Xinwu Liu. *The Wounded: New Stories of the Cultural Revolution, 77–78*. Trans. Germie Barmé, and Bennett Lee. Hong Kong: Joint, 1979. Print.

Lü Hai Yan. *Bian yi jing cha* [*Plainclothes Policeman*]. Beijing: People's Literature, 1985. Print.

MacCormack, Geoffrey. *The Spirit of Traditional Chinese Law*. Athens: U of Georgia P, 1996. Print.

___. *Traditional Chinese Penal Law*. Edinburgh: Edinbugh UP, 1990. Print.

Mair, Victor H. *Columbia History of Chinese Literature*. New York: Columbia UP, 2001. Print.

Mo Yan. *The Republic of Wine: A Novel*. Trans. Howard Goldblatt. New York: Arcade, 2000. Print.

Qiu Xiaolong. *A Case of Two Cities*. New York: St. Martin's, 2006. Print.

___. *Death of a Red Heroine*. New York: Soho, 2001. Print.

___. *A Loyal Character Dancer*. New York: Soho, 2002. Print.

___. *Red Mandarin Dress*. New York: St. Martin's, 2007. Print.

Sampson, Catherine. *The Pool of Unease*. London: Macmillan, 2007. Print.

___. *The Slaughter Pavilion*. London: Macmillan, 2008. Print.

See, Lisa. *Flower Net*. New York: Harper, 1997. Print.

___. *The Interior*. New York: Harper, 1999. Print.

Shapiro, Sidney. *The Law and the Lore of China's Criminal Justice*. Beijing: New World, 1990. Print.

Shi Yukun. *Tales of Magistrate Bao and His Valiant Lieutenants: Selections from Sanxia Wuyi*. Trans. Susan Blader. Hong Kong: Chinese UP, 1998. Print.

Sprenkel, Sybille van der. *Legal Institutions in Manchu China: A Sociological Analysis*. London: Athlone, 1962. Print.

Tam, King-fai. "The Detective Fiction of Ch'eng Hsiao-ch'ing." *Asia Major* 3rd ser. 5.1 (1992): 113–32. Print.

Tanner, Harold M. *Strike Hard! Anti-crime Campaigns and Chinese Criminal Justice, 1979–1985.* Ithaca: East Asia Program, Cornell U, 1999. Print.

Wang Shuo. *Playing for Thrills.* Trans. Howard Goldblatt. New York: Morrow, 1997. Print.

Wang Xiaoying. *Ni wei shui bianhu* [*Whom Do You Defend?*]. Beijing: Zuojia Chubanshe, 1988. Print.

Weisl, Annabella. *Cheng Xiaoqing (1893–1976) and His Detective Stories in Modern Shanghai.* Norderstedt: Verlag, 1998. Print.

West, Stephen H., and Wilt L. Idema, trans. and eds. *Monks, Bandits, Lovers, and Immortals: Eleven Early Chinese Plays.* Indianapolis: Hackett, 2010. Print.

Widmer, Ellen, and David Der-wei Wang, eds. *From May Fourth to June Fourth: Fiction and Film in Twentieth-Century China.* Cambridge: Harvard UP, 1993. Print.

Williams, Philip F., and Yenna Wu. *The Great Wall of Confinement: The Chinese Prison Camp through Contemporary Fiction and Reportage.* Berkeley: U of California P, 2004. Print.

Wong, Timothy C., ed. and trans. *Stories for Saturday: Twentieth-Century Chinese Popular Fiction.* Honolulu: U of Hawaii P, 2003. Print.

Zhang Xianliang. *Getting Used to Dying.* Ed. and trans. Martha Avery. New York: Harper, 1991. Print.

___. *My Bodhi Tree.* Trans. Martha Avery. London: Secker, 1996. Print.

Assimilation, Innovation, and Dissemination: Detective Fiction in Japan and East Asia _____

Amanda Seaman

Introduction

Stories of mystery and crime have a long pedigree in Japan. It was not until the late nineteenth century, however, that "detective fiction" as it is commonly understood came into being. As a result, debates about the definition of "Japanese detective fiction," and the degree to which detective fiction in Japan is an imported genre, have often served as stalking horses for broader debates about Japanese modernization itself and Japan's relationship to the West. As Japan changed from an agricultural, militarily governed polity with closed borders to a bureaucratic, industrial nation seeking its place among powerful Western countries—such as England, the United States, France, and Germany—Japanese statesmen, merchants, and artists identified what they believed defined those nations as "modern" and sought to emulate and adapt them for their own uses. Detective fiction, so deeply rooted in and reflective of urban society, scientific rationalism, the bureaucratic state, and individual subjectivity, offered fertile literary soil for Japan's efforts at "modern" self-definition and exploration, efforts that continued apace as Japan established itself as a legitimate imperial power.

After the devastation of World War II, Japan's gradual transformation from military to economic superpower—marked by the rise of a vibrant consumer culture, a burgeoning middle class, and challenges to prewar social mores—was chronicled by detective writers whose stories addressed the personal and political consequences of unbridled development, corruption, and social decay. In the late 1980s and 1990s, moreover, this sociocritical brand of detective fiction was given a new energy and impetus by increasing numbers of female crime writers. This boom of women's detective fiction cast light into previously unexplored shadows of Japanese society, highlighting the corrosive effects of sexism, the unraveling of family institutions, and the gender imbalances implicit in Japan's postwar economic transformation.

As the preceding paragraph suggests, therefore, this chapter will attempt to trace the history of detective fiction in Japan in two senses—namely, the chronological development of the genre and the writers who created it, and the ways in which detective fiction itself was shaped by and responded to social, cultural, and economic change over time. In turn, I will briefly survey the development of detective fiction in Taiwan and Korea, two countries whose twentieth-century history has been deeply and traumatically implicated with that of Japan. As two of the first acquisitions in Japan's modern imperial project, Taiwan and Korea were heavily influenced by Japanese culture, a culture that included popular genres such as detective fiction. After their liberation from Japanese control in 1945, however, Japanese literature was rejected as an artifact of colonial exploitation; moreover, as I will suggest, the military and autocratic regimes that dominated both countries in subsequent decades created a social and artistic environment in which detective fiction found only slow, and grudging, acceptance.

Detective Fiction as Genre

Detective fiction is, in many ways, a quintessentially modern genre constructed on a series of historically contingent pillars including the (ideally) impartial justice system; empirical observation; the regime of private property ownership; an ideology of scientific inquiry, ratiocination, and problem solving; and the rise of large, socially diverse, and economically vibrant urban centers. Further, as critic John Cawelti has suggested, it is the literary genre most dependent upon representational verisimilitude, or the appearance of reality (34–35).

What we now know as detective fiction is a uniquely urban literary genre, one that was born amid the rapid expansion of the city in the nineteenth century. The accompanying transformation of the city's economic and social roles, and the influx of new people to it, engendered new spatial regimes, new ways of seeing and ordering people and the spaces they inhabit. The figure of the detective, as created and elaborated by Edgar Allan Poe and others, was an impresario of these new regimes; he was able, as Margaret Crawford puts it, to "penetrate below the surface to discover the meanings hidden in the city streets" (120). The detective was not only able to navigate the city's jumble of new buildings, thoroughfares, and inhabitants with ease, but also to make sense of that jumble by recognizing and categorizing its details and in particular its denizens as "types" (the drunk, the bawd, the drifter, and so on). The detective thus was presented to readers as a kind of urban professional, analogous to practitioners of the new *-logies* coming into being at the time, each of whom claimed special competence to recognize, discriminate among, and productively organize the seemingly random and disparate elements of the natural and cultural world.

The detective's intimate knowledge of the city's streets and alleyways was not an end in itself. Rather, it helped him to overcome crime (disorder) and restore affairs to their "proper" disposition. The detective became the conservator of justice, of law and order, and of the private property that the criminal so desperately wanted to subvert or possess. The figure of the detective is ambiguous, however, since he ultimately is aloof from the institutions and practices that he is committed to maintain. The detective is tasked with upholding the law (although he often bends its rules to his own ends), a law founded upon the notion of individual agency, responsibility, and guilt. At the same time, his investigations frequently reveal flaws in the system that produces that law and thus force the reader to confront the social conditions of criminal behavior. Thus, the image we have of the detective is of someone who stands at an ironic distance from the established order, a distance that allows him to comment on its problems and injustices and to expose its corruption and malfeasance, even while he contributes to its preservation and replication.

Detective Fiction in Japan: Beginnings

The Japan in which detective fiction made its first tentative appearance was one of rapid and dramatic social, cultural, and economic transformation. Throughout the Edo period (1603–1867), Japan had been ruled by a highly developed military government with the shogun at its head, its well-ordered civil society defined in terms of a strict occupational and social class structure. It was, moreover, largely cut off from the rest of the world through a conscious policy called *sakoku* (literally, "locked country"); with the exception of the Dutch, who were permitted access to a small island near Nagasaki, foreigners were prohibited from entering Japan, and most Japanese were banned from leaving the country. While this policy was put to the test by various Western nations making colonial inroads into Asia, it was only in 1853 that sakoku was successfully challenged by Commodore Matthew Perry, who convinced the shogun and his advisers to open two ports, Shimoda and Hakodate, to foreign ships and then to sign trade treaties (Gordon 52–53). Within a decade, the shogunate was dissolved and replaced by a constitutional monarchy with its capital in Edo (now Tokyo) and the previously fainéant emperor, Meiji, at its head.

Whereas for centuries the Japanese ruling classes had spurned, at least in principle, any influences from Europe or America, the new elites actively engaged with the West in search of political, economic, and cultural models. Over the next four decades of Meiji's reign (1868–1912), Japanese society underwent a rapid process of modernization dubbed *bunmei kaika* ("civilization and enlightenment"), marked by the establishment of material and cultural infrastructure ranging from a railroad system to a compulsory education system for boys and girls to a number of daily newspapers (Gordon 108). In turn, Japanese statesmen and educators worked to reform their language, create a national literature, and develop a university system. They also strove to create a comprehensive and rule-based justice system like those of their Western counterparts—both to put themselves on an equal legal footing with the world's "civilized" nations and to gain international acceptance of Japanese jurisdiction over crimes committed on Japanese soil (see Kayaoğlu).

All of these changes were critical for the development of detective fiction. The imposition of compulsory education during the Meiji period, combined with an already substantial literacy rate at the end of the Edo regime, produced a growing reading public with a desire for new materials. The burgeoning newspaper industry both responded to and fed that desire in a variety of ways. Particularly popular were serialized stories of scandal and crime, often drawn from real-life events, foremost among them *dokufu* ("poison woman") narratives, a genre with roots in the late Edo period. The most famous of these concerned Takahashi Oden, who fled justice after killing her husband but was eventually captured, tried, and executed. Her story, as told by the Japanese satirist and social critic Kanagaki Robun with equal degrees of reportage and scandal mongering, proved irresistible to the popular reading public. Its success encouraged writers and publishers alike to seek out similar tales not just from home but also from abroad, already a rich source of literature extolling the virtues and rewards of entrepreneurial individualism. European and American detective stories fit the bill perfectly, leading to a spate of translations of texts such as Edgar Allan Poe's "Murders in the Rue Morgue," Anna Katharine Green's *XYZ: A Detective Story*, and the novels of French writers Émile Gaboriau and Fortuné du Boisgobey (Silver 58).

The literary scholar Mark Silver has argued that Japanese detective fiction has its roots in this Meiji-era world of translators, journalists, and cultural middlemen; it is, in other words, a literary import, adopted by the Japanese and adapted by them as part of a broader process of Westernization and modernization during the Meiji period. As a result, Japanese detective fiction in this view was initially derivative and imitative, only slowly developing its own voice as authors began to distance themselves from Western models and examples. Sari Kawana takes a quite different position, emphasizing at the outset the indigenous antecedents to later detective fiction. As Silver himself notes, the nineteenth-century Japanese reading public already was familiar with stories of crime and its resolution before the introduction of Western literature (22). These took the form of the Edo-era genres of criminal biography and *torimono-cho* ("crime reports"), in the latter of which a criminal's guilt was established and a punishment imposed by an infallible magistrate, able to see through the machinations of the criminal (Yoshida 276). Kawana thus argues that the Japanese interest in Western detective fiction was less a case of cultural importation and adoption than a result of shared sociocultural conditions: namely, that detective fiction evolved in both the West and in Japan as a result of each society's experience of modernity, in what Kawana dubs "global simultaneity" (6). Ultimately, however, both scholars agree on one fundamental point—that Japanese detective fiction is an emphatically "modern" genre, whose development depended upon a particular set of historical conditions in which the West played a critical, if not exclusive, role.

Translation and Adaptation: Kuroiwa Ruikō and His Legacy

The figure responsible for transforming the Edo-era literature of mystery and crime into what we now recognize as "Japanese detective fiction" was Kuroiwa Ruikō (1862–1920), whose translations and adaptations of famous Euro-American detective fiction did much to increase the popularity of the genre. Ruikō was a well-known newspaper journalist and self-described muckraker, who assembled a progressive stable of writers for his social reform–oriented newspaper *Yorozu chōhō* ("Morning report for the masses") (Silver 63). He was also a prolific translator of foreign detective fiction in Japanese: during one three-year period in the late nineteenth century, Ruikō produced three-quarters of the translations available to Japanese readers (six out of eleven translations in 1888, twenty-two of twenty-nine in 1889, and fourteen of seventeen in 1890) (59).

Ruikō not only introduced his readers to Western stories, but also taught them how to read them by offering lengthy introductions to each work that explained aspects of detective fiction—in particular, the notion that a mystery should not be solved until the story's end— that were alien to the Japanese literary tradition. As Mark Silver suggests, this effort reflected Ruikō's belief that the genre could be used to educate people, not only about the ways of the Western world, but also about Western literature more broadly (61). Ruikō's translations served his own social and political agenda as well, by being put into editorial contexts within his newspaper that highlighted particular aspects of the story. These aspects were further emphasized by "adding didactic prefaces, inserting direct addresses to the reader, grafting in wholly new material, and—in the pages of the tabloid he founded— juxtaposing against his translations news coverage that had an obvious thematic connection to them" (62). This strategy of creative appropriation and assimilation was reflected in Ruikō's own practice of translation. Although he retained the settings found in his original text, Ruikō changed the names of the characters into roughly homophonous Japanese ones, providing a chart of the original names and their new versions at the beginning of the volumes. Likewise, Ruikō re-presented objects used in daily life in Japanese form: parlors, for example, were turned into *zashiki* (Japanese tatami-covered sitting rooms), while dresses and suits became *kimono* and *hakama*. Such transformations, however, were not confined to terminology or surface details: in one novel, Ruikō rewrote the ending in such a way that the heroine's self-sacrifice in order to save her beloved became the popular Japanese literary device of *shinjū* (double suicide of lovers).

The efforts of Ruikō and others gained a growing audience for detective fiction. At the turn of the twentieth century, for example, "the vast majority of books" borrowed from one booklender in Tochigi Prefecture "were not 'pure' literature but *kōdan sokkibon* (transcriptions of storyteller performances) and detective novels" (Mack 45). This audience was reached by a new group of authors in the early Taishō era (1912–26) via the booming medium of niche-market periodicals. Detective stories became a frequent feature in the pages of new journals devoted to women's issues, political debate, youth culture, and more, most prominent among them *Shinseinen* (New youth), and offered young writers an entrée into literary life. A notable case in point was Tanizaki Jun'ichirō, whose later contributions to the canon of Japanese literature were preceded by forays into mystery writing. Tanizaki's early story "Himitsu" (1911; "The Secret," 1993) was deeply indebted to detective fiction and in particular to the works of Kuroiwa Ruikō, while his 1918 "Yanagi-yu no jiken" ("The Incident at the Willow Bath House," 1997) offered an eerie and perverse investigation into the mysterious death of a young woman. Other authors, better known for their work in different genres, also experimented with detective fiction, drawn in no small part by the money they could make writing popular fiction. Hirabayashi Taiko, for example, a noted left-wing writer and activist, supported herself by churning out standard, puzzle-oriented detective stories such as "Supai jiken" (The spy incident) and "Irezumi jiken no shinsō" (The truth about the tattoo affair) (Seaman 5).

The Nostalgic Detective: Okamoto Kidō's Hanshichi

As the twentieth century began, Japan's rapid importation of things Western as a means to modernize was supplanted by an increasing sense of Japanese identity, particularity, and power. Military victories in the Sino-Japanese War of 1894–95 and the Russo-Japanese War of 1904–5, followed by the annexation of Korea in 1910, heralded Japan's emergence as a player on the world stage. External expansion was accompanied by internal turmoil, however: public dissatisfaction with the terms of the Western-brokered Treaty of Portsmouth (1905) boiled over into rioting in Tokyo, bringing down the government and ushering in over a decade of public unrest, increasing political conflict, and labor activism (Gordon 134–35).

The detective fiction that emerged from this period of discontent reflected Japan's new sense of itself, its historical trajectory, and its place in the world, as Ruikō's open-armed embrace of everything Western gave way to efforts at producing indigenous interpretations of and experiments with the genre. The leading figure in this regard was Okamoto Kidō (1872–1939), whose stories featuring the wily Inspector Hanshichi enjoyed enormous popularity. Beginning in 1917 and running through 1937 (with an eight-year sabbatical in the late 1920s and early 1930s), the sixty-plus installments of the Hanshichi series featured a retired *okappiki* (literally, "thief catcher"), who served the function of a private detective in the employ of the old Edo police force (Okamoto xvii–xviii). Many of Okamoto's stories follow a similar pattern, first remarking on how much Tokyo has changed and then establishing the historical context of the story. In "The Mystery of the Fire Bell," for example, the story opens with the narrator coming to visit Inspector Hanshichi, who recalls an incident from his past that then makes up the rest of the narrative. Hanshichi interrupts his story, however, to lecture his interlocutor (and the reader) about the importance of fire bells during the Edo period, when fire constantly threatened to devour the city's closely packed wooden neighborhoods. As he points out, ringing the fire bell when there was no fire was a very serious crime (Okamoto 130). The purpose of this digression becomes clear in the course of the narrative, which concerns a case of repeated burglaries and attacks seemingly facilitated by false fire alarms. Hanshichi, brought in to identify the guilty party, determines that the man fingered by the local residents cannot have been the sole perpetrator, although he was responsible for one petty theft. Instead, he sets a trap and snares the real culprit: a large monkey. As he explains to the narrator at the end of the story, "How did I figure out the culprit was a monkey? Well, when I inspected the bell, I noticed that there were claw marks all over the ladder. Somehow I didn't think they could've been made by a cat, but it suddenly struck me that that monkey might have got up to such tricks" (Okamoto 150).

Okamoto was inspired by the oeuvre of Arthur Conan Doyle, and his stories, like those of Sherlock Holmes, focus upon a singular detective who is able to solve crimes by applying his superior intellectual powers to a small number of clues (Silver 99). Despite the Holmesian inspiration, however, Okamoto took great pains to create a unique character. Hanshichi is more human, and humane, than the forbidding Holmes, and more empathetic to the people around him. In turn, Hanshichi is an emphatically Japanese figure, whose accounts of his long career highlight the transformation of old Edo into new Tokyo and the special nature of the city and its inhabitants. This nostalgic quality would prove particularly attractive in the years following the Great Kantō Earthquake of 1923, as readers found in Okamoto's stories a link to vanished people and places. As Mark Silver notes, then, Okamoto's decision to situate his stories in the recent past was an ideological as well as artistic one, offering an antidote to the tumultuous present and celebrating the "charm of a lost but easily comprehensible and culturally pure Japan, a charm that depended heavily on that Japan's difference from the very modernity that Holmes so effectively embodied" (100).

Imperial Anxieties: Edogawa Rampo

Of all the figures in the history of Japanese detective fiction, by far the best known and most read is Edogawa Rampo (1894–1965). Born Hirai Tarō, Edogawa Rampo's pen name—a homonym for the name Edgar Allan Poe—served as a clear symbol of his dedication to the genre. He was celebrated not only for his brilliant detectives and ingenious plots, but also for his embodiment of the intellectual and cultural zeitgeist of 1920s and 1930s Japan. After the end of World War II, moreover, Rampo was instrumental in reviving detective fiction in Japan and encouraging its growth, efforts that led to his name being given to the premier literary award for detective fiction in Japanese.

Rampo made an immediate splash with the 1923 publication of his first story, "Ni-sen dōka" (Two-sen copper coin), in *Shinseinen*, and for the next several years, Rampo published a number of stories that confirmed his growing reputation as the first Japanese author who could hold his own against better-known Western detective fiction writers (Silver 136). Rampo's style quickly evolved, as he imbued his genre writing with the sensibility of the new "*ero-guro-nonsense* ('erotic, grotesque, non-sense')" artistic movement of the time and mined the new media of film and radio for devices that would help him titillate and terrify his readers (Kawana 10; italics in orig.). Two stories first published in 1925 illustrate this aesthetic: "Ningen-isu" ("The Human Chair," 1956), the tale of an ugly furniture maker who sews himself into one of his own chairs in order to be close to the woman of his dreams, and "Akai heya" ("The Red Chamber," 1956), in which the wild tales told by members of a mystery club are trumped by the horrible true story of a stranger in their midst. Rampo was also fascinated by dwarves, twins, and doubles, characters that recur in many of his works.

In addition to its role within Japanese cultural modernism, Rampo's detective fiction also was shaped by Japanese imperialism and militarism in the 1930s. Beginning in 1931, when Japanese agents staged an attack on the South Manchurian Railway in order to justify the military occupation of Manchuria itself, Japan's government pursued an aggressive expansionist policy designed to make it the dominant imperial power in Asia (Gordon 188). This colonial impulse was reflected in the foreign settings of many of Rampo's novels, which, for dramatic effect, exploited Japanese anxiety about their new foreign possessions and about the disruptive impact of the non-Japanese Other upon the homeland's culture and values. This can be seen as early as the 1930 novel *Kotō no oni* (Demon of the desert isle), where a remote Pacific island is the site for horrific experiments on kidnapped Japanese, as well as in the 1935 novella *Zakuro* (The pomegranate), in which a murderer evades Japanese justice by fleeing to the cosmopolitan chaos of Shanghai.

Boom and Busts: Matsumoto Seichō and the Postwar

During the Pacific War, official censorship and disapproval of "frivolous" literature led to the near-disappearance of detective fiction in Japan, as Rampo and others either pursued other literary projects or stopped writing altogether. After the war, however, detective fiction reemerged in occupation-era magazines such as *Hoseki* (The jewel), which assumed the mantle of talent promoter from *Shinseinen*, even though it struggled to earn enough money to pay its writers (Seaman 6; Yoshida 281). By the 1950s, a new style of detective fiction had emerged, championed by the writer Matsumoto Seichō (1909–92). Commonly referred to as *shakai-ha* ("social school") fiction, Matsumoto's stories and novels explored crime not simply as a matter of individual wrongdoing or as a puzzle to be solved, but as a social phenomenon, proceeding from and reflecting corruption, injustice, and economic inequality (Seaman 9). In Matsumoto's best-selling novels *Ten to sen* (1958; *Points and Lines*, 1970) and *Suna no utsuwa* (1961; translated as *Inspector Imanishi Investigates*, 1989), as well as his collection of short stories "Koe" ("The Voice"), intricate storytelling and engaging mysteries are built around a framework of real-world Japanese economic and political institutions and relationships. These true-life elements provide the author with a forum in which to critique government bureaucracy and its collusive relationships with corporations and other business interests, the seedy underbelly of Japan's trumpeted "economic miracle."

While Matsumoto's socially engaged detective fiction continues to attract readers (notably, *Points and Lines* was adapted for television in 2007 and starred the Japanese impresario "Beat" Takeshi Kitano), its popularity waned by the late 1970s with the rise of another, less political form of the genre known as *shin-honkaku-ha*. This "new orthodox school" emphasized puzzle solving and the detective's reasoning skills rather than the socioeconomic context in which the plot took place. A leading exponent of this approach is Higashino Keigo, whose novels of mystery and suspense often explore supposedly supernatural phenomena through the lens of scientific reason, as in *Dying Eye* (translated as *Naoko*), in which a man's dead daughter appears to be communicating with her parents. Higashino's most celebrated works feature the duo of Detective Kusanagi and Yukawa Manabu, a dedicated, if frazzled, police officer and a hyperrational, sometimes misanthropic physicist.

Other popular Japanese mystery writers recently translated into English include Natsuhiko Kyogoku, whose 1994 novel *Ubume no natsu* (*The Summer of the Ubume*, 2009) features a Shintō priest-turned-exorcist who runs a small bookstore while taking on quasi-supernatural cases, which prove to be the result not of malevolent spirits but of everyday human greed and envy.

A New Voice: Women's Detective Fiction

Although women have been writing and reading detective fiction since the genre first appeared in Japan, it was only after World War II that female authors began to take a leading role. In the 1970s, authors like Togawa Masako (b. 1933) and Natsuki Shizuko (b. 1938) produced best-selling works that combined intricate emplotment with compelling female protagonists, features that later gained them a substantial readership overseas; see, for example, Togawa's *The Master Key* (1985) and *Slow Fuse* (1995) and Natsuki's *Murder at Mt. Fuji* (1984). In the 1980s, women's detective fiction experienced a boom paralleling that of the Japanese economy more generally. With the passage of the Equal Employment Opportunity Law in 1986, women entered the workforce in greater numbers and increasingly deferred or rejected childbearing, leaving them freer to pursue careers and with more disposable income of their own. It was this generation of single, career-minded women who provided both the audience for and the authors of the new women's detective fiction. Two writers in particular dominated the best-seller lists in the early 1990s, Takamura Kaoru (b. 1953) and Miyabe Miyuki (b. 1960), sometimes referred to by the Japanese press as the Queen and the Princess of Mystery writing. While Takamura ultimately left detective fiction behind in favor of more "serious" literary pursuits, Miyabe has continued to write mysteries of a sociocritical bent, which address what she sees as the excessive consumerism and decline of traditional communal values in contemporary Japan. A signal example of this is Miyabe's best-known novel, *Kasha* (1992; English: *All She Was Worth*, 1996), in which a no-nonsense detective investigates the disappearance of a young woman whose life was destroyed by debt in the pursuit of a materialistic "good life." Miyabe has enjoyed some success in the American market, with five of her mystery novels translated into English.

A number of other female authors have enjoyed similar success as detective writers. Aoi Natsumi (b. 1960), for example, has launched a series featuring a crime-solving midwife whose clients are pregnant women. Nonami Asa (b. 1960) created a memorable motorcycle-riding police detective, Otomichi Takako, in her novel *Kogoeru kiba* (1996; English: *The Hunter*, 2006). Her 1993 novel *Anki* was also translated into English, appearing as *Now You're One of Us* (2007). Kirino Natsuo (b. 1951) also has established herself as a leading figure in the mystery literature world. Her 2002 novel *Out*, a harrowing tale of four female factory workers who begin a side business dismembering and disposing of corpses, was translated into English only a year after its publication in Japan and was nominated for the Edgar Prize, the top American honor for detective fiction. Kirino's reputation has continued to grow over the last decade, with the appearance of a number of mystery novels, including *Grotesque* (2007) and *Real World* (2008). Thus, while the boom of women's mysteries has subsided, replaced by a surge in romance and other popular genres, female authors are now an established and important element within the world of contemporary Japanese detective fiction.

Colonialism and Crime: Korea and Taiwan

Korea and Japan have had a long and fraught relationship. In the late sixteenth century, the powerful general Toyotomi Hideyoshi (ca. 1537–98) invaded Korea twice before his death; neither effort was successful, however. Thus, the Korean kingdom remained free from overt Japanese control for another four centuries. With Japan's victories over China and Russia, however, Korea found itself a pawn in the political games of its powerful neighbors: in 1905, Korea became a Japanese protectorate under the terms of the Treaty of Portsmouth, followed by its outright annexation to the Japanese empire five years later. During the following four decades, Japan sought to transform Korea into another Japan, imposing Japanese as the official language and, in 1938, outlawing the use of the Korean language in any context (Park n11). While Korean writers were allowed to publish under the Japanese regime, strict censorship led to a straitened literary culture, with an emphasis upon traditional Korean poetry or carefully veiled satirical stories about relations between colonizer and colonized (see, for example, Ch'ae). Nevertheless, Japanese efforts to introduce mass media to the Korean colony spurred the creation of numerous newspapers and magazines, in Japanese as well as in Korean, which disseminated literature, music, sports, and new ideas from the Japanese metropole and the wider world (Chong). Like in Japan a few decades earlier, detective fiction found a receptive audience through the new Korean media—not only in the form of translated stories from English, French, and Japanese, but also in critical discussions of famous authors, such as *Detective Novels of the World: Western*, the April 1936 special issue of the magazine *Chogwang* (Kim).

The popular culture that characterized colonial Korea quickly dissolved, however, with the end of World War II and the departure of the defeated Japanese army and its colonial apparatus. Following years of conflict between the Communist north and the American-supported south, an independent Republic of South Korea was established in 1953 and, until 1987, was ruled in large part by repressive military governments. The new national project in Korea was based not only on the positive assertion of Korean culture and institutions, but on the rejection of Korea's colonial past. This was accomplished through policies such as *sooipseon tabyunwha jeongchaek* ("imports source diversification"), which aimed to restrict the influence of Japanese culture by curtailing the import of Japanese products as a whole (Han 196). As a result, the reinvigoration of detective fiction in postwar Japan had little opportunity to influence writers in South Korea. Korean authors turned their attention to the legacy of the Korean War and the peninsula's partition, the challenges faced by Korean families, and issues of isolation and individualism (Borchardt). Within the realm of popular literature, spy thrillers—such as Kim Young-ha's *Pit ŭi cheguk* (2006; *Your Republic is Calling You*, 2010) about a North Korean agent activated by his handlers after years of quiet life in the south—have enjoyed the greatest popularity, a preference due, perhaps, to South Korea's uneasy relationship with its bellicose northern neighbor and the real-life threat posed by infiltrators and espionage. Nevertheless, in recent years, Korean literary scholars have begun to reexamine the works of colonial-era authors such as Ch'ae Man-shik, Yom Sang-sop, and Kim Tong-in as early examples of a native mystery novel tradition (Kim). In turn, police procedurals have begun to grow in popularity, particularly on the small and large screen, suggesting that detective fiction may still have a future in the Korean literary world.

Detective fiction has played an even smaller role in the literary history of Taiwan, another of Japan's former imperial territories. Occupied by the Portuguese and Dutch before becoming a part of the Qing Empire, Taiwan was long a focus of Asian trade and political maneuvering. The Japanese officials who took possession of Taiwan at the end of the Sino-Japanese War in 1895, following its surrender by the Qing emperor as war reparations, found a population made up of Han Chinese from the mainland and a smaller indigenous population, whom the Japanese disparagingly referred to as "aboriginals" (Kono 85). Despite a pattern of active resistance against Japanese rule, punctuated by major uprisings in 1915 and 1930 (Katz), the Japanese colonial authorities persisted in their efforts to transform the relatively undeveloped island into a "model colony," modernizing its society, culture, and economy (Simon 113–15). One key element in this program was the introduction of a compulsory system of education (Simon 113), which produced a high degree of literacy and a vibrant literary scene. Mass media from Japan, novels, and popular fiction, including contemporary detective stories, rubbed elbows with literary journals in the vernacular Chinese that featured literature written about the colonial experience, as well as humanism and individuality (Ching 770–75; Kleeman 119–96).

At the end of World War II, Taiwan was "returned" to China, which at that time was governed by the Chinese Nationalist Party (Kuomintang or KMT) of Chiang Kai-shek. When Mao Zedong's forces took control of the mainland, the KMT fled to Taiwan and set up a provisional government there. The ruling government, dominated by the military, held a near monopoly on power until 1987, when President Chiang Ching-kuo insisted on democratic reforms. In 1996, the KMT candidate won the first presidential elections, and Taiwan has continued to democratize since then (Wachman 128–67). As a result of this political history, most scholars of Taiwanese literature identify the year 1987 as the true beginning of Taiwan's postcolonial period. Ironically, this period also was marked by a growing curiosity about and eventual embrace of Japanese culture, as Taiwan began to orient itself culturally and economically with Japan rather than mainland China (Ching 785). At the same time, more positive appraisals of Japan's role in Taiwan's national development gained increasing traction (Simon 119–24).

While the Taiwanese have continued to import and enjoy Japanese cultural products such as movies, television, anime, and manga, however, detective fiction has enjoyed only minor popularity; even police procedurals, a longstanding staple of Japanese primetime television, seem to have little appeal for the Taiwanese viewing public, which prefers indigenous as well as imported romances and "idol dramas." One notable exception is *Detective Conan*, a Japanese manga, anime, and 2006 live-action television movie that gained a considerable following in Taiwan for its tale of a high school boy mysteriously transformed into a first grader. Its protagonist's dogged pursuit of clues about his condition and its cure leads him to assume a new name (Conan Edogawa), paying homage to the master mystery writers of England and Japan.

As this introduction to detective fiction in Japan, Korea, and Taiwan has demonstrated, detective fiction requires a certain set of historical

conditions to flourish. Despite debates over the origins of detective fiction, most critics agree that detective fiction has long provided a forum
for discussing and calling attention to social, cultural, and economic
problems. Kuroiwa Ruikō's works pointed out the flaws in Japanese
justice system, while Okamoto Kidō's works demonstrate a retrench-
ment in Japanese culture after a period of intense modernization. In the
postwar period, Matsumoto Seichō's works offered a trenchant critique
of government corruption and bureaucratic and business collusion,
while the women writers of the 1990s called attention to gender dis-
crimination, workplace harassment, and the dissolution of community
and family ties in the face of consumerism and atomistic individualism. Notably, detective fiction has never occupied a comparable place
within the popular literary imagination of Japan's former colonies; Korea turned away from Japanese culture for a number of years while
developing its own interest in spy fiction and police dramas, while Taiwan, although ultimately embracing Japanese cultural products, was
drawn to a different set of texts and influences. Farther afield, however,
Japan has established itself as an important contributor to the growth
and transformation of detective fiction in the twenty-first century, help-
ing to define the genre as a truly global one.

Works Cited

Borchardt, Katharina."Korean Literature in Flux." *Sign and Sight.* Sign and Sight.
    com, 18 Oct. 2005. Web. 18 May 2012. Trans. of "Der Wandel ist greifbar." *Frank-
    furter Rundschau*, 12 Oct. 2005.
Cawelti, John. *Adventure, Mystery, and Romance: Formula Stories as Art and Popu-
    lar Culture*. Chicago: U of Chicago P, 1976. Print.
Ch'ae Manshik. "My Innocent Uncle." *Modern Korean Fiction: An Anthology*.
    Ed. Bruce Fulton and Youngmin Kwon. New York: Columbia UP, 2005. 95–
    112. Print.
Chong Chin Sok. "Development of Mass Media and Modernity in the 1920s." Tap-
    estry of Modernity: Urban Cultural Landscapes of Colonial Korea, 1920s–1930s.
    Center for Korean Studies, U of Hawaii at Manoa. Center for Korean Studies
    Auditorium, U of Hawaii at Manoa. 16 Feb. 2012. Address.
Ching, Leo. "'Give Me Japan and Nothing Else!': Postcoloniality, Identity, and the
    Traces of Colonialism." *South Atlantic Quarterly* 99.4 (2000): 763–88. Print.

Crawford, Margaret. "Investigating the City—Detective Fiction as Urban Interpretation: Reply to M. Christine Boyer." *The Sex of Architecture*. Ed. Diana Agrest, Patricia Conway, and Leslie Kanes Weisman. New York: Abrams, 1996. 119–26. Print.

Gordon, Andrew. *A Modern History of Japan: From Tokugawa Times to the Present.* New York: Oxford UP, 2003. Print.

Han, Seung-Mi. "Consuming the Modern: Globalization, Things Japanese, and the Politics of Cultural Identity in Korea." *Globalizing Japan: Ethnography of the Japanese Presence in Asia, Europe, and America*. Ed. Harumi Befu and Sylvie Guichard-Anguis. London: Routledge, 2001. 194–208. Print.

Kamada, Mamie. "The Awkward Writer: Opinions about and Influence of Matsumoto Seichō." *Japan Interpreter: A Journal of Social and Political Ideas* 12.2 (1978): 149–70. Print.

Katz, Paul. *When Valleys Turned Blood Red: The Ta-pa-ni Incident in Colonial Taiwan*. Honolulu: U of Hawaii P, 2005. Print.

Kawana, Sari. *Murder Most Modern: Detective Fiction and Japanese Culture*. Minneapolis: U of Minnesota P, 2008. Print.

Kayaoğlu, Turan. "Japan's Rapid Rise to Sovereignty." *Legal Imperialism: Sovereignty and Extraterritoriality in Japan, the Ottoman Empire, and China*. New York: Cambridge UP, 2010. 66–103. Print.

Kim, Jina. Message to the author. Mar. 2012. E-mail.

Kirino Natsuo. *Grotesque*. Trans. Rebecca Copeland. New York: Knopf, 2007. Print.

___. *Out*. Trans. Stephen Snyder. New York: Kodansha, 2003. Print.

___. *Real World*. Trans. Philip Gabriel. New York: Knopf, 2008. Print.

Kleeman, Faye Yuan. *Under an Imperial Sun: Japanese Colonial Literature of Taiwan and the South*. Honolulu: U of Hawaii P, 2003. Print.

Kono, Kimberly Tae. "Writing Colonial Lineage in Sakaguchi Reiko's 'Tokeisō.'" *Journal of Japanese Studies* 32.1 (2006): 83–117. Print.

Mack, Edward. *Manufacturing Modern Japanese Literature: Publishing, Prizes, and the Ascription of Literary Value*. Durham: Duke UP, 2010. Print.

Matsumoto Seichō. *Inspector Imanishi Investigates*. Trans. Beth Cary. New York: Soho, 1989. Print.

___. *Points and Lines*. Trans. Makiko Yamamoto and Paul C. Blum. Tokyo: Kodansha, 1970. Print.

___. *The Voice and Other Stories*. Trans. Adam Kabat. New York: Kodansha, 1989. Print.

Miyabe Miyuki. *All She Was Worth*. Trans. Alfred Birnbaum. New York: Kodansha, 1996. Print.

Natsuki Shizuko. *Murder at Mt. Fuji*. Trans. Robert Rohmer. New York: St. Martin's, 1984. Print.

Nonami Asa. *The Hunter: A Detective Takako Otomichi Mystery*. Trans. Juliet Winters Carpenter. New York: Kodansha, 2006. Print.

___. *Now You're One of Us*. Trans. Michael Volek and Mitsuko Volek. New York: Vertical, 2007. Print.

Okamoto Kidō. "The Mystery of the Fire Bell." *The Curious Casebook of Inspector Hanshichi: Detective Stories of Old Edo*. Trans. Ian MacDonald. Honolulu: U of Hawaii P, 2007. 128–51. Print.

Park Yuha. "Victims of Imperial Discourse: Korean Literature under Colonial Rule." Trans. Gavin Walker. Ed. Melissa Wender. *Asia-Pacific E-Journal: Japan Focus* 42 (2008): 6. *TOC Premier*. Web. 24 Oct. 2012.

Seaman, Amanda. *Bodies of Evidence: Women, Society, and Detective Fiction in 1990s Japan*. Honolulu: U of Hawaii P, 2004. Print.

Silver, Mark. *Purloined Letters: Cultural Borrowing and Japanese Crime Literature, 1868–1937*. Honolulu: U of Hawaii P, 2008. Print.

Simon, Scott. "Contesting Formosa: Tragic Remembrance, Urban Space, and National Identity in Taipak." *Identities: Global Studies in Culture and Power* 10.1 (2003): 109–31. Print.

Shinseinen-dokuhon (Shinseinen Reader). Tokyo: Sakuhinsha, 1988. Print.

Tanizaki Jun'ichirō. "The Secret." Trans. Anthony Hood Chambers. *New Leaves: Studies and Translations in Honor of Edward Seidensticker*. Ed. Aileen Gattan and Anthony Hood Chambers. Ann Arbor: U of Michigan P, 1993. 157–73. Print.

___. "The Incident at the Willow Bath House." Trans. Phyllis I. Lyons. *Studies in Modern Japanese Literature: Essays and Translations in Honor of Edwin McClellan*. Ed. Dennis Washburn and Alan Tansman. Ann Arbor: U of Michigan P, 1997. 321–39. Print.

Togawa Masako. *The Master Key*. Trans. Simon Grove. Harmondsworth: Penguin, 1985. Print.

___. *Slow Fuse*. Trans. Simon Prentis. New York: Pantheon, 1995. Print.

Wachman, Alan M. *Taiwan: National Identity and Democratization*. Armonk: Sharpe, 1994. Print.

Yi Nam-ho, U Ch'an-je, Yi Kwang-ho, and Kim Mi-hyŏn. *Twentieth-Century Korean Literature*. Trans. Youngju Ryu. Ed. Brother Anthony of Taizé. Norwich: Eastbridge, 2005. Print.

Yoshida, Kazuo. "Japanese Mystery Literature." *Handbook of Japanese Popular Culture*. Ed. Richard Gid Powers and Hidetoshi Kato. Westport: Greenwood, 1989. 275–99. Print.

Latin American Crime Fiction _____

Natalia Jacovkis

Early Period

Detective fiction made its first appearance in Latin America at the end of the nineteenth century in Argentina, with short stories such as "La huella del crimen" (The traces of crime, 1877), written by Luis Vicente Varela under the pseudonym Raúl Waleis; "La pesquisa" (The inquiry, 1844) by Paul Groussac; and "La bolsa de huesos" (The bag of bones, 1896) by Eduardo L. Holmberg. However, what prevailed in the region until the 1940s was British classical detective fiction in translation. The reason for this was that the genre had little prestige within the Latin American literary field. During this period, most Latin American practitioners of the genre wrote under a pseudonym and/or set their stories in a foreign setting as a way to make them more popular to the public.

This situation started to change in Argentina in the 1930s due to the influence of Jorge Luis Borges. Probably the most influential Argentine writer from the twentieth century, he wrote numerous essays defending the genre. In 1942, he and Adolfo Bioy Casares, another prestigious writer, published *Seis problemas para Don Isidro Parodi* (*Six Problems for Don Isidro Parodi*, 1981) under the pseudonym H. Bustos Domecq. Borges also wrote several stories that can be categorized as detective fiction, including "La muerte y la brújula" (1944; "Death and the Compass," 1954) and "El jardín de los senderos que se bifurcan" (1941; "The Garden of Forking Paths," 1948). The latter became the first of Borges's stories to appear in English translation when it was published in the August 1948 issue of *Ellery Queen's Mystery Magazine*. Borges was also the director of the collection *El Séptimo Círculo* (The seventh circle) for Emecé, a publishing house, from 1943 to 1956. The works published in this collection disseminated throughout Latin America the most important examples of classic analytical detective fiction.

Another early practitioner of the genre was Antonio Helú of Mexico, who wrote a series of detective stories in the 1920s. His detective protagonist is Máximo Roldán, a thief, inspired in part by the character Arsenio Lupin created by Maurice Leblanc. Helú's detective fiction takes place in Mexico DF, and Roldán is often joined by another thief, Carlos Miranda. Roldán uses his intelligence not only to solve the mysteries but also to trick law-enforcing agents and keep the loot. One difference between Helú's fiction and other detective fiction is its national orientation. Amelia Simpson, in her seminal book *Detective Fiction from Latin America*, explains that in Mexico, the tendency was to use detective models "to express and explore national culture and problems" (82). As a result, "the use of pseudonyms and the adoption of foreign settings and characters is less frequent in Mexico" (82–83). For a long period of time, however, Mexican literary criticism would consider detective fiction only a minor genre, and consequently its development was more sporadic in this country.

Latin American political upheavals had a great influence in how the genre developed in the region during the twentieth century. The breakdown and failure of liberal democratic governments, the imposition of dictatorships, and the corruption of the forces in charge of preserving the law made classical detective fiction, with its emphasis on restoring law and order within a liberal bourgeois society, incompatible with the national realities of Latin American nations. With variations within each country, Latin American authors have increasingly adopted the United States' hard-boiled model. Argentina is the country with the strongest tradition in detective fiction within the region, and it was the first country where the genre started being practiced systematically. Borges's seal of approval meant that it became an accepted mode of narration among Argentinean literary circles. Though Borges vehemently disapproved of the American hard-boiled model, the genre became increasingly politicized in parallel with the breakdown of liberal democracies and the increasing repression and authoritarianism on the part of the state. *Operación masacre* (Operation massacre, 1957), a nonfiction investigative novel by Rodolfo Walsh, is the precursor of the politicization of the genre in Argentina. *Operación masacre* narrates the investigation carried on by the author regarding the massacre of José León Suárez on June 6, 1956. That day, a group of civilians accused of supporting the pro-Peronist uprising of General Tanco and General Valle were executed by members of the army without trial. In *Operación masacre*, the crime is committed by the state. This book marks the beginning of the politicization of crime fiction in Latin America.

Latin American Hard-Boiled Fiction

In Latin America, the 1970s and 1980s mark a clear shift from the whodunit to the hard-boiled detective model. It coincides, as Glen S. Close points out, with a "moment . . . defined generally by the exhaustion of the import-substitution model of State-directed modernization, the resurgence of authoritarian military regimes in the Southern Cone and elsewhere, and the beginning of the imposition of neoliberal economic policies in nearly all countries" ("Detective is Dead" 147). Latin American crime writers did not just mechanically use the conventions of the genre. On the contrary, they adapted it to the Latin American reality and criminal nature of the state in most countries of the region. This suggests the first difference between Latin American hard-boiled fiction and its US counterpart. In an essay on American author Raymond Chandler, Frederic Jameson notes:

> The federal system and the archaic federal Constitution developed in Americans a double image of their country's political reality, a double system of political thoughts which never intersect with each other. On the one hand, a glamorous national politics whose distant leading figures are invested with charisma. . . . On the other hand, local politics with its odium, its ever-present corruption . . . . The action of Chandler's books takes place inside the microcosm, in the darkness of a local world without the benefit of the federal Constitution, as in a world without God. (129–30)

In contrast, the universe that arises from most Latin American hard-boiled fiction written after the 1970s describes a society in which the whole system is corrupt and the state is the biggest criminal of all. In that sense, Glen S. Close suggests that the Latin American crime novel's "principal distinction was its attempt to modify the essentially individualistic and populist orientation that rendered the US hard-boiled novel, for all its disenchanted skepticism, ideologically integrative" ("Detective is Dead" 145). The conventions of the genre will serve its practitioners to critically map contemporary society and/or to question official, hegemonic discourses about the national past. Therefore, as Ana María Amar Sánchez suggests in her book *Juegos de seducción y traición*, the best practitioners of the genre in Latin America break with the ideological fiction in which legality triumphs and order is restored. The Latin American texts destroy the harmonious relationships between society, justice, and law by representing crime as a product of political and social institutions. As a result, there is no legal and legitimate body that can mediate between citizens and crime (Amar Sánchez 60).

In the 1970s and the 1980s, Mexico and Chile saw the creation of two of the most famous literary Latin American detectives: Héctor Belascoarán Shayne and Heredia. Héctor Belascoarán Shayne is the creation of Mexican writer and public intellectual Paco Ignacio Taibo II. It is impossible to understand crime fiction in Mexico without paying attention to this figure. Paco Ignacio Taibo II is not only a well-known writer but also a public figure, a political activist, and an intellectual who has been immersed in different cultural and political debates in his country. He was also marked by the experience of the massacre of Tlatelolco in 1968.[1] He is the driving force behind the popularity the genre has achieved in Mexico since the late 1970s, having created what he has denominated the trend of the *neopolicial*. Héctor Belascoarán Shayne is a one-eyed, melancholic, and lonely private detective. He first appeared in the novel *Días de combate* (Days of combat, 1976). He has appeared in ten novels written by Taibo, including *Muertos incómodos: Falta lo que falta* [2005; *The Uncomfortable Dead (What's Missing is Missing): A Novel by Four Hands*, 2006], cowritten by Subcomandante Marcos.[2] The detective is an electromechanical engineer who worked for many years as a supervisor in a corporation. However, he one day decides to leave behind his middle-class routine, quits his job, and becomes a private detective. This move causes his marriage to disintegrate and isolates him from his friends.

In every Taibo novel in which Belascoarán Shayne is the protagonist, two elements are key to the narration: the chaotic and omnipresent Mexico City and the solidarity among its working-class residents. Jorge Hernández Martín explains that in these texts, solidarity is "the key word in the citizens' strategy for survival. In a city where the forces of order are often the forces of oppression and disorder, citizen action ensures that what needs to be done is carried out with a minimum of waste, self-interest, or interference of the profit motive" (171). Furthermore, Taibo's novels often dwell with Mexican historical events, all part of a past that was many times hidden or repressed by hegemonic-accepted narratives and that is crucial to explain the events of the narrative. An example is *No habrá final feliz* (1981; *No Happy Ending*, 2003), in which Belascoarán Shayne's investigation involves Los Halcones, a paramilitary group responsible for the deaths of students during a 1970 demonstration in Mexico City. Analyzing the role that the past plays in Taibo's novels, William Nichols suggests that "through the investigative process [the detective], not only uncovers 'truth' in post-1968 Mexico but also attempts to reclaim a past appropriated by the power structure. Through memory, then, the detective attempts to protect 'history' from the silence, omissions, and absences" (239). Taibo's novels, then, are an attempt to present an alternative discourse to that articulated by the hegemonic classes.

Heredia is the literary creation of Chilean writer Ramón Díaz Eterovic. The first novel in which the character appears is *La ciudad está triste* (The city is sad), published in 1987. Heredia has been the protagonist of ten novels and a number of short stories. Similar to

Belascoarán Shayne, he also has a middle-class past that he has rejected. He chooses a life of marginality that refuses to participate in the free-market capitalist economy, a product of the economic policies of Pinochet's dictatorship. Unlike most of his former classmates in college, he has not given up on his left-wing ideals. He is willing to pay the consequences and endure isolation because it is the only way he feels that he has freedom. As with the novels of Paco Ignacio Taibo II centering on his nation's capital city, in Díaz Eterovic's novels, the city of Santiago is an essential element of the narration. Heredia lives in a small apartment near Plaza de Armas—the traditional square in the city center—a neighborhood with a lot of history that represents a Santiago that does not exist anymore. Benjamin B. Fraser explains how in the Heredia series, "the city becomes an expression of the inner emotional state of the protagonist" (202). Santiago is also a city dominated by fear, violence, and corruption, a victim of political repression and savage neoliberalism. At the same time, Heredia's novels explore the crimes committed by the Pinochet dictatorship and investigate its legacy in contemporary Chile.[3] Heredia is also a loner. While he has numerous romantic relationships throughout the series, they never seem to work and he always ends up alone in his apartment. His sidekick is Simenon, his cat, with whom he sustains dialogues that form a substantial part of the novels.

The other important hard-boiled detective worth mentioning is Mario Conde, the protagonist of a series of detective novels written by Cuban author Leonardo Padura Fuentes. The first novel of the series is *Pasado Perfecto* (1991; *Havana Blue*, 2006); a later novel of the series is *La neblina del ayer* (2005; *Havana Fever*, 2009). Because of Cuba's history, these novels constitute a unique case within the canon of Latin American detective literature. The detective novel began to develop in Cuba in the 1970s, encouraged by the socialist government. The plots were schematic and obvious. The good guys were always police officers devoted to the success of the socialist revolution, while the bad guys were usually acting on behalf of the CIA to sabotage and overthrow the Castro government. Leonardo Padura Fuentes's novels break with this model, openly criticizing errors of the past and foregrounding the disillusion that many Cuban citizens have with their government in the present. They highlight some of the darkest moments of the Castro dictatorship, such as the persecution of homosexuals, the corruption of high government officials, and the trauma of the veterans of the Angola war. They question official narratives about the Cuban Revolution. They do not represent, however, a complete break with the ideology of the Castro government, since the novels are always pointing out the positive sides of the revolution and the improvement it brought to many people's lives. Mario Conde is a melancholic police officer with a cynical view of reality. He is a heavy drinker, and he is incapable of forming a lasting relationship with women, even though he desires one. From the first pages of *Pasado Perfecto*, the reader is made aware of the weaknesses of the character: the novel first introduces Mario Conde in his apartment, fighting a hangover, and finally vomiting in the toilet. He does not like his profession, nor does he feel like a real detective. He is a loner whose only respite is the companionship of a cadre of loyal (male) friends.

Unlike the examples mentioned above, it is very rare to find a detective protagonist in Argentinean hard-boiled fiction.[4] On the contrary, it is "gangsters, professional assassins, common murderers, corrupt policemen, and lesser delinquents [who] have usually served as protagonists of the Argentine *novela negra* [noir novel]" (Close, "Detective is Dead" 153). At the beginning of the 1970s, parody was the preferred discursive strategy in hard-boiled novels like *Los asesinos las prefieren rubias* (Murderers prefer blondes, 1974) by Juan Martini or *Triste, solitario y final* (Sad, lonely, and final, 1973) by Osvaldo Soriano. Later, during the 1976–83 dictatorship, the most notable trait of Argentinean crime fiction is an atmosphere of omnipresent violence and paranoia. The best examples of these kinds of texts are *Últimos días de la victima* (Last days of the victim, 1979), written by José Pablo Feinmann, and *El cerco* (The siege, 1977), by Juan Carlos Martini.

Since the return to a democratic government in 1983, the novela negra in Argentina has "retained much of its vigor as a medium for reflection on the legacies of State terrorism, the criminal ramifications of political power, and the persistence of social violence" (Close, "Detective is Dead" 154), as exemplified by novels such as *Luna caliente* (1983; *Sultry Moon*, 1998) by Mempo Giardinelli and *Una sombra ya pronto serás* (1990; *Shadows*, 1993) by Osvaldo Soriano.

Neoliberalism and Latin American Crime Fiction

The 1990s witnessed the implementation of free-market neoliberal economic policies in most Latin American countries. Among the consequences, there was a rise in social fragmentation and a crisis of public security in many Latin American cities due to the increase in crime. In his book *Contemporary Hispanic Crime Fiction* (2008), Glen S. Close suggests what marks Latin American crime fiction during this period is a "turn toward a 'dirtier' and more lawless urban social realism reflecting the 'dramatic rise in criminality'" (23). The importance of local realities is reinforced. In the case of Colombia, for example, while the novel *Perder es cuestión de método* (Losing is a question of method, 1997), by Santiago Gamboa, is an excellent example of novela negra in a country that has virtually no tradition in the genre, what flourished there were the so-called *sicariato* novels.[5]

Colombia has had waves of violence throughout its history. One of these waves had its peak during the 1980s and 1990s and involved turf wars between different drug cartels. One of the most dramatic expressions that came out of it was the phenomenon of the *sicario*, particularly in the city of Medellín. The sicario is a hit man—often just a teenager—who kills under the order of his boss. Sicarios often come from the most marginalized neighborhoods in Colombian cities. Particularly in Medellín, Pablo Escobar Gaviria, drug lord of the Medellín cartel, provided social services and economic support to the impoverished sectors of the population in exchange for obedience. His death in 1993 created a power vacuum. Thousands of teenagers were left without means of subsistence, so they resorted to robbery and murder as a mean of survival. This phenomenon was articulated in literature through what is called *novela del sicariato*; some prime examples include *La virgen de los sicarios* (1994; *Our Lady of the Assassins*, 1999) by Fernando Vallejo and *Rosario Tijeras: Una novela* (1999; *Rosario Tijeras: A Novel*, 2004), by Jorge Franco Ramos.

Central American countries—Guatemala, El Salvador, and Nicaragua in particular—are not known for having a tradition of crime fiction. In these nations, extreme poverty, an economy dominated by a few powerful elites, and the repression of peaceful demands gave rise in the 1960s and 1970s to a radicalization of social movements that led citizens to armed struggle. These rebellions, however, were only successful in Nicaragua.[6] In El Salvador and in Guatemala, the government resorted to atrocious massacres and human rights violations to fight against the guerrillas. In the realm of literature and nonfiction, the hybrid genre of *testimonio* was predominant during this period.

It was only after the end of the civil wars that something akin to crime fiction emerged in the region. Some examples are *De vez en cuando la muerte* (Once in a while death, 2002) and *Cualquier forma de morir* (Any form of dying, 2006), by Salvadoran writer Rafael Menjívar Ochoa; *Managua, salsa city* (2000), by Salvadoran-born Nicaraguan resident Franz Galich; *Que me maten si . . .* (Kill me if . . . , 1996), by Guatemalan writer Rodrigo Rey Rosa; and *La diabla en el espejo* (The she-devil in the mirror, 2000), by Salvadoran author Horacio Castellanos Moya. These are all very different works in style and topic, but they have some traits in common. In his analysis of these postwar narratives, Misha Kokotovic explains how most of them share "a noir sensibility characterized by a pervasive sense of corruption, decay, and disillusionment, in which the social order itself, and particularly the state, is the ultimate source of criminality, rather than justice" (15). Central American crime fiction expresses "a deep disillusionment with the outcome of revolutionary struggles and marks its distance from the Left more categorically" (Kokotovic 16). One of the ways in which this type of novel marks this distance is by recycling, in parodic fashion, the genre of testimonio. As a result, it represents "a sharper break with the preceding regional tradition than do its Latin American noir counterparts" (16).[7] Most of the aforementioned novels denounce the neoliberal era, marked by the alliance of the historical national oligarchies with transnational forms of capitalism, but an attitude of cynicism is prevalent in the universe that these texts present.

Within the Latin American region, another interesting case is Brazil. Brazilian crime fiction from the past thirty years is mostly urban. It has a special interest in the urban imaginaries that arose from the internal migrations of the rural population into the cities—and the subsequent rise in poverty and crime. Although the best-known international writers of crime fiction were available in translation in bookstores since the 1930s, Brazil did not have a strong detective fiction literary tradition until the late 1980s. According to Simpson, "*literatura policial* remain[ed] a relatively unassimilated product, receiving little attention either as a foreign ingredient of Brazilian culture, as a set of conventions of formal, critical interest, or as a form to be cultivated [by writers]" (62). This situation changed dramatically in the 1990s, and the genre experienced a boom in sales with such authors as Rubem Fonseca, Patrícia Melo, and Luiz Alfredo García-Roza.

The commercial success of *A grande arte: Romance* (1983; *High Art*, 1986), by Rubem Fonseca, is considered the main precedent of the explosion in popularity of the genre. The book appeared in the middle of a resurgence of Brazilian literature in a market that had mostly been dominated by foreign best sellers. *A grande arte* was also controversial among academic circles, a group that had not paid much attention to the genre until then. Flora Süssekind, for example, considers that the novel is just a reinforcement of traditional European liberal values, in consonance with a national context of a country that was undergoing a transition to democracy after a dictatorship that had lasted twenty years (164). Nelson Vieira, on the other hand, considers *A grande arte* as an example of the fusion of "high" and "low" culture. He interprets this fusion as "a self-conscious Brazilian politics for internal and structural change away from exclusively bourgeois ideal or extremes and towards the inclusion of interests from 'othered' groups such as women, blacks, underprivileged, ethnic, gays, and other minorities" (Vieira 111).

More than in any other Latin American country, Brazilian publishing houses and the Brazilian market have played a crucial role in the dissemination and promotion of detective fiction. In a paper for the 2003 Brazilian Congress of Communication Sciences, Marco Antônio de Almeida explained the importance that publishing houses have had in building a new status for the genre: putting together and publishing special collections dedicated only to crime fiction. While many of the authors included in the collections are international best-selling novelists (e.g., John Grisham and Michael Connelly), Brazilian writers are an important part of this commercial strategy. However, not all Brazilian authors have received the same kind of marketing from the publishing houses. Echoing the academic dichotomy that opposes "high literature" to "popular literature," the covers of the books from the most prestigious authors—including Rubem Fonseca and Patrícia Melo—emphasize the authors, with their names in bold print being the most important graphic element of the covers (Almeida). In contrast, the novels of such authors as Luiz Alfredo Garcia-Roza and Tony Bellotto, considered only commercial best-seller writers, have been released with covers that make an emphasis on the genre and not on the name of the writer.

What links all these authors is how the topic of violence is represented—or, as in the case of Garcia-Roza, hidden—within the narrative. For example, Rubem Fonseca's stories question the multiple fictional and nonfictional discourses circulating in Brazilian society that try to explain the phenomenon of violence that spiked in Brazil during the past twenty years. His texts also interrogate the ethics of writing, questioning what limits are posed by language to render this phenomenon comprehensible. In Patrícia Melo's works, on the other hand, there is no such reflection of the link between the formal narrative and the content. Her texts reproduce everyday slang and official hegemonic discourses without questioning their validity or what lies behind them.

Female Detective Fiction Writers

Latin American detective fiction is a predominantly male universe. Most of its practitioners are men and so are the protagonists of these narratives. In Belascoarán Shayne and Heredia's series, the female character loved by the detective only appears briefly. The women are portrayed as the Other, elusive objects of affection or seductive temptresses. However, female Latin American detective fiction writers do exist. One pioneer was Mexican author María Elvira Bermúdez (b. 1916). Among her publications are the anthologies *Los mejores cuentos policíacos mexicanos* (The best Mexican detective stories, 1955) and *Muerte a la zaga* (Death follows, 1987). She also published the novel *Diferentes razones tiene la muerte* (Death has different reasons, 1987).

In addition, Bermúdez created the character of María Elena Móran, the first female detective in Latin American literature. Móran first appeared in the story "Detente, sombra" (Stop, shadow) in 1961. Describing this character, J. Patrick Duffey states, "Morán owes much of her detective abilities not only to cold, hard logic, but also to her restless, endlessly creative imagination" (25). The detective is also a writer and reader of detective fiction. Although the narratives are rather formulaic, Bermúdez's female detective stories celebrate "the female self by proudly showing that women are perfectly capable of performing any job they set their minds to: lawyer, judge, writer, critic, detective, reporter, or taxi driver" (25). This was certainly unusual at the time. Within literary critic circles, though, Bermúdez has been more appreciated for her role in spreading Mexican detective fiction through her two anthologies than as a writer.

Most of the contemporary female detective fiction writers appear in the genre only occasionally. Among them is Marcela Serrano, a well-known Chilean writer. Her works often explore the lives of women in contemporary Chile. For her fifth novel, *Nuestra Señora de la Soledad* (Our Lady of Solitude, 1999), she experiments with the detective genre, creating the character of the private detective Rosa Alvallay. Alvallay is assigned to investigate the disappearance of crime writer Carmen Lewis Avila. Rosa Alvallay is a fifty-four-year-old woman and a divorced mother of two. Contrary to the cases of Belascoarán Shayne and Heredia, she feels no particular attachment to her profession but has taken it up after a series of failures in other aspects of her life. Central to the case is Alvallay's increasing empathy with the figure of Carmen Lewis Avila, as well as her belief that it is not objective investigation but rather subjective feelings that are crucial to solving the case. This counters conventional genre tradition, which tends to value objectivity over subjectivity.

Another prestigious writer who has made incursions into detective fiction is Cuban-born Puerto Rican resident Mayra Montero. In *Son de Almendra* (2005; *Dancing to "Almendra,"* 2007), she uses the genre to explore a very particular moment in Cuba's past. The text re-creates the universe of 1957, prerevolutionary La Havana, and narrates the story of a young journalist investigating a corrupted underworld that is trying to turn the city into a Caribbean version of Las Vegas.

Two other exceptions, female writers whose literary production is mostly dedicated to crime fiction, are Argentinean writer Claudia Piñeiro and Brazilian writer Patrícia Melo. Piñeiro has created, with her novels *Tuya* (*All Yours*, 2005), *La viudas de los jueves* (2005; *Thursday Night Widows*, 2009), and *Betibú* (2011), narratives that highlight the hypocrisy and fragmentation of Argentinean society under the axis of neoliberalism. Melo repeatedly explores the topic of the extreme violence that ravaged Brazil in the 1990s and beyond in novels like *Elogio da mentira* (1998; *In Praise of Lies*, 1999) and *O matador* (1995; *The Killer*, 1998). Before publishing her first book in 1994, Melo was a television screenwriter. Her aesthetic is very close to television, and in her novels, what is important is usually not the solution of the crime, but rather the harshness and brutality of the scenes that are being narrated.

Conclusion

The popularity of detective fiction in Latin America has been on the rise since the 1980s. It has been used as a medium to denounce society's ills, shed light on the local urban realities brought about by neoliberal policies, and explore the legacy of the dictatorships and human rights violations that ravaged the region until the 1990s. This popularity means, too, that it is impossible to discern a definitive trend to describe contemporary Latin American detective fiction. Hard-boiled fiction has continued to flourish, with stories such as *Puerto Apache* (Port Apache, 2002) and *Santería* (2008), written by the Argentinean writers Juan Martini and Leonardo Oyola respectively. In Mexico, the growth of violent crime during the 1990s and its increasing importance in transnational drug trafficking produced a decentralization of hard-boiled detective fiction. Since most drug cartels are based in border cities, the capital was no longer the predominant setting. A new wave of authors located their fiction in such cities as Puebla, Monterrey, Tijuana, and Ciudad Juárez. Some authors that are representative of this trend are Gabriel Trujillo Muñoz, Elmer Mendoza, and Eduardo Antonio Parra.

At the same time, there has been a resurgence of the classical analytical detective fiction. In 2003, Argentinean mathematician-turned-writer Guillermo Martínez published *Crímenes imperceptibles* (*The Oxford Murders*, 2005), which became an instant best seller.[8] The novel is set in Oxford, England, and starts with the violent death of an elderly woman. It is narrated in first person, from the point of view of a young Argentinean mathematician who is there for a year on a fellowship. The murderer goes on a crime spree and, at each of the crime scenes, leaves cryptic messages that allude to mathematical problems and to the history of the field. These messages are the key to solving the crimes.

Mexican writer Jorge Volpi Escalante also uses the conventions of detective fiction in his 1999 novel *En busca de Klingsor* (*In Search of Klingsor*, 2002). The novel takes place mostly in Europe immediately after World War II. Francis "Frank" Bacon, a young US mathematician and physicist, is sent to Germany to uncover the identity of the physicist—code name Klingsor—who was rumored to have been in charge of all of the Reich's scientific projects, including attempts to develop the atomic bomb. Unlike in a classical detective novel, there is no definite answer that solves the mystery. One suspect is arrested, but it is never clear whether he was in fact Klingsor or not.

Another name worth mentioning is Pablo de Santis, also from Argentina, whose novels include *La traducción* (Translation, 1998) and *Filosofía y letras* (Philosophy and letters, 1998). His novel *El enigma de París* (2007, *The Paris Enigma: A Novel*, 2008) clearly evokes the origins of the genre. It is set in Paris in 1889, where the world's twelve greatest detectives converge to investigate a string of murders during the Universal Exposition (World's Fair).

To sum up, detective fiction is thriving in Latin America, having experienced a boom over the past thirty years. Each country has adapted and developed the genre in a unique way, as a product of their national realities. Once a marginalized genre, it has become an accepted mode of narration within literary circles in Latin America. Consequently, each writer has adopted and used the conventions of the genre for his or her own literary project with remarkable results throughout the region.

Notes

1. The Tlatelolco massacre took place in Mexico DF (Mexico City), the capital of the country, days before the celebration of the Olympic Games in that city. It had been preceded by months of political instability and police repression against the protests of the student movement. Weeks before the massacre, Mexican president Gustavo Díaz Ordaz had ordered the army to occupy the campus of the National Autonomous University of Mexico. This episode only increased the tension. On October 2, 1968, more than fifteen thousand students congregated in Tlatelolco Square in protest against the military occupation of the university. That night, police and military forces opened fire against the multitude. The exact number of deaths remains unknown, although most sources estimate that between two hundred and three hundred people died that night. After the massacre, the combative force of the student and other antigovernment movements weakened for many years.

2. Subcomandante Marcos is the spokesman for the Zapatista Army of National Liberation (EZLN), a Mexican rebel movement born as a reaction to the North American Free Trade Agreement (NAFTA), a free-trade agreement between the United States, Mexico, and Canada. The group made its first appearance on January 1, 1994, when NAFTA became effective. An anti-neoliberal social movement based in the southern state of Chiapas, the Zapatistas fight for indigenous control and to improve the lives of indigenous people in Mexico.

3. For example, in *Nadie sabe más que los muertos* (No one knows more than the dead, 1993), his third novel, Heredia is hired to discover the location of a young child born in a detention center to a young woman who had been arrested and later executed by Pinochet's troops. The child had been appropriated by a torturer. In *El ojo del alma* (The soul's eye, 2001), Heredia investigates the disappearance of a university friend who had been suspected of being an informant for the Pinochet regime.

4. One exception is Etchenique, the detective protagonist of Juan Sasturain's *Manual de perdedores* (Loser's guide, 1985).

5. The term, first coined by Colombian writer Héctor Abad Faciolince, refers to a specific subgenre of Colombian crime fiction centered on *sicarios*, the young hit men employed first by the Medellín drug lords and later by other criminal organizations (Close, *Contemporary* 60).

6. Only in Nicaragua were these revolutionary movements successful, with the overthrow of the Somoza dictatorship in 1979. The Sandinista revolutionaries stayed in power for a decade, fighting the Contras, a counterrevolutionary group that received financial backing from US government.

7. One notable exception is the Nicaraguan author and politician Sergio Ramírez, Nicaragua's vice president between 1986 and 1990. Ramírez later published his memoirs of this period, *Adiós muchachos: Una memoria de la revolución sandinista* (2007; *Adiós Muchachos: A Memoir of the Sandinista Revolution*, 2012), in which he lays out his disillusionment and criticism of the Sandinista Revolution. Parallel to this, he developed a prestigious career as a writer. He had made incursions into the genre with his remarkable novel *Castigo divino* (Divine punishment, 1988). In 2008, Ramírez published *El cielo llora por mí* (Heaven weeps for me), a more conventional example of crime fiction, which expresses the melancholy of old revolutionary fighters within neoliberal society and the treason and corruption of old comrades. The novel still fits, from a thematic point of view, within the trend of contemporary Central American crime fiction focusing on transnational forms of organized crime, such as the link between Colombian and Mexican drug trafficking cartels.

8. The novel was republished in Barcelona in 2004 as *Los crímenes de Oxford*, and it was translated into English as *The Oxford Murders* the following year. A film version of *The Oxford Murders* was released in English in 2008, directed by Álex de la Iglesia and starring Elijah Wood, John Hurt, and Leonor Watling.

Works Cited

Almeida, Marco Antônio de. "Estratégias de legitimidade e distinção no mercado editorial, algumas considerações a partir da literatura policial no Brasil" [Strategies and legitimacy distinction in publishing: Some considerations from crime fiction in Brazil]. *Anais do 26. Congresso Brasileiro de Ciências da Comunicação.* São Paulo: Intercom, 2003. *Intercom.* Web. 18 Oct. 2012.

Amar Sánchez, Ana María. *Juegos de seducción y traición: Literatura y cultura de masas* [*Games of seduction and betrayal: Literature and mass culture*]. Rosario: Viterbo, 2000. Print.

Close, Glen S. *Contemporary Hispanic Crime Fiction: A Transatlantic Discourse on Urban Violence.* New York: Macmillan, 2008. Print.

___. "The Detective is Dead. Long Live the Novela Negra!." *Hispanic and Luso-Brazilian Detective Fiction: Essays on the Género Negro Tradition.* Ed. Renée W. Craig-Odders, Jacky Collins, and Glen S. Close. Jefferson: McFarland, 2006. 143–62. Print.

Duffey, J. Patrick. "María Elvira Bermúdez (1916–1988)." *Latin American Mystery Writers: An A-to-Z Guide.* Ed. Darrell B. Lockhart. Westport: Greenwood, 2004. 24–28. Print.

Fraser, Benjamin R. "Narradores contra la ficción: La novela detectivesca como estrategia política" [Storytellers against fiction: The detective novel as political strategy]. *Studies in Latin American Popular Culture* 25 (2006): 199–219. Print.

Hernandez Martin, Jorge. "Paco Ignacio Taibo II: Post-Colonialism and the Detective Story in Mexico." *The Post-Colonial Detective.* Ed. Ed Christian. London: Macmillan, 2001. 47–67. Print.

Jameson, Frederic. "On Raymond Chandler." *The Poetics of Murder: Detective Fiction and Literary Theory.* Ed. Glen W. Most and William W. Stowe. San Diego: Harcourt, 1983. 122–48. Print.

Kokotovic, Misha. "Neoliberal Noir: Contemporary Central American Crime Fiction as Social Criticism." *Clues: A Journal of Detection* 24.3 (2006): 15–29. Print.

Nichols, William John, II. *Social Crisis, Economic Development and the Emergence of the "Novela Negra" in Mexico and Spain: The Case of Paco Ignacio Taibo II and Manuel Vázquez Montalbán.* Diss. Michigan State U, 1999. Print.

Simpson, Amelia S. *Detective Fiction from Latin America.* Rutherford: Fairleigh Dickinson UP, 1990. Print.

Süssekind, Flora. *Vidrieras astilladas: Ensayos críticos sobre la cultura brasileña de los sesenta a los ochenta* [*Stained glass windows splintered: Critical essays on the Brazilian cultural of the sixties to eighties*]. Buenos Aires: Corregidor, 2003. Print.

Vieira, Nelson H. "'Closing the Gap' between High and Low: Intimations on the Brazilian Novel of the Future." *Latin American Literary Review* 20.40 (1992): 109–19. Print.

Criminal Welfare States, Social Consciousness, and Critique in Scandinavian Crime Novels _____

Sara Kärrholm

There has been a remarkable upswing in the international awareness about Scandinavian crime fiction since the 1990s, with the novels of Swedish author Henning Mankell as the main example. For a long time, German readers presented the largest audience for Scandinavian crime fiction outside of Scandinavia. In later years, though, the international awareness and translations of Scandinavian crime writers have taken on entirely new proportions, mostly as a result of the great fame held by the now-deceased Swedish author Stieg Larsson and his Millennium trilogy. In less than ten years, since the first English translation of *The Girl with the Dragon Tattoo* was published in 2008, the trilogy has become a best-seller phenomenon comparable to Dan Brown's *The Da Vinci Code*. The success of Stieg Larsson's novels and the film adaptations of these novels has resulted in more translations of novels by Scandinavian authors than ever before. During the last couple of years, Scandinavian crime novels, films, and television series have sold well in the United Kingdom, the United States, Germany, France, and Spain, as well as in the authors' home countries.

The concept "Scandinavian crime fiction" may be confusing since Scandinavia normally only includes the three countries of Sweden, Norway, and Denmark, while the concept sometimes seems to include crime literature by, for example, Finnish author Matti Rönkä and Icelandic author Arnaldur Indriđason. However, the use of the term "Scandinavian" has changed in recent years toward including Finland and Iceland, making it work as a synonym to the term "Nordic." It may also be stressed that there are national traditions in the development of crime fiction in all these countries and that this makes it difficult to talk about a specifically Scandinavian tradition. Some may argue that most of the writing included in the brand of Scandinavian crime fiction found outside of Scandinavia is actually Swedish and that one should thus speak of a Swedish tradition rather than a Scandinavian one. Even if it is true that the Scandinavian crime fiction tradition has been dominated by Swedish authors, however, non-Swedish authors such as Dane Peter Høeg and Norwegian Jo Nesbø, as well as the Danish television series *Forbrydelsen* (2007; *The Killing*, 2011), have contributed greatly to how Scandinavian crime fiction is perceived in other countries as well as in Scandinavia.

The Scandinavian countries have a history of influencing each other culturally through their proximity and through the likeness between some of the major languages in the area. Their similar developments of universal welfare states after the end of World War II also makes it useful to talk about Scandinavian crime fiction as a unifying concept, as the crime genre since then has developed in close relation to the development of the welfare state in all Scandinavian countries (Nestingen and Arvas, Introduction 6–9). That said, there are also several areas in which the nation-states have developed in different directions because of their different histories, different political climates, and different geographical positions. Finland's geographical closeness to and long history of being occupied by Russia has, for instance, made it natural to use the Russian as the Other in Finnish crime writing (Arvas). While Norway and Denmark were occupied by Germany during World War II, Iceland was occupied by the Allied forces. The countries' different stances in relation to this war are a subject that crime fiction of the different countries often draws upon as material for revisiting and re-examining their national histories (Nestingen and Arvas, Introduction 8). Different positions toward the European Union have also marked political differences between the nations of Scandinavia. Iceland and Norway are not members, while Sweden, Denmark, and Finland have all joined.

Even if several of the Scandinavian countries have examples of authors writing in the genre as early as the end of the nineteenth and the beginning of the twentieth centuries, the genre did not develop into a major writing scene for Scandinavian authors until the later decades of the twentieth century. In fact, Norway had some very early attempts in the genre: *Mordet på maskinbygger Roolfsen* (The murder of machine builder Roolfsen), written by Mauritz Hansen in 1840, and *Grevens Datter* (The count's daughter), written by Hanna Winsnes in 1841 (Skei 33; Hejlsted 8). These and other early attempts, however, carried nowhere near the same impact on the genre as the stories about detective C. Auguste Dupin, written by Edgar Allan Poe starting in 1841. Most early examples, such as the novels by the Norwegian Stein Riverton (pseudonym for Sven Elvestad) and Swedes S. A. Duse, and Frank Heller (pseudonym for Gunnar Serner) in the early 1900s, were influenced by the adventure novel, combining elements from this with the logical problem solving of the detective genre. During the 1940s and 1950s, the genre inspired new homegrown authors in several of the Scandinavian countries, most of them writing in the clue-puzzle subgenre made famous by authors such as Agatha Christie and John Dickson Carr. In Sweden, some of the most celebrated authors of the period that is sometimes called the first golden age of Swedish crime fiction (1945–65) were Stieg Trenter, Maria Lang (pseudonym for Dagmar Lange), and Hans-Krister Rönblom (Kärrholm 7).

The dominant subgenre within the Scandinavian tradition is the police procedural, a crime narrative in which a group of police officers work together to investigate a crime or several crimes. Connected to the genre is also a realistic mode of storytelling that has become one of the characteristic ingredients for Scandinavian crime fiction, focusing on a realistic dialogue as well as giving a detailed description of ordinary police work and an up-to-date depiction of the most involved problems in contemporary Scandinavian society. Many of the protagonists of Scandinavian crime novels are known specifically for being so normal and recognizable from everyday life. These and other characteristic traits for the Scandinavian type of crime fiction will be elaborated on in the following paragraphs, ingredients such as critique of the welfare state, the melancholic policeman character, issues of equality between the sexes, and the importance of the Scandinavian setting.

Scandinavian crime fiction is often described as specifically interested in issues of social awareness. The reason for this will be discussed throughout this article, which will eventually end with the outline of some current trends and possible futures for the genre.

Crime and the Scandinavian Welfare State(s)

One of the most salient features of Scandinavian crime fiction is its often close relationship to the development and history of the Scandinavian welfare state. That said, it must be noted that there is no such thing as one singular Scandinavian welfare state. The different countries in northern Europe have all developed their own models of the welfare state even if there are also common features. The Swedish version of the welfare state—often mentioned in terms of the People's Home (a concept used by the social democrats in Sweden since the 1930s as a metaphor for Swedish society) and sometimes as the "Swedish model"—has long been the version with the most impact on how the "typical" Scandinavian welfare state has been perceived outside of Scandinavia.

The Swedish crime writers Maj Sjöwall and Per Wahlöö and the tradition formed in their wake have been imperative for making Scandinavian crime fiction a genre with a growing international appeal. This writing couple has also been at least partly responsible for making the police procedural the preferred subgenre in Scandinavia. Their ten novels, gathered under the title *Historien om ett brott* (*The Story of a Crime*) and published during the period from 1965 to 1975, are about Martin Beck and his police team. Beck is depicted as an everyday man, with a great deal of social consciousness and good detective skills. Yet it is not Beck's own skills that are most important for solving the crimes in these novels, but rather the collective work of and the different skills represented by the team's members. The first novel in the series, *Roseanna* (1965), breaks decisively with the former tradition of the clue-puzzle story in earlier Swedish crime fiction by taking an interest in societal injustices as well as in the murder mystery involving an American girl killed by a sex offender.

Sjöwall and Wahlöö's impact on the genre, both in Sweden and in the Scandinavian region as a whole, has been crucial in several aspects. Their proclaimed ambition to use a less well-regarded literary genre as a sociological tool to critically dissect the Swedish welfare state also served to make the genre more accepted among the literary critics and other parts of the cultural elite. This shift in the genre's critical awareness was one of the features that formed a tradition and later became a trademark for Swedish and, eventually, Scandinavian crime fiction. Many of today's most best-selling Scandinavian authors—such as the Swedes Börge Hellström and Anders Roslund, Norwegians Gunnar Staalesen, Anne Holt, and Karin Fossum, and Icelanders Arnaldur Indriðason—have claimed to be influenced by their writing in some way or another.[1] Sjöwall and Wahlöö were highly regarded both as writers and as social commentators; this contributed to creating a new role for crime writers in the Swedish society, with the possibility of making themselves heard and seen in the media to an unprecedented and much greater degree. The new public space that these two authors helped to create for crime writers contributed to make the genre attractive to authors with other ambitions than to just entertain their audience as effectively as possible. This is one of the major explanations for why the Scandinavian tradition of crime writing often stands out in other countries as a specifically serious take on the crime genre.

Even though Sjöwall and Wahlöö's critique of the Swedish welfare state and contemporary social democratic politics was directed from a radical left-wing angle, many readers shared their indignation toward the government politics that were often criticized as based on values that by the 1960s and 1970s had become obsolete in Swedish society. Sjöwall and Wahlöö were often considered to show high skills in storytelling, while also sometimes being criticized for being too explicit with their radical political agenda. The highly symbolic ending of their series, in the novel *Terroristerna* (1975; *The Terrorists*, 1976), is the utterance of the word "Marx" by Beck's friend and former colleague Lennart Kollberg. Readers of the series greatly appreciated the authors' very dry sense of humor in their novels and the characterization of the team leader, Martin Beck. The character, together with some other characters from the series, later inspired a very popular television series, called simply *Beck* (1997–98, 2001–2, 2006–7).

Sjöwall and Wahlöö were also the ones who introduced a particular sense of social awareness to the Scandinavian crime writing tradition by putting the issue of who is to be blamed for the crime under debate. In most of their novels, the criminal is less responsible for his or her crime(s), and the ultimate responsibility is instead placed on society and the different governmental failures to provide the promised safety and nurture of the People's Home to its members. The title for the whole series, *The Story of a Crime*, is to be interpreted as this crime of the Swedish welfare state failing to protect its citizens, rather than the individual crimes committed by the different killers portrayed in the novels. The novels were published at a time when the state's role toward criminality was up for debate—a debate that eventually resulted in a new governmental approach toward criminals, in which different kinds of medical and psychological treatment were considered more beneficial ways to deal with criminals than the more traditional forms of punishment, such as years in prison.

The tradition formed by Sjöwall and Wahlöö of writing police procedurals with an explicitly leftist critique of the Swedish welfare state has since developed further in Swedish crime fiction through the writing of novelists such as Henning Mankell, Olov Svedelid, Liza Marklund, Leif G. W. Persson, Arne Dahl (pseudonym for Jan Arnald), and the writing duo Roslund and Hellström.[2] There are, as already mentioned, many crime writers from other Scandinavian countries who claim to have been influenced by them as well. In making the genre a forum for discussing political problems and the direction that welfare politics sets out for Swedish society, their work continues to influence Scandinavian crime writing.

The Melancholic Policeman

In the wake of Sjöwall and Wahlöö's *The Story of a Crime*, it has become more common within Scandinavian crime fiction to write about a policeman with a pronounced melancholic, and sometimes even straight-out depressed, state of mind. The melancholic policeman as a literary character can be found already in the novels by the Belgian author Georges Simenon about French detective Commissaire Maigret (stories published from 1931 to 1972) and thus cannot be regarded as a Scandinavian invention. The character type has nevertheless become one of the trademarks for the Scandinavian brand, perhaps because the melancholia takes on a special character when placed in a typical Scandinavian setting and related to a critique of the welfare state.[3] This tradition has sometimes also been referred to as the "ulcer tradition," based on the psychosomatic symptoms of the male protagonists, starting with Martin Beck's ulcer in Sjöwall and Wahlöö's crime novels (Lundin and Wopenka 6).

The most notable example of the melancholic policeman is Kurt Wallander, the protagonist of the series by another Swedish author, Henning Mankell. Wallander is a divorced policeman with a teenage daughter. His personal problems are often examined thoroughly in the stories alongside the narration of his criminal investigations, making Wallander a complex character whose professional life is constantly influenced by his private life. These personal problems, combined with the state of the human lives that Wallander connects with through the murder cases he investigates, fuel his often depressed thoughts and gloomy worldview.

Wallander may be the best example of this type of character, but there are also other notable examples: namely, the Swedish author Håkan Nesser's main character, Inspector Van Veeteren, in the Maardam series, Swede Kristian Lundberg's Inspector Nils Forsberg, and Norwegian Karin Fossum's Inspector Konrad Sejer, to mention a few. Interestingly, it is decidedly more difficult to describe female detectives within Scandinavian crime fiction as melancholic to the same extent. Possible exceptions to this rule are Monika Pedersen in the novels of Swedish author Åsa Nilsonne and Ann Lindell in the crime series by Kjell Eriksson, another Swede; both Nilsonne and Lindell show sure signs of a depressed state of mind.

One of the main appeals of these characters to an audience outside of Scandinavia seems to be their ordinariness, which promotes the possibilities for identification between reader and protagonist. Unlike many American and British detectives, for example, the Scandinavian melancholic policemen are not very heroic or gentlemanlike but rather everyday men and women in recognizable situations and moods (Miller, "The Strange Case"). The melancholic policeman is also a preferred vessel for expressing the social awareness that is pronounced in the crime novels where the character is present. Already in Sjöwall and Wahlöö's characterization of Martin Beck, Beck stands out through his compassionate ways of treating suspects while interviewing them, showing that he cares about the circumstances that led them to committing crime rather than just finding out who did it. His dark view of society makes his stomach hurt precisely because of his great empathy with the victims of society's ills. The same can be said about Kurt Wallander, Van Veeteren, Sejer, and others among Beck's successors in the melancholic policeman tradition.

The Great Breakthrough of Women Authors

Women authors were few in the early days of Scandinavian crime fiction. There are, however, some exceptions, Maj Sjöwall being one of them. Norwegian Hanna Winsnes has already been mentioned, writing as early as 1841, and in Sweden, Fanny Alving wrote a book about a female detective in 1918. During the 1940s and especially the 1950s, several women were successful within the genre in Sweden, Denmark, and Norway. Among them were Kjerstin Göransson-Ljungman, Maria Lang (pseudonym for Dagmar Lange), Helena Poloni (pseudonym for Ingegerd Stadener), and Elisabet Kågerman in Sweden; Karen Blixen (writing under the pseudonym Pierre Andrezél) and Else Faber in

Denmark; and Karin Bang, Lalli Knudsen (writing under several different pseudonyms) and Gerd Nyquist in Norway (Hejlsted 8).

Among the women authors emerging in the 1950s, Swedish author Kerstin Ekman deserves special mention. Her career within the genre started with classical whodunits or clue-puzzle mysteries. During the 1960s, she wrote a couple of psychological murder stories, but the novel that was to attract international attention was *Händelser vid vatten* (*Blackwater*, 1993). The novel is a psychological crime novel in which the landscape in northern Sweden plays a suggestive and important part. When *Blackwater* was published, it was received as a remarkable crime novel because of the way it paired great literary qualities with a carefully plotted murder mystery. Together with Peter Høeg's *Frøken Smillas fornemmelse for sne* (1992; *Smilla's Sense of Snow*, 1993), the novel has often come to represent the best that can be accomplished— a perfect merger between popular culture and literariness—within the crime genre in Scandinavia.[4] Ekman's authorship can thus also be connected both to the golden era of the 1950s and to the greater wave of women authors emerging during the 1990s in several of the Scandinavian countries.

Although there were several women writing crime novels in the Scandinavian countries during the following decades—some examples are Norwegians Ella Ormhaug and Kim Småge; Swedes Jenny Berthelius, Kerstin Ekman, and Inga Thelander; and Danes Helle Stangerup and Kirsten Holst—it was not until the early 1990s that women authors were to experience a large-scale breakthrough as Scandinavian crime writers. This time, the Norwegians were the forerunners. Norwegian Kim Småge started writing as early as the 1980s with *Nattdykk* (Night diving, 1983) and introduced her female investigator Anne-Kin Halvorsen in the early 1990s. Even though Småge's *Nattdykk* is generally considered more of a psychological thriller than a classic murder mystery, it is often mentioned as an important inspiration for the wave of women authors in the Norwegian crime genre that followed in the 1990s (Skei 81, 83).

Anne Holt is the woman author who has been the most successful internationally among the Norwegian crime writers. Holt's career as a crime writer started with her first novel about police officer Hanne Wilhelmsen, titled *Blind gudinne* (1993; *Blind Goddess*, 2013). A later novel in the series, *1222* (2007; English translation, 2011), features Wilhelmsen in a wheelchair after being wounded in a previous murder case and is set in a classical Nordic milieu, the alpine mountain. Parallel to the different stories of her life as an inspector, the novels also examine Wilhelmsen's personal life and her relationship to her lesbian partner, Cecilie. Holt has also written several novels in a crime series about the partnership between criminologist Johanne Vik and policeman Yngvar Stubo. Holt has had a career as a journalist and politician and was a well-known public figure in Norway before her debut as a crime writer. She served as minister of justice for the Norwegian Labor government during the years 1996 and 1997.

Other Norwegian women who started writing crime novels with successful outcomes during the 1990s were Kjersti Scheen, Karin Fossum, and Unni Lindell, to name a few. Several of them have written about male detectives; Fossum, as already mentioned, created Inspector Konrad Sejer, and Unni Lindell created Inspector Cato Isaksen. Lindell has also introduced a woman as a partner for Isaksen and thus created a more dynamic police group with a lot of internal conflicts. Even though Lindell's novels have yet to be translated into English, she is well known and widely read in the Nordic countries, and her novels have been translated into Spanish and German, among other languages.

The success of Norwegian women crime writers eventually inspired a similar development in Sweden and in Denmark. In Sweden, the mystery magazine *Jury* and the publishing house Ordkonst together initiated this wave by instituting the Poloni prize, an award given to prominent new women authors in the genre from 1998 and onward. Only four years later, however, the Poloni prize was cancelled since it was no longer deemed necessary in order to promote women writing crime fiction. After Liza Marklund won the award in 1998, more than a dozen new women authors emerged on the Swedish market. Among these were Camilla Läckberg, Mari Jungstedt, Anna Jansson, Aino Trosell, Karin Wahlberg, Åsa Larsson, Eva-Marie Liffner, and Karin Alvtegen.

Liza Marklund's winning of the Poloni prize in 1998 was the general breakthrough for the so-called *femikrimi* to the Scandinavian readership (Hejlsted 10; Egholm Andersen 30). The femikrimi has been defined as crime fiction written by, for, and about women. The concept also often implies writing with some kind of feminist agenda (Hejlsted 1). In Denmark, women authors also emerged on a larger scale during the second half of the 1990s, with authors such as Ditte Birkemose, Birgitte Jørkov, Lis Wagner, and Susanne Staun (Hejlsted 10). Norwegians Pernille Rygg and Finn Leena Lehtolainen can also be said to pertain to this general breakthrough of women authors in Scandinavia during the 1990s. Lehtolainen has not had as much competition as the others in their own home countries, however. In Iceland, Yrsa Sigurðadóttir has had an international breakthrough since her debut novel *Þriðja táknið* (2005; *Last Rituals*, 2008).

The new wave of women authors in the 1990s and beginning of the 2000s continued to challenge the former patterns in the crime genre, introducing more female protagonists and more focus on issues such as motherhood and career opportunities for women. Liza Marklund, who became a trendsetter for women authors in Sweden, has used her series about crime reporter Annika Bengtzon to comment on issues of equality between men and women through the nature of the crimes in her novels—often involving domestic abuse, for instance—and through the focus on women's work situations in male-dominated workplaces. Her debut novel, *Sprängaren* (1998; *The Bomber*, 2000), is a good example of this, as it describes the difficult situations of three women: Annika, the murder victim, and the murderer, all hold positions of power in male-dominated workplaces. Marklund was also among the first authors in Sweden to write about the difficulties of balancing family life with building a career for oneself as a workingwoman. Other authors that have continued this discussion in their own ways are Helene Tursten, in her series about Irene Huss, and Åsa Nilssonne, with her investigator Monika Pedersen. In Denmark, Elsebeth Egholm's detective and journalist, Dicte Svendsen, struggles with the same career-life balance, while the novels about Karin Sommer, the retirement-aged detective and journalist created by Gretelise Holm, present these issues from a somewhat different perspective.

Even if the concept of femikrimi has proved itself useful in the academic discussions about women crime writers, female investigators, and feminist crime fiction, the term also has some shortcomings. Like the Swedish use of the term *deckardrottning* ("crime queen"), femikrimi has sometimes come to connote the quality of the fiction described, mostly in a negative way. It is also unclear to what extent a novel written by a woman needs to have a feminist agenda in order to qualify as a femikrimi. Because the original meaning has been watered down by a too liberal use of it, in much the same way as the Swedish concept, the term has lost some its analytical usefulness (Klitgaard Povlsen 40–41).

It should also be noted that the Scandinavian development of interesting female characters and writing within a feminist discourse has not solely been a concern of women writers. An early example of an interesting woman investigator is Danish author Peter Høeg's Smilla Jaspersen, the protagonist of his best-selling crime novel *Frøken Smillas fornemmelse for sne* (1992; *Smilla's Sense of Snow*, 1993). Smilla is a Greenlander and an expert on snow, making her specifically well equipped to solve the murder of a young boy who is also Smilla's friend. She is tough and hard boiled, as well as feminine and compassionate.

Lisbeth Salander in Stieg Larsson's novels, working together with the journalist Mikael Blomkvist, is another interesting woman character and one of the protagonists in a story with an explicit feminist agenda. In fact, the uniqueness of Salander as a character is often mentioned as the main reason for the huge success of Larsson's novels.[5]

Other Scandinavian male authors who have used a woman investigator as a main character are Swede Kjell Eriksson, writing about the policewoman Ann Lindell, and Henning Mankell, who makes Wallander's daughter, Linda, the protagonist of some of the later novels in his Wallander series, starting with *Innan frosten* (2002; *Before the Frost*, 2005). After Larsson's success with Salander, it has become more legitimate than ever for male authors to write about women detectives, as shown in the novels about detective Jeanette Kihlberg by the Swedish cowriters Jesper Eriksson and Håkan Axlander Sundquist and in those of Swede Mons Kallentoft about criminal investigator Malin Fors.

The Scandinavian Setting

That all Scandinavian countries are relatively small and "safe" when compared to other parts of the world appears to be a reason for the widespread fascination with Scandinavian crime literature. "Today's Scandinavian societies are famously stable, peaceable and orderly, although not, it seems, anywhere near perfect," wrote Laura Miller for the *Wall Street Journal* in January 2010 (Miller, "The Strange Case"; Forshaw 35).

The Nordic landscape is often focused on in the marketing of Scandinavian crime novels outside of Scandinavia, revealing that it is one of the features that publishers deem to be particularly interesting to an outside audience. While not all covers have pictures of Scandinavian landscapes, in those that do, the choice of landscape seems to depend on which audience is being targeted in the marketing campaign. In Germany, many Scandinavian crime novels feature an idyllic rural summer landscape, preferably with a red cottage on the cover, while American-produced covers more often have winter landscapes with ice or snow on them. These choices for marketing strategies suggest that the landscape plays an important role in the international reception of Scandinavian crime fiction, enticing readers by adding an exotic touch or, in the German case, perhaps a familiar touch (since many Germans spend summer vacations in Sweden). The installation of tourist trails following in the footsteps of Wallander in Ystad, Patrik and Erika Lundell in Fjällbacka (the setting in Camilla Läckberg's novels), and Mikael Blomkvist and Lisbeth Salander in Stockholm is another sign of this exoticism of the landscapes in Scandinavian crime fiction.

Even if there are some common features between landscapes in the different Scandinavian countries, there are also many differences, and the authors are often well aware of the uniqueness and specifics of the landscapes they have chosen as settings for their fictional crimes. Most Scandinavian crime writers use the landscape to create a symbolic effect in their novels. Small, secluded societies are often used in the genre at large as the perfect setting for a murder mystery of the clue-puzzle type. The great abundance of these types of milieus is one of the circumstances that make the Scandinavian setting so suitable for the crime genre. The populations of Scandinavian countries are generally a great deal smaller and have a greater distance between inhabitants than in most other countries, making it easier to provide a sense of loneliness and desertedness.

Many of the most translated authors, such as Henning Mankell, Camilla Läckberg, Johan Theorin, also use small towns or islands as their main setting, further emphasizing the differences between these secluded societies and life in the big cities. In the Icelandic crime fiction of Arnaldur Indriðason, Yrsa Sigurðadóttir, and Viktor Arnar Ingólfsson, for example, the whole country of Iceland—an island secluded from the rest of the Nordic countries as well as from the rest of the world—serves as a version of this type of setting. In Indriðason's novel *Mýrin* (2000; *Jar City*, 2004), the isolation of the Icelanders plays a central part in the murder case. The murder investigation involves a databank holding the DNA of all Icelanders, registering, among other things, diseases that are inherited within families and that only occur on Iceland. Another author who has already been mentioned here, Henning Mankell, uses Ystad in highly symbolic ways, underscoring its small-town feeling while also utilizing the fact that it is a town placed at the very southernmost tip of Sweden, forming a link to Europe and to the rest of the world. Mankell often makes the world come to Ystad and play a part in the murder investigations, in a way made possible by the town's geographical position (Nestingen 251).

Current Trends and Possible Futures for Scandinavian Crime Writing

Apart from issues of the abuse of and emancipation of women, other areas of special interest in the Scandinavian crime genre in recent years have been child abuse and issues having to do with immigration. Many of the crime novels published in the last twenty years have discussed pedophilia and other types of child abuse. Some examples are Swede Kristina Ohlsson's debut novel *Askungar* (*Unwanted*, 2009), Swedish writing duo Anders Roslund and Börge Hellström's novel *Odjuret* (2004; *The Beast*, 2005), and Danish duo Lene Kaaberbøl and Agnete Friis's *Drengen i kufferten* (2008; *The Boy in the Suitcase*, 2011). Globalization offers one explanation for the increasing awareness about child abuse of all kinds. The internet's expansion has made it more difficult to reach the people responsible for spreading child pornography, while also making it easier for pedophiles to organize in larger groups, increasing the risk for criminal behavior. Crime fiction provides a narrative forum in which the general anxiety raised by new threats from a globalized society can be dealt with, while also giving the comforting reading experience of a good ending with the apprehension of the criminal(s).

Another significant feature in Scandinavian crime writing is the attention given to issues of social minorities and immigration. The social reality depicted in the crime novels is often related to immigration politics and societal and individual attitudes toward immigration. In recent years, anti-immigration movements have grown stronger in most of the Scandinavian countries, while the immigrant population has become both a more salient and a more integrated part of everyday life, at least in the big cities. Criminal gangs consisting of immigrants, racists, or antiracists, represent a growing part of society's crime rate;

this fact is utilized by many crime writers, often as a means to raise the reader's awareness about racism and its consequences.

In Høeg's best-selling crime novel about Smilla Jaspersen, the situation of Denmark's relation to Greenland and to its Greenlandic population is brought into focus. Henning Mankell often writes about the relationship between Swedes, Swedish society, and the Other by incorporating elements of Otherness in the Scandinavian landscape he uses for his plots (McCorristine). Another novel that brings issues of racism to the fore is Karin Fossum's novel *Elskede Poona* (2000; *The Indian Bride*, 2005), which has been translated into many languages.

Even though antiracism was one of Stieg Larsson's most cherished subjects in his career as a journalist, the subject gave way to the subject of men's abuse of women in his world-conquering trilogy. One reason for Stieg Larsson's fiction being the first to engage broadly with an international audience may be the ways that Larsson flirts with ingredients from American popular culture that are easily recognized by a large-scale international audience. He, for instance, uses several genre traits from spy agent thrillers recognizable from films such as the James Bond series or *The Bourne Identity*, which he mixes with some of the ingredients of the classical clue-puzzle fiction of many British mystery writers. The casual mixing of genres and the filmic qualities of his fiction are part of how it departs from the realist trademark of the Scandinavian tradition and heads in a new direction. There still are, however, examples of realistic storytelling in his novels and a link back to the Scandinavian crime fiction tradition formed by Sjöwall and Wahlöö in the 1960s and 1970s. By blurring the former boundaries between the typical Scandinavian and American ways of narrating crime, Larsson has in this way managed to "introduce" the Scandinavian tradition to the American audience, an audience known for being skeptical toward translated literature. The result is more translations of Scandinavian crime fiction into English than ever before and an international market ready to embrace any new Scandinavian authors that have proven themselves worthy of attention in their own countries.[6]

This is part of what has sometimes been referred to as the "Stieg Larsson effect" on Scandinavian crime fiction: a new audience has become available to the Scandinavian writers, changing not only these authors' sales figures but also how they write. It is not only the influence of Larsson's own writing that can be discerned in new crime fiction in Scandinavia, but also the targeting of this new audience.[7] Recent Scandinavian crime fiction not only shows more tendencies to blur boundaries between typically Scandinavian and other crime fiction ingredients, while also respecting regional conventions less when coming up with new detective characters and plots, for instance. One example is the work of Lars Kepler, the joint pseudonym of the married couple Alexandra Coelho Ahndoril and Alexander Ahndoril, who write about Inspector Joona Linna, an expert in martial arts and, according to the authors' official homepage, a Scandinavian version of James Bond. In Kepler's second novel, *Paganinikontraktet* (2010; *The Paganini Contract*, 2012), Linna is joined in his investigation by the secret agent Saga Bauer, who is lethal and intelligent but has the appearance of a Nordic fairy.

Another up-and-coming author with a style of his own in comparison to the Scandinavian tradition is Swede Jens Lapidus, whose novels about the underworld of Stockholm are written in a style comparable to American hard-boiled fiction of Dennis Lehane and James Ellroy. Lapidus has had a long career as a criminal defense lawyer, which informs his crime writing. He is also a well-known public figure in Sweden, figuring as an expert on the Swedish version of *America's Most Wanted*, the television show *Efterlyst*. His first crime novel in his Stockholm noir series, *Snabba cash* (2006; *Easy Money*, 2011) has been adapted to the screen in Sweden. The series portrays different personalities within the criminal gangs of Stockholm as well as police officers, keeping the line between good and evil constantly blurred.

In Denmark, the author that has drawn the most attention in recent years is Jussi Adler-Olsen. He created the burned-out policeman Carl Mørck, who works on cold cases for the small-scale Department Q of the Danish police force. The first novel in the Department Q series, *Kvinden i buret* (2007; *Mercy*, 2011), has turned into an international best seller. Denmark has also become a respected producer of crime fiction for television, since the Danish television series *Forbrydelsen* (*The Killing*, 2007–) earned huge numbers of viewers when aired on the BBC network in Britain. Other notable Danish television series are *Ørnen: En krimi-odyssé* (The eagle, 2004–6), *Rejseholdet* (Unit 1, 2000–2004), and *Livvagterne* (The protectors, 2008–), among others.

Another result of the expanded market for Scandinavian crime fiction is discernible in some of the new crime novels that are published in Scandinavia, in which the Scandinavian setting has been forfeited for new playgrounds. Some examples include the most recent publications by Swedish author Arne Dahl in the Intercrime series, such as *Viskleken* (The whispering game, 2011), wherein the formerly Swedish setting has been replaced with a European one. Another Swedish author, Ingrid Hedström, sets her Martine Poirot crime novels in Belgium, starting in 2008 with *Lärarinnan i Villette* (The teacher in Villette). The change of setting is a sign that Scandinavian authors are taking themselves more seriously in the international competition for readers' attention. As a strategy, it may nevertheless be a gamble, since the Scandinavian setting has up until now played a major part in gaining the attention of readers outside of Scandinavia.

The Stieg Larsson effect—as well as BBC's current interest in Scandinavian crime fiction, not least shown by their recording of a British version of the Wallander series starring Kenneth Branagh—has opened new channels for the Nordic noir that will most certainly have long-lasting effects. As a contemporary trend, the interest in just about anything Scandinavian within the genre might fade, but it is safe to say that the Scandinavian authors will still have had time to leave their mark in the international field of crime fiction. Among the wave of fiction now being translated into all major languages, there are works by a number of authors that will continue to raise people's eyebrows while breaking the reader's expectations. As with any kind of crime fiction, it is also safe to conclude that when the readers like a concept, they always want more.

Notes

1. See interviews with these respective authors in Forshaw: 83–85, 111, 114, 122, and 142.
2. Some of the most notable writers of this tradition and the tradition itself are thoroughly handled in Tapper.
3. See, for example, Jefferson and Crace.
4. The receptions of both these novels are discussed in Persson.
5. See, for example, the contributions by Miller and McPhee in *Secrets of the Tattooed Girl*.
6. Many critics have commented on the effect that the success of Larsson's trilogy has had on the level of interest directed toward other Scandinavian crime authors. Among them are Burstein in *Secrets of the Tattooed Girl* and Forshaw in *Death in a Cold Climate*.
7. Kerstin Bergman, Bo Lundin, Per Svensson, and I held a discussion about these effects in the Swedish newspaper *Sydsvenska dagbladet* in December 2011. For the full discussion, see Svensson.

Works Cited

Agger, Gunhild, and Anne Marit Waade, eds. *Den skandinaviske krimi: Bestseller og blockbuster* [*The Scandinavian 'krimi': Best seller and blockbuster*]. Göteborg: Nordicom, 2010. Print.

Arvas, Paula. "Next to the Final Frontier: Russians in Contemporary Finnish and Scandinavian Crime Fiction." Nestingen and Arvas 115–27. Print.

Burstein, Daniel. "The Profound Prescience of Stieg Larsson." Burstein, De Keijzer, and Holmberg 3–15. Print.

Burstein, Daniel, Arne J. De Keijzer, and John-Henri Holmberg, eds. *Secrets of the Tattooed Girl: The Unauthorised Guide to the Stieg Larsson Trilogy*. London: Weidenfeld, 2011. Print.

Crace, John. "Move Over, Ian Rankin." *Guardian* [London]. Guardian News and Media, 23 Jan. 2009. Web. 23 Oct. 2012.

Egholm Andersen, Frank. *Den nordiske femikrimi: Læbestiftslitteratur eller fornyelse af en genre* [*The Nordic femikrimi: Lipstick literature or the renewal of a genre*]. Frederiksberg: Her, 2008. Print.

Forshaw, Barry. *Death in a Cold Climate: A Guide to Scandinavian Crime Fiction*. New York: Macmillan, 2012. Print.

Hejlsted, Annemette. "Den skandinaviske femi-krimi – definition og historiske aner" [The Scandinavian femikrimi – definition and history]. *Krimi og kriminaljournalistik i Skandinavien* [*Crime fiction and crime journalism in Scandinavia*]. Krimiforsk.aau.dk, 2009. Web. 23 Oct. 2012.

Jefferson, Margo. "Murder in a Cold Climate." *New York Times.* New York Times, 14 Apr. 2002. Web. 23 Oct. 2012.

Klitgaard Povlsen, Karen. "*Anna Pihl* – Mor(d) på Bellahøj Politistation" [Anna Pihl – murder (and/or mother) at Bellahøj police station]. Agger and Waade 37–48. Print.

Kärrholm, Sara. *Konsten att lägga pussel: Deckaren och besvärjandet av ondskan i folkhemmet* [*The art of doing a jigsaw puzzle: The detective novel and the conjuring up of evil in the Swedish welfare state*]. Diss. Stehag: Brutus Östlings Bokförlag Symposion, 2005. Print.

Lundin, Bo, and Johan Wopenka. *Århundradets svenska deckare* [*The Swedish detective novels of the century*]. Bromma: Jury, 1993. Print.

McCorristine, Shane. "The Place of Pessimism in Henning Mankell's Kurt Wallander Series." Nestingen and Arvas 77–88. Print.

McPhee, Jenny. "Lisbeth Salander, the Millennium Trilogy, and My Mother." Burstein, De Keijzer, and Holmberg 25–29. Print.

Miller, Laura. "The Girl Who Conquered the World." Burstein, De Keijzer, and Holmberg 21–25. Print.

___. "The Strange Case of the Nordic Detectives – The Growing Appeal of Scandinavian Crime Fiction; Existential Malaise and Bad Coffee." *Wall Street Journal.* Dow Jones, 15 Jan. 2010. Web. 23 Oct. 2012.

Nestingen, Andrew K. *Crime and Fantasy in Scandinavia: Fiction, Film, and Social Change.* Seattle: U of Washington P, 2008. Print.

Nestingen, Andrew K., and Paula Arvas, eds. *Scandinavian Crime Fiction.* Cardiff: U of Wales P, 2011. Print.

___. Introduction. Nestingen and Arvas 1–17. Print.

Persson, Magnus. *Kampen om högt och lågt: studier i den sena nittonhundratalsromanens förhållande till masskulturen och moderniteten* [*The battle for high and low: studies in the late twentieth-century novel's relationship to mass culture and modernity*]. Diss. Eslöv: Brutus Östlings Bokförlag Symposion, 2002. Print.

Skei, Hans H. *Blodig alvor: Om kriminallitteraturen* [*Dead serious: About crime literature*]. Trondheim: Aschehoug, 2008. Print.

Svensson, Per. "Samtal om kriminallitteraturen" [Talks on forensic literature]. *Sydsvenskan.* Sydsvenska dagbladet AB, 4 Dec. 2011. Web. 23 Oct. 2012.

Tapper, Michael. *Snuten i skymningslandet: Svenska polisberättelser i roman och film 1965–2010* [*The cop in the land of twilight: Swedish police narratives in novels and films 1965–2010*]. Lund: Nordic Academic, 2011. Print.

From "Hard-Boiled" Detective to "Fallen Man": The Literary Lineage and Postwar Emergence of Film Noir _____

Joseph Paul Moser

The heroic male archetype becomes increasingly ambiguous in 1930s and 1940s "hard-boiled" fiction, from the detectives of Dashiell Hammett and Raymond Chandler—descendants of the Ernest Hemingway code hero—to the corruptible protagonists of James M. Cain (who rose to literary prominence before Chandler) and the authors that came in his wake. This development had an enormous impact on the themes and style of film noir in Hollywood, the heyday of which stretched from 1941 up through the mid-1950s, as well as subsequent noir and detective fiction, including the work of Cornell Woolrich, David Goodis, Geoffrey Homes, and Jim Thompson, among others.

While classic noir fiction reflects the desperation of the Great Depression, (direct and indirect) film noir adaptations of this fiction echo that desperation while confronting the profound disillusionment and social devastation of World War II. Thus, noir fiction and film can be viewed as a fascinating countercurrent in American culture, one that reveals a bleak and fatalistic outlook on an increasingly violent world. Viewed from this perspective, World War II is not simply a glorious triumph for the United States and its allies, but also a physically and morally devastating experience that followed on the heels of another great calamity, that of the Depression.

Though critics often lump them into one literary movement, detective and noir fiction of the 1930s to 1950s can be productively approached as complementary genres that sometimes intersect. Both have roots in the hard-boiled tradition, which is best epitomized by the work of three seminal fiction writers: Dashiell Hammett, Raymond Chandler, and James M. Cain. In this chapter, I will distinguish the two types of fiction and explain how both genres influenced the film noir movement in 1940s and '50s Hollywood cinema. Furthermore, I will outline some of film noir's predominant stylistic elements, narrative fixations, themes, and character types, including the fallen man and the femme fatale, citing examples of quintessential film noir from 1944 to 1949.

From Delicate Moral Order to Social Chaos: The Fiction of Hammett, Chandler, and Cain

In retrospect, both Dashiell Hammett (1894–1961) and Raymond Chandler (1888–1959) can be mistaken for writers mainly concerned with upholding and celebrating a rigorous ideal of tough, virile, intelligent American masculinity in the figure of the principled detective. It is perhaps this façade of resolute bravado that gave rise in the 1920s and '30s to the term "hard-boiled" in the first place, but turbulent emotions lie beneath that surface. These characters' complex motivations serve to undercut their aggressive confidence.

Although, like many Hemingway heroes, Hammett's and Chandler's private-eye protagonists are willing to die to uphold a code of honor, their relationships to their communities—and to society—are deeply ambiguous, their adherence to a professional code becoming an end in itself, a borderline obsession, rather than a means to contributing to the greater good. In addition, these characters frequently confront and angrily resist the temptations of erotic love and fatalism, which represent pervasive threats to their identities. In the fiction of James M. Cain (1892–1977), we encounter hard-boiled figures with cynical attitudes similar to those of Hammett's and Chandler's characters; in contrast, however, Cain's nondetective protagonists lack a strong professional identity and ultimately succumb to temptation and corruption.

In this way, hard-boiled detectives are a deliberate contrast to their counterparts in the detective fiction of the nineteenth century. The latter are typified by Edgar Allan Poe's C. Auguste Dupin of "The Purloined Letter" and other 1840s stories and by Arthur Conan Doyle's Sherlock Holmes, popularized in stories and novels published between 1887 and 1927. These characters are eccentric geniuses of deductive reasoning and Enlightenment rationality, unraveling clearly solvable mysteries and safely dividing the world into perpetrators and victims. As scholar Robert Porfirio notes, "In reaction to this classic detective, Dashiell Hammett helped create the modern 'hard-boiled' private eye, whose allegiance was only to a highly personal and private code, whose style was virtually everything, and who attempted to survive in a universe as chaotic as anything in Poe" (xi). Praising Hammett in 1944, Raymond Chandler wrote that he "took murder out of the Venetian vase and dropped it into the alley . . . Hammett wrote at first . . . for people with a sharp, aggressive attitude to life. They were not afraid of the seamy side of things; they lived there. Violence did not dismay them; it was right down their street" (qtd. in Polito xiii).

Hammett: Godfather of Hard-Boiled Fiction

Beginning in 1915 and before embarking on his literary career in the mid-1920s, Hammett worked as a Pinkerton detective for several years, an experience that informed both his fiction and eventually his public image as a writer. Detractors and some historians have likened Pinkertons to a force of disciplined vigilantes, rather than an agency of auxiliary law enforcement officials, as these detectives frequently worked for large companies to quell labor disputes and disrupt the efforts of laborers on strike in mining and other industries. As he later told his life companion, writer Lillian Hellman, while working for the Pinkerton Agency in Montana, Hammett was "offered $5,000 by the Anaconda Copper Mining Company to assassinate [Frank] Little" (Polito xvii). Although Hammett apparently had no part in any action against the labor leader, in August 1917, six armed men kidnapped Little from a boardinghouse in the middle of the night, murdered him, and left him hanging from a railroad trestle as a warning to other labor leaders in Montana; no one was ever brought to justice for the murder ("I. W. W. Strike Chief").

Thus, Hammett's personal background acquainted him with conflicts that had no clear-cut resolutions. This lack of moral certitude informs all of his fiction, haunting his characters and frequently driving them to compulsively assert control over people and situations. In one telling episode in Hammett's third novel, *The Maltese Falcon* (1930), his most famous protagonist, detective Sam Spade, recounts the tale of an identity-shifting man named Flitcraft to Brigid O'Shaughnessy, the darkly alluring woman employing him. The gist of the story is that one day, Flitcraft, a wealthy man (probably in his thirties) with a wife and children, walks past a construction site and comes within half a step of being crushed by a falling beam; this experience leads him to completely reevaluate his life. As Spade explains, "'He was scared stiff . . . but he was more shocked than really frightened. He felt like somebody had taken the lid off his life and let him look at the works'" (Hammett 65). Upon recognizing that the world he lived in was really not the "clean orderly sane responsible affair" (65) he had taken it to be, Flitcraft's response is to immediately leave his family and job and permanently move away, which he seems to view as his only means of regaining some semblance of control: "Life could be ended for him at random by a falling beam: he would change his life at random by simply going away" (66). Spade has no reason to tell Brigid this story other than to kill time, and he begins it out of the blue, "without an introductory remark of any sort" (63), perhaps revealing that the specters of chaos and randomness, and Flitcraft's oddly sensible response to these threats, are never very far from the detective's mind.

In Spade's own world, he struggles to remain one step ahead of his adversaries and gain possession of the eponymous falcon while resisting the corrupting influence of Brigid O'Shaughnessy, the employer who turns out to have murdered his no-good partner. Coming near the end of the novel, in reply to Brigid's plaintive pleas for protection from the law, Spade's assertion of his professional code of ethics may come across as cold-hearted and excessively macho, as his principled stand necessitates her likely execution. Underpinning his speech, however, is the desperation of a man who has nothing else to believe in:

> "Listen. When a man's partner is killed he's supposed to do something about it. It doesn't make any difference what you thought of him. He was your partner and you're supposed to do something about it. Then it happens we were in the detective business. Well, when one of your organization gets killed it's bad business to let the killer get away with it. It's bad all around . . . I'm a detective and expecting me to run criminals down and then let them go free is like asking a dog to catch a rabbit and let it go. . . . . I don't even like the idea of thinking that there might be one chance in a hundred that you'd played me for a sucker." (Hammett 221)

Debating aloud the alternatives before him, he continues:

> Now on the other side we've got what? All we've got is the fact that maybe you love me and maybe I love you. . . . But I don't know what that amounts to. Does anybody ever? But suppose I do? What of it? Maybe next month I won't. . . . Then I'll think I played the sap. . . ."

> Spade set the edges of his teeth together and said through them: "I won't play the sap for you." (222–23)

Thus, Spade's resistance to "playing the sap" is driven both by deep principle and by great fear. In the final analysis, Spade simply cannot relinquish control and leave himself vulnerable to a woman or to professional humiliation.

Tilting Toward Macho Hysteria: Raymond Chandler's Marlowe

Raymond Chandler's private-eye protagonist, Philip Marlowe, clearly follows in the footsteps of Hammett's Spade. Marlowe's tight but tenuous hold on his detective identity and his resistance to the charms of women, however, take on more extreme forms in Chandler's first novel, *The Big Sleep* (1939). Like Spade, Marlowe has occasion to plainly state his professional code, in this case to Los Angeles district attorney Taggart Wilde. Near the middle of the novel, after Marlowe has been scrambling to cover the tracks of Carmen and Vivien, the two willful daughters of Marlowe's employer General Sternwood, Wilde asks Marlowe why he's willing to make enemies of "half the law enforcement of this county" for only "twenty-five dollars a day and expenses." To this, Marlowe replies:

> "I don't like it. . . . But what the hell am I to do? I'm on a case. I'm selling what I have to sell to make a living. What little guts and intelligence the Lord gave me and a willingness to get pushed around in order to protect a client. It's against my principles to tell [you] as much as I've told tonight, without consulting [my employer] the General. As for the cover-up, I've been in police business myself, as you know. They come a dime a dozen in any big city. . . . And I'm not through. I'm still on the case. I'd do the same thing again, if I had to." (Chandler 113–14)

While the detective might seem morally dubious in his willingness to bend rules and flout the law, he obviously does so not out of greed, but out of a very high-minded sense of duty to his clients.

Marlowe's fealty is comparable to the devotion of a medieval knight to his king, and Chandler underscores this point with symbolic imagery from the very start of the novel. When Marlowe first enters the Sternwood mansion, he wryly observes: "Over the entrance doors, which would have let in a troop of Indian elephants, there was a broad stained-glass panel showing a knight in dark armor rescuing a lady who was tied to a tree and didn't have any clothes on but some very long and convenient hair" (3). What initially seems like a mocking joke at the expense of nobility actually speaks to Marlowe's most profound, abiding desire: to be the one good gun for hire in a dirty, venal, corrupt city.

In one of the most striking and significant scenes of *The Big Sleep*, Marlowe resists the advances of the aggressively, compulsively sexual

Carmen Sternwood, a woman he believes has "made saps of" several other men (89); this scene reveals his fear of female sexuality and of his own frailty. Carmen slips into his apartment and lies naked in his bed, and when Marlowe returns home, he—first gently, then emphatically—tells her to get dressed and get out. As Marlowe tries to reason with Carmen, he first cites his "professional pride," the fact that he is "working for [her] father," and at this moment, the knight imagery returns, as Marlowe regards his solo game of chess and his last move on the board: "The move with the knight was wrong. I put it back where I had moved it from. Knights had no meaning in this game. It wasn't a game for knights" (156). Again, though, his dismissal of the knights' relevance is ironic: by suggesting that their values and qualities no longer apply in a moment of moral crisis, he indicates how integral these ideals are to his identity as a detective and as a man.

Marlowe's refusal of Carmen's advances very quickly turns to disgust—at her, but also at himself and his own isolation and vulnerability: "This was the room I had to live in. It was all I had of a home. In it was everything that was mine . . . anything that took the place of a family. Not much; a few books, pictures, radio, chessmen, old letters, stuff like that. Nothing. . . . I couldn't stand her in that room any longer." Thus, the value of Marlowe's material possessions is "nothing," and therefore, all he has is who he believes himself to be. After Marlowe threatens to put her out in the street naked, Carmen finally relents, dresses, and leaves, but not before repeatedly emitting a "hissing noise" that "was sharp and animal." Her rage in response to rejection is vitriolic and grotesque, yet Marlowe's composure cracks as well— though only after Carmen leaves: "I went back to the bed and looked down at it. The imprint of her head was still in the pillow, of her small corrupt body still on the sheets. I put my empty [liquor] glass down and tore the bed to pieces savagely" (158–59). As we will see even more clearly in the work of James M. Cain, the hard-boiled male protagonist makes sense of his own frailty and sexual desire by projecting in onto a concupiscent woman, often a femme fatale.

The repercussions of Marlowe's repulsion of Carmen and his commitment to absolute professional integrity converge in the climax and resolution of the novel. After Carmen attempts to shoot Marlowe, he orders Carmen's more levelheaded sister, Vivien, to take her away from Los Angeles; when Vivien suggests that Marlowe intends to blackmail her family, Marlowe counters with sarcasm and genuine indignity at her accusation:

> "I haven't a feeling or a scruple in the world. All I have the itch for is money. I am so money greedy that for twenty-five bucks a day and expenses, mostly gasoline and whiskey, I do my thinking myself, what there is of it; I risk my whole future, the hatred of the cops . . . [and gangsters], I dodge bullets and eat saps, and say thank you very much, if you have any more trouble, I hope you'll think of me" (227–28).

In the same vein as Sam Spade's final speech to Brigid, Marlowe explains his actions as a necessary consequence of his detective's code, but his repeated self-justifications also reveal the chinks in his knight's armor.

Considering my close comparison of the hugely influential literary figures of Spade and Marlowe, one might be tempted to look upon the revered film adaptations of the two novels and the casting of Humphrey Bogart in both roles as equally compatible with the tone and themes of hard-boiled detective literature. However, while Bogart effectively portrays the tortured but resolute Sam Spade in *The Maltese Falcon* (1941), a film that stays fairly true to the spirit of Hammett's fiction, the actor's suave take on Philip Marlowe in *The Big Sleep* (1946) bears little resemblance to the Marlowe of Chandler's novel, who is a fairly uptight man barely able to conceal his self-doubt. Furthermore, the affirmatively romantic ending of the latter film elides the sacrifice of Chandler's detective as a tragically constrained code hero, one who must give up on the possibility of intimacy and love for the sake of his professional (and human) identity. Bogart's Hollywood persona, from

1942 on, had key qualities that were incompatible with the hard-boiled tradition, broadly speaking, and more specifically with the thematics of noir (more on this point below).

James M. Cain: Maestro of Noir

While Sam Spade and Philip Marlowe ultimately manage to keep the wolves of their own frailty, women's sexual power, social chaos, and nothingness at bay, James M. Cain's male protagonists are studies in agonizing dissolution, as they inevitably fall prey to temptation and desire. Whereas Spade and Marlowe stare into the abyss of moral corruption and recoil from it, Cain's male figures are drawn to the abyss, teeter at the brink, and plummet into the void of moral depravity. His protagonists are figures epitomizing what film scholar Janet Staiger has labeled "the fallen man" of noir. Particularly in *The Postman Always Rings Twice*, Cain suggests this social failure is bound up with the desperation and privation of the Great Depression. At the same time, the writer sketches noir's other signature archetype, the femme fatale, in a manner that is horrifying but perversely sympathetic. In this way, Cain can be viewed as noir fiction's most influential writer and film noir's most essential literary touchstone.

Cain's introduction to Frank Chambers in *The Postman Always Rings Twice* (1934) immediately establishes his protagonist as a down-on-his-luck, itinerant no-account; he is a drifter with little investment in professional success or in stability. As the novel opens, Chambers has recently returned to California after a three-week jaunt to Tijuana, Mexico—spent, presumably, drinking and loafing—and he has just been ejected from a hay truck, on which he had stowed away to hitch a ride north from the border. Characteristically, he takes this humiliation in stride: "I tried some comical stuff [with the drivers], but all I got was the dead pan, so that gag was up. They gave me a cigarette, though, so I hiked down the road to find something to eat." Chambers happens upon "a roadside sandwich joint, like a million others in California" (3), and at this random destination, he meets the man and his wife,

Nick and Cora Papadakis, who will embroil him very willingly in the torrid love triangle and murder plot that drive the conflict of the novel.

Although Frank Chambers lives in the same state and during the same decade as Philip Marlowe, he exists in a very different world—that of the Depression-bound, marginally employed, fatalistic noir "loser," as opposed to that of the hard-boiled detective, who usually manages to solve his cases and maintain some control of his destiny. As editor and publisher Otto Penzler argues, noir fiction "is about losers," and the main characters in "a noir story (or film) [are] driven by greed, lust, jealousy or alienation, a path that inevitably sucks them into a downward spiral from which they cannot escape. . . . It is their own lack of morality that blindly drives them to ruin." By contrast, Penzler defines hard-boiled detective fiction by its reliance on a protagonist "with a moral center," citing Sam Spade and Philip Marlowe as prime examples ("Noir Fiction Is."). Prevailing social and economic conditions in 1934 essentially define Frank Chambers, and in this way, Cain challenges the core American beliefs in upward social mobility and rugged individualism.

Double Indemnity (1935–36) is a fascinating variation on the love triangle/domestic murder plot of *Postman*. In his second novel, Cain deliberately toys with reader expectations. He establishes his noir anti-hero, Walter Huff, as a man who, at first glance, seems to have a strong professional identity as a cautiously cynical insurance salesman. Huff's commitments to professional propriety and personal morality, however, are instantly compromised when he meets the intoxicating Phyllis Nirdlinger. She initially appears "sweet" but "washed-out" to him—that is, until he notices the contours of her body: "I saw something I hadn't noticed before. Under those blue pajamas was a shape to set a man nuts, and how good I was going to sound when I started explaining the high ethics of the insurance business I didn't exactly know" (5–6). Huff catches on to Phyllis's scheming during their first encounter, and he castigates himself for falling under her spell: "I got in the car bawling myself out for being a fool just because a woman had given me one sidelong look" (7). Nevertheless, he allows Phyllis to draw him deeper into her plot to kill her husband and collect on the "double indemnity" clause of his accident insurance. Rather than insulating him from temptation, Huff's professional identity becomes a source of hubris, as he applies all of his expert knowledge to rigging the insurance system for a maximum payout.

In contrast to the many noir writers and filmmakers who resort to crude misogyny in portraying women, Cain represents his female characters as little, if at all, worse than the moral equals of his male protagonists in *Postman* and *Indemnity*. (Later, in *Mildred Pierce*, published in 1941, Cain's titular hard-boiled protagonist is a businesswoman struggling to protect her family, despite her own deep self-delusions.) These women corrupt men, but men corrupt them in equal measure. Although *Double Indemnity*'s Phyllis Nirdlinger seems genuinely sociopathic in her murderous tendencies, particularly when it is revealed that she has most likely killed before, she, like Cora Papadakis, warrants some sympathy as a woman trapped in a loveless marriage with an incompatible older man.

Living in the midst of the Great Depression, these women have striven for security by marrying for money in a male-dominated world, but they remain deeply dissatisfied, leaving them as vulnerable to temptation as the lustful men who show up on their doorsteps. Particularly in his characterization of Cora, Cain depicts a woman full of greed and cruelty who finally has real capacity to change and to love. Chambers makes the first pass at her, and later, in their initial tryst, the two exude sadomasochistic passion, as Cora cries out for him to bite her lips as they kiss, and he obliges: "I sunk my teeth into her lips so deep I could feel the blood spurt into my mouth. It was running down her neck when I carried her upstairs" (11). Their pattern of combining pleasure with pain continues in the wake of their murder of Cora's husband, but just before the novel's end, Cora is pregnant and willing to forgive Chambers for all the wrongs he has done to her and with her. She declares, "The devil has left me," and then promises him "kisses that come from life, not death"

(110). Things do not end well for the two killers, and though they are very much defined by their place and time, they do exhibit some growth and humanity by finally making peace with each other—before bad luck and bad decisions catch up with them once more.

Film Noir as a Cinematic Movement: Landmark Films, Stylistic Patterns, Icons, Themes, and Archetypes

Noir fiction, which shares roots with the detective novels and stories of Hammett and Chandler but finds its truest expression in Cain's compact, lurid novels, provided the creative foundation for film noir's alluringly toxic cocktail of dark, subversive characters and themes. Film noir takes viewers into a liminal realm beyond the normal, comfortable confines of what scholar Thomas Schatz terms "genres of order." According to Schatz, classic detective and western films (genres of order) create similar fictional worlds in which a lone hero, who is both committed to protecting order in a community (civilized) and adept at using violence to counter his villainous adversaries (and thereby savage), ultimately succeeds in restoring order to a town or city threatened by ruthless gunmen: "The detective, like the Westerner, represents the man-in-the-middle, mediating the forces of social order and anarchy, yet somehow remaining separate from each. He has opted to create his own value system and behavioral code, which happens (often, almost accidentally) to coincide with the forces of social order" (26). While archetypal film detectives and westerners are agents of order who prevail over antisocial thieves and murderers, noir protagonists and femmes fatales are often those who are molded by social dysfunction and who contribute to the perpetuation of crime, vice, and the fracturing of families.

Thus, adapting Schatz's term, one might consider film noir a genre of disorder, as its narrative world frequently lacks an obvious moral center or pro-social mediator. Film noir, like noir fiction, tends to blur distinctions between the civilized and the savage, the principled and the corrupt, through its emphasis on morally ambiguous, impulsive male protagonists and seductive, dangerous women, or femmes fatales. The femme fatale in film noir can be interpreted as American culture's fearful response to female empowerment during World War II, when many women went to work and became heads of household while millions of American men were serving overseas. As noir literature, which came of age during the 1930s, heavily influenced film noir even when its stories did not serve directly as source material for movies, we can view film noir as a cinematic response to both the Great Depression and to World War II, successive calamities that undermined American faith in man's rationality and social and technological progress.

Furthermore, a number of significant noir films in the mid-to-late 1940s, including *The Blue Dahlia* in 1946 (scripted by Raymond Chandler), *Act of Violence* in 1948, and *The Breaking Point* in 1950—center on the malaise and disillusionment of American soldiers returning from the war. In addition, one significant but often overlooked development of some later noir films is their tendency to shift the emphasis from the femme fatale to the *homme fatal* (fatal man) as the corruptor of the vulnerable protagonist. *The Third Man* (a 1949 British film with Hollywood stars) and 1951's *The Prowler* and *Strangers on a Train* all hinge on a main character's relationship with an homme fatal. Still further on in its development, noir spotlights embittered, rampaging police detectives in such daringly bleak films as *Where the Sidewalk Ends* (1950), *On Dangerous Ground* (1952), and *The Big Heat* (1953). These lawmen, in a manner similar to Cain's literary noir characters, become tainted products of their depraved environments, as opposed to conventional detective or western heroes, whose principles tend to transcend their communities. Such deviant characters and ambiguous themes help account for noir's disorienting effect on its readers and viewers, a key element of its enduring appeal.

Cain's Long Shadow Falls on Landmark Film Noir: *The Postman Always Rings Twice* and *Double Indemnity*

It can be useful to approach film noir as a target with several rings surrounding its bull's-eye. Many films that have only one or two noirish qualities—a good proportion of hard-boiled detective movies and thrillers—are perhaps mistakenly viewed as central to the movement. In considering some landmark films and iconic stars, however, we gain a better sense of the qualities and features, including the plots, themes, visual elements, and characters types, most integral to noir. An excellent place to begin is with two mid-1940s adaptations of James M. Cain's work: Billy Wilder's *Double Indemnity* (1944), which was coscripted by none other than Raymond Chandler, and Tay Garnett's *The Postman Always Rings Twice* (1946). Beyond those touchstones, I will briefly consider the screen personas of Robert Mitchum, Burt Lancaster, and John Garfield—noir actors through and through—with that of the more traditional star Humphrey Bogart, who is often closely, and somewhat misleadingly, associated with noir. Finally, I will closely analyze two films that reflect slightly divergent but parallel tendencies of the noir movement: *Out of the Past* (1947) and *Criss Cross* (1949).

Critic and later screenwriter-director Paul Schrader, in his influential 1972 article "Notes on Film Noir," cites *Double Indemnity* as a cinematic "bridge to the post-war phase of film noir." As Schrader explains, the film's "unflinching noir vision" was shocking in its time, and its release "was almost blocked. . . . Three years later, however, *Double Indemnitys* were dropping off the studio line" (12). With writer-director Billy Wilder at the helm, the darkly cynical tone and attitude of Cain's story was in good hands. Summing up one of the most constant themes of his work in 1976, Wilder cuts straight to the sick heart of the noir: "People will do anything for money—except some people, who will do almost anything for money" (107). The director never flinches from revealing the sheer avarice and ruthlessness of Walter Huff (Fred MacMurray) and Phyllis Nirdlinger (Barbara Stanwyck). In the murder scene, for example, which Wilder places almost exactly at the film's midpoint, in keeping with its tragic narrative structure, the director focuses on Phyllis's reaction to Walter's strangling of her husband, a crime that Wilder refrains from showing onscreen and conveys to viewers only via sound. During the murder itself, he employs a striking close-up of Phyllis's eyes and mouth, bracketing them with darkness, to highlight her steely resolve and determination, as she remains absolutely steady at the wheel of the car.

Beyond its compelling take on the noir archetypes of the fallen man (Walter) and the femme fatale (Phyllis), *Double Indemnity* offers signature noir stylistics in its use of visual elements and narration. As Schrader defines it, the fundamental noir style can be boiled down to seven techniques:

1. "The majority of scenes are lit for night";
2. "As in German expressionism, oblique and vertical lines are preferred to horizontal," and "Oblique lines tend to splinter a screen, making it restless and unstable";
3. "The actors and setting are often given equal lighting emphasis," as "An actor is often hidden in the realistic tableau of the city at night, and, more obviously, his face is often blacked out by shadow as he speaks";
4. "Compositional tension is preferred to physical action," and "the actor [frequently does not] control the scene by physical action";
5. "There seems to be an almost Freudian attachment to water";
6. "There is a love of romantic narration," creating "a mood of *temps perdu*: an irretrievable past, a predetermined fate and an all-enveloping hopelessness"; and
7. "A complex chronological order is frequently used to reinforce the feelings of hopelessness and lost time" (Schrader 11).

In the bravura opening twelve minutes of *Double Indemnity*, Wilder's visual and narrative arsenal includes six of these seven techniques. The film begins with Walter staggering to his office to tape his confession (the integration of technique 6, "romantic narration"), and his voiceover cues a flashback to the main events of the plot (establishing element 7, "complex chronological order"), starting with his first meeting with Phyllis on a routine insurance sales call. When Walter enters Phyllis's home (in flashback), even though it is daytime, all the lights are off, setting the stage for high-contrast lighting and looming shadows throughout the scene (technique 1, "scenes are lit for night"). The set design of Phyllis's dark living room is consistently just as prominent as the two actors are, sometimes receiving more light, particularly in the background, which receives a few stray sunbeams (element 3, "equal lighting emphasis" for actors and setting).

Furthermore, the physical placement of the actors within the set and in relation to each other takes on much greater significance (technique 4, "compositional tension is preferred") than any of their characters' actions do at this point. Phyllis stands at the top of the stairs wrapped in a towel as she greets Walter, standing far below her, and after she dresses, he seats himself on the arm of a sofa, looking down at her, while she nestles in the corner of a plush chair. The use of water (item 5) can be also extended to "mirrors, windows, and other reflective surfaces," according to Schatz (116). Here, Phyllis has just been "taking a sunbath," presumably by the poolside, and a mirror figures prominently in this scene as well: after Phyllis has dressed and joined Walter in the living room, she puts on her lipstick in the mirror, as he stands close behind her. Thus, the soon-to-be treacherous couple are immediately shown as doubled—with their backs to the camera in the right foreground and only their reflections in the background at left revealing their full facial expressions—a strong visual cue to their capacity for duplicity and manipulation.

The only missing element of noir style in *Double Indemnity*'s opening reel, and throughout much of the film, is the second technique that Schrader identifies: the preference for "oblique and vertical lines." Wilder and his cinematographer, John Seitz, tend to emphasize horizontal lines, particularly in the many scenes featuring venetian blinds, which cast distinctive patterns on the sets and characters. Even so, one could argue that the brief prominence of the oblique line of the staircase railing effectively "splinters" the screen as Phyllis descends to talk insurance with Walter, initiating the sequence of events that will lead to the fracturing of her family and the destruction of three lives.

Although it elides much of the novel's Depression-era grit in favor of Hollywood glamour, *The Postman Always Rings Twice* preserves, to a great extent and despite the severe limitations of the censorial Hollywood Production Code, the raw desire and desperation of Cain's fictional characters. Though Lana Turner initially seems out of place working at a roadside lunch counter, she effortlessly conveys Cora's ruthless ambition and yearning to escape the marital/professional rut of her husband's service station. John Garfield's face, while ruggedly handsome, looks very appropriately as if it has been battered dozens of times, and his wiry physicality complements Turner's cold poise with seething restlessness. Additionally, in a development indicative of the morally ambiguous world of noir, the distinguished character actor Leon Ames, who portrays the canny prosecutor unraveling Frank and Cora's murder scheme in *Postman*, would go on to play an equally skillful and coolly unscrupulous criminal defense attorney working for a couple (Robert Mitchum and Jean Simmons) implicated in a Cainian murder plot in *Angel Face* (1952).

Finally, both of these adaptations of Cain's work effectively employ what scholar Dennis Broe, drawing on the work of Murray Smith, terms a "structure of sympathy" for their principal characters, another typical aspect of noir, as opposed to the "structure of antipathy" often used in gangster films. The former narrative strategy functions to promote viewer "alignment" and "allegiance" with characters, specifically through film noir's frequent reliance on voiceover confessions and focus on illicit couplings and schemes (Broe xxv–xxxii). In other words, the noir formula provides a cathartic outlet for social misfits and outcasts to reveal their most shocking secrets in a plaintive plea to readers and viewers. Such narrative elements are Cain's métier and the main attraction of these films, which both enact a tight bond between viewers and contemptible but comprehensible protagonists who take part in extramarital yet extremely desirable couplings. This type of relationship between viewers and film characters, however, is rarely enacted by more mainstream genre films, which rely on structures of identification and Othering. In other words, the typical genre film asks the viewer to identify with aggressive, heroic, socially acceptable figures, like those often played by Humphrey Bogart, John Wayne, and Clint Eastwood, while condemning to misery and/or death socially undesirable characters, who are often the "heroes" of noir stories.

Noir Icons: Bogart vs. Garfield, Mitchum, and Lancaster

Humphrey Bogart is a pivotal star, not just because of his mid-career jump from gangster-thug roles to romantic leads and his iconic work in such films as *Casablanca* and *The African Queen*, but for the way he tempers the more subversive qualities of detective and noir films. Bogart's composed, traditional, macho screen presence—as, typically, a man who asks for no sympathy and offers none—is in many ways antithetical to the core characterizations and themes of noir as an artistic movement. Particularly in *Casablanca* (1942), *To Have and Have Not* (1944), *The Big Sleep* (1946), *Dead Reckoning* (1947), and *Key Largo* (1948), Bogart plays a resourceful, triumphant, romantic hero, and once again, "noir is about losers" (Penzler).

By contrast, John Garfield, Robert Mitchum, and the young Burt Lancaster embody the epitome of noir on screen. I will discuss performances by Mitchum and Lancaster in some detail below. As for Garfield, his roles as Frank Chambers in *The Postman Always Rings Twice* and Harry Morgan in *The Breaking Point* (the obscure, underrated 1950 adaptation of Hemingway's homage to noir fiction *To Have and Have Not*) masterfully capture the anguish and alienation of the quintessential noir protagonist.

In a key scene of *The Breaking Point*, Harry Morgan's wife, Lucy (Phyllis Thaxter), looks from her kitchen into the dining room and, via a reflection in a mirror, catches Harry (Garfield) loading a pistol. He is preparing to take part in a shady venture with gangster smugglers (in what is to be the film's climactic sequence), and she asks about his intentions. Morgan's explanation, which he gives while standing in shadow with his back turned to his brightly lit wife, goes a long way toward explaining the bitter legacy of World War II for many struggling veterans, as well as the socially ambivalent attitude of the noir protagonist: "I am doing right. . . . This is my business, this is what I'm good at. It's a job, like any other job. I did worse in the Philippines, and I got a medal for it." Failing to heed Lucy's warning to put the safety of his family (and himself) above a chance at some quick but dirty money, Harry is shot twice when the deal with the smugglers turns into a double cross. As the film nears its ambiguous ending, Harry lies prone and bandaged, perhaps mortally wounded, and with Lucy by his bedside, he offers his own eulogy, a truncation of the climactic, semidelirious speech from Hemingway's novel: "Like passing cars on a hill. With luck? Yeah, maybe. No luck, no luck. . . . A man alone ain't got no chance." This reckless but vulnerable character, and Garfield's sensitive performance in the role, stands as a stark repudiation of the overcome-all-odds, self-defining Bogart heroes—including the latter's own portrayal of Harry Morgan in the earlier adaptation of *To Have and Have Not*, which is a romantic adventure with a few noir twists and shadings and shares a title with the book but little else. Like few other actors before or since, Garfield embodies the agony and allure of the all-American guy gone tragically wrong.

Out of the Past and *Criss Cross*: Paragons of the Mature Noir Sensibility

In a similar fashion, the sublime allure of surrendering to material and fleshly temptations animates the late-1940s personas of Robert Mitchum and Burt Lancaster, and both became stars by virtue of their performances in film noir. *Out of the Past* (1947), featuring Mitchum, and *Criss Cross* (1949), starring Lancaster, capture the core noir theme: "a passion for the past and the present" combined with "a fear of the future" (Schrader 11). Once again, we can draw a sharp contrast between this influential noir sensibility and stereotypical ideas of triumphant, prosperous post–World War II America.

Jeff Markham (Mitchum), protagonist of *Out of the Past*, both re-calls the hard-boiled detectives of Hammett and Chandler and evinces the corruptibility of a Cainian loser. The dark past referenced in the film's title encompasses Markham's work as a detective and his der-eliction of duty to his partner and a client, who had hired him based on his reputation for being "smart" and "honest." Markham has the skills and savvy of Sam Spade, but when he is put to the test by Ka-thie (Jane Greer), the gorgeous femme fatale he has been charged with bringing back to his gangster employer, he delivers the signature line "Baby, I don't care," indicating that he will turn his back on his profes-sional identity if that is what it takes to keep her. Then he kisses Kathie, their faces darkly lit as they crouch before huge, ominous fishing nets looming behind them on the beach. This statement and decision make Markham the antithesis of Sam Spade and Philip Marlowe: he is now a once-principled detective who has traded his macho integrity for a wild shot at romance, willingly leaving himself vulnerable to a trap.

Much of the conflict of *Out of the Past* stems from Markham's ill-fated attempts at redemption. Three years after his fall from grace, Markham strives to build a new life in the idyllic mountains and forests of northeastern California, but his personal and professional sins ulti-mately overtake and destroy him. In the process, Markham commits the further offense of infecting a pastoral American small town with big-city (San Francisco) crime. After Markham reunites with Kathie, the woman who helped precipitate the end of his former life, she asks Markham's forgiveness for fleeing the scene of his partner's murder with all their money by offering the lame excuse of "I couldn't help it." The pithy expression of contempt he fires back at her, however, could just as well be interpreted as self-castigation: "You're like a leaf that the wind blows from one gutter to another. You can't help anything you do, even murder." Throughout the film, Mitchum's disaffected bari-tone voice and bone-tired expression find their feminine counterpart in the calculating half-smile and semidead eyes of Jane Greer as Kathie. Echoing the sentiments of Frank and Cora near the end of Cain's *The*

Postman Always Rings Twice, Kathie's final attempt to draw Markham back into her criminal life comes down to this pitch: "You're no good, and neither am I. That's why we deserve each other."

Like Jeff Markham, *Criss Cross*'s Steve Thompson (Lancaster) has an ambiguous relationship to law and order. Thompson works as a driver/guard for an armored truck service, and when the time comes that he can use his inside knowledge to lure his mercenary ex-wife, Anna (Yvonne De Carlo), back into his arms, he jumps at the opportunity. Thompson sells out his colleagues by participating with Slim Dundee, a brutal small-time gangster and Anna's current husband, in a heist, a botched crime that leads to the death of Thompson's elderly partner.

Whereas about a third of *Out of the Past* consists of an extended flashback, more than half of *Criss Cross* is viewed through the demented prism of the protagonist's obsession with his troubled past. Thompson's flashback-cuing voiceover could be interpreted as the noir outlook in microcosm: "But then, from the start, it all went one way. It was in the cards, or it was fate, or a jinx, whatever you want to call it. But right from the start . . ." This tortured rationalization serves to explain his reasons for reconnecting with Anna, despite the repeated warnings of his devoted family and friends. Near the climax of the film, Anna, in words reminiscent of Kathie, offers Thompson an equally fatalistic account of her reasons for leaving him in the lurch:

> "Love, love—you have to watch out for yourself. That's the way it is, I'm sorry. What do you want me to do, throw away all this money? You always have to do what's best for yourself. That's the trouble with you, it always was, from the beginning. You just don't know what kind of a world it is. . . . Well, people get hurt, I can't help it. . . . I'm not like you, I wasn't born that way. . . . I'm sorry, I can't help it."

Though their motives differ, the two are equally stunted in their capacity to focus on any concerns beyond their own selfish whims and desires. In this dark cinematic world, Thompson's naive obsession with tempestuous, unrequited love is no less tawdry than Anna's fixation on money, rendering them, like Markham and Kathie, as perfect representations of noir's fallen man and femme fatale.

Conclusion: Noir's View of the Present through the Dark Lens of the Past

Both *Out of the Past* and *Criss Cross* have been plundered creatively and turned into inferior Hollywood remakes. These films, *Against All Odds* (1984) and *The Underneath* (1995), fail artistically, not simply because of their inferiority in terms of thematic and stylistic coherence, but because they are set in the present and lack the social immediacy of their predecessors, which acted as direct reflections of two successive periods of anguish in American society, the Great Depression and World War II. The most successful neo-noirs of recent years—the Coen brothers' *Miller's Crossing* (1990), *The Man Who Wasn't There* (2001), and *No Country for Old Men* (2007)—reflect on and are firmly grounded in specific historical contexts: the Prohibition era (late 1920s and early 1930s), the post–World II period (1949), and the nascent expansion of the international drug trade in 1980, respectively. In addition, the first two films are virtual adaptations of the fiction of Hammett (*Miller's Crossing*) and Cain (*The Man Who Wasn't There*), while *No Country* is a direct adaptation of a Cormac McCarthy noir novel. Therefore, the Coens' neo-noirs are firmly enmeshed in the movement's tradition of specific, subtle social commentary, complex characterization, and psychological realism.

Thus, at their most powerful and sophisticated, noir fiction and film still hold an unflattering mirror up to Americans and call into question our most cherished beliefs about our society and ourselves. These stories eschew conventional heroes and villains in favor of more identifiable characters who fail, like so many of us, in their quests for love, wealth, and security. In this way, the characters function as cautionary tales with vitally important messages about human frailty and relationships, rather than flattering the audience with comforting illusions of success and invulnerability and pandering to our delusions of grandeur. Noir exposes the afflicted heart and tainted soul beneath the veneer of the American dream.

Works Cited

Act of Violence. Dir. Fred Zinnemann. Warner Bros., 1948. DVD.
Against All Odds. Dir. Taylor Hackford. Columbia Tristar, 1984. DVD.
Angel Face. Dir. Otto Preminger. Perf. Robert Mitchum, Jean Simmons, and Leon Ames. Warner Bros., 1952. DVD.
The Big Heat. Dir. Fritz Lang. Perf. Glenn Ford. Columbia Tristar, 1953. DVD.
The Big Sleep. Dir. Howard Hawks. Perf. Humphrey Bogart. Warner Bros., 1946. DVD.
The Blue Dahlia. Dir. George Marshall. Screenplay by Raymond Chandler. Paramount, 1946. DVD.
The Breaking Point. Dir. Michael Curtiz. Perf. John Garfield and Phyllis Thaxter. Warner Bros., 1950. DVD.
Broe, Dennis. *Film Noir, American Workers, and Postwar Hollywood*. Gainesville: UP of Florida, 2009. Print.
Cain, James M. *The Postman Always Rings Twice*. 1934. New York: Vintage, 1992. Print.
___. *Double Indemnity*. 1936. New York: Vintage, 1992. Print.
___. *Mildred Pierce*. 1941. New York: Vintage, 2011. Print.
Casablanca. Dir. Michael Curtiz. Perf. Humphrey Bogart. Warner Bros., 1942. DVD.
Chandler, Raymond. *The Big Sleep*. 1939. New York: Vintage, 1992. Print.
Criss Cross. Dir. Robert Siodmak. Perf. Burt Lancaster, Yvonne DeCarlo, and Dan Duryea. Universal, 1949.
Dead Reckoning. Dir. John Cromwell. Perf. Humphrey Bogart. Columbia Tristar, 1947. DVD.
Double Indemnity. Dir. Billy Wilder. Screenplay by Billy Wilder and Raymond Chandler. Universal, 1944. DVD.
Hammett, Dashiell. *The Maltese Falcon*. 1930. *The Maltese Falcon, The Thin Man, Red Harvest*. New York: Knopf, 2000. 1–226. Print.
Hemingway, Ernest. *To Have and Have Not*. 1937. New York: Scribner, 2003. Print.
"I. W. W. Strike Chief Lynched at Butte." *New York Times*. New York Times, 2 Aug. 1917. Web. 25 Oct. 2012.
Key Largo. Dir. John Huston. Perf. Humphrey Bogart. Warner Bros., 1948. DVD.
The Maltese Falcon. Dir. John Huston. Perf. Humphrey Bogart. Warner Bros., 1941. DVD.
The Man Who Wasn't There. Dir. Joel Coen. Prod. Ethan Coen. Universal, 2001. DVD.
Miller's Crossing. Dir. Joel Coen. Prod. Ethan Coen. 20th Century Fox, 1990. DVD.
No Country for Old Men. Dir. Joel and Ethan Coen. Miramax, 2007. DVD.

On Dangerous Ground. Dir. Nicholas Ray. Perf. Robert Ryan. Warner Bros., 1952. DVD.

Out of the Past. Dir. Jacques Torneur. Screenplay by Geoffrey Homes. Perf. Robert Mitchum and Jane Greer. Warner Bros., 1947. DVD.

Penzler, Otto. "Noir Fiction Is about Losers, Not Private Eyes." *Huffington Post*. TheHuffingtonPost.com, 10 Aug. 2010. Web. 25 Oct. 2012.

Phillips, Gene D. "Billy Wilder." *Billy Wilder: Interviews*. Ed. Robert Horton. Oxford: UP of Mississippi, 2001. 99–109. Print.

Polito, Robert. Introduction. *The Maltese Falcon, The Thin Man, Red Harvest*. By Dashiell Hammett. New York: Knopf, 2000. xi–xxx. Print.

Porfirio, Robert. Foreword. *The Philosophy of Film Noir*. Ed. Mark T. Conrad. Lexington: UP of Kentucky, 2006. ix–xiii. Print.

The Postman Always Rings Twice. Dir. Tay Garnett. Perf. John Garfield, Lana Turner, and Leon Ames. Warner Bros., 1946. DVD.

The Prowler. Dir. Joseph Losey. Perf. Van Heflin and Evelyn Keyes. VCI Video, 1951. DVD.

Schatz, Thomas. *Hollywood Genres: Formulas, Filmmaking, and the Studio System*. New York: Random, 1981. Print.

Schrader, Paul. "Notes on Film Noir." *Film Comment* 8.1 (1972): 8–13. Print.

Staiger, Janet. "Film Noir as Male Melodrama: The Politics of Film Genre Labeling." *The Shifting Definitions of Genre: Essays on Labeling Films, Television Shows, and Media*. Ed. Lincoln Geraghty and Mark Jancovich. Jefferson: McFarland, 2008. 71–91. Print.

The Third Man. Dir. Carol Reed. Perf. Joseph Cotten and Orson Welles. Criterion, 1949. DVD.

To Have and Have Not. Dir. Howard Hawks. Perf. Humphrey Bogart. Warner Bros., 1944. DVD.

The Underneath. Dir. Steven Soderbergh. Universal, 1995. DVD.

Where the Sidewalk Ends. Dir. Otto Preminger. Perf. Dana Andrews. 20th Century Fox, 1950. DVD.

The Metaphysical Detective Story

Susan Elizabeth Sweeney

The first detective story, Edgar Allan Poe's "The Murders in the Rue Morgue" (1841), is "metaphysical"—that is, concerned with abstract and philosophical thought—because it focuses not only on a brutal crime but also on the mental processes entailed in solving it. Investigating this particular crime, moreover, leads to provocative questions about the nature of language. The story also prompts readers to pay attention to their own thinking as they read, especially because Poe's sleuth partly unravels the mystery by studying newspaper articles and reference volumes. All detective stories are "metaphysical," in fact, to the extent that they emphasize (and make readers aware of) the acts of thinking, reading, and analyzing.

A true metaphysical detective story, however, is less concerned with crimes, or even solutions, than with the very idea that mysteries can be solved. Typically, the detective discovers in the end that his explanation for the crime was incomplete, random, misguided, or fatally flawed—an outcome that led one critic, Stefano Tani, to choose *The Doomed Detective* as his title for a book on such fiction. The editors of another volume, *Detecting Texts*, define the metaphysical detective story as "a text that parodies or subverts traditional detective-story conventions—such as narrative closure and the detective's role as surrogate reader—with the intention, or at least the effect, of asking questions about mysteries of being and knowing which transcend the mere machinations of the mystery plot" (Merivale and Sweeney 2).

To encourage readers to consider such questions, metaphysical detective stories are often self-reflexive—that is, they refer to writing or reading the text within the text itself. Inevitably, this practice makes readers uncomfortably aware of their struggles to decipher the mystery and comprehend the story. In some metaphysical detective stories, the real detective or criminal or victim turns out to be the reader, in the literary equivalent of those lithographs by artist M. C. Escher in which one level of reality turns into another. This is what happens, for example, in Julio Cortázar's short story "Continuidad de los parques" (1963; "Continuity of Parks," 1965), which describes a man in a green velvet armchair, reading the final chapters of a detective novel. In that novel, a criminal steals through the grounds of a country estate, into the house, up the stairs, and into a study—where his victim sits in a green velvet armchair, reading a novel.

Because the metaphysical detective story emphasizes reading texts—especially detective stories, as in "Continuity of Parks"—in this fashion, it seems appropriate to trace its development according to the relationships among writers and books from the beginning of detective fiction itself.

The Plot Thickens: Nineteenth-Century Metaphysics

Indeed, many of these elements (especially the detective's failure and the story's self-reflexivity) appear in what might be considered the first metaphysical detective story, "The Man of the Crowd" (1840). Not only did Poe write this tale, but, more surprisingly, he did so before composing "The Murders in the Rue Morgue." The story opens by comparing crime solving to reading; according to Poe, however, the human heart is a text that "does not permit itself to be read. . . . And thus the essence of all crime is undivulged" (*Poetry* 388). The scene that follows this statement anticipates the beginnings of many later detective stories. The investigating protagonist—who also narrates the tale—sits in a coffee shop while idly deducing the occupation, status, and character of passersby based on their appearance, just as Sherlock Holmes might do. When he glimpses a sinister old man who defies such categorization, the narrator begins to follows him, but after a day and a half, he has discovered nothing except that the old man seems desperate to disappear into the crowd. Eventually, the narrator abandons his pursuit: Although the old man may indeed be "the type and genius of deep crime. . . . It will be in vain to follow; for I shall learn no more of him, nor of his deeds" (396). The story ends by repeating once more that the human heart is a book that cannot be read. "The Man of the Crowd" might be considered the first metaphysical detective story, then, because it not only compares crime solving to reading, but it also describes its investigator as a failed reader. In a sense, all metaphysical detective stories are texts that do not allow themselves to be read because they advocate and illustrate an interpretive methodology that leads nowhere.

When Poe published "The Man of the Crowd" in the early nineteenth century, other American writers, especially Nathaniel Hawthorne and Herman Melville, were also composing allegorical crime stories that questioned the nature of evil and the limits of knowledge. In Hawthorne's fiction, in particular, characters try unsuccessfully to penetrate the mysteries of the human heart. Hawthorne even compares such detection to reading a text whose meanings cannot be fully understood; consider, for example, Chillingworth's efforts to detect Dimmesdale's secret sin in Nathaniel Hawthorne's *The Scarlet Letter* (1850). And in England, not long afterwards, Robert Louis Stevenson wrote *The Strange Case of Dr Jekyll and Mr Hyde* (1866), another crime narrative with disturbing implications about humanity's hidden wickedness.

By that point, of course, Poe himself had already produced several remarkable tales, including not only "The Murders in the Rue Morgue," "The Mystery of Marie Rogêt" (1842–43), and "The Purloined Letter" (1844), all featuring C. Auguste Dupin, but also "The Gold-Bug" (1843). These tales established the detective genre at the same time that they emphasized its self-reflexive aspects, as when Dupin finds a missing text in "The Purloined Letter" or Legrand deciphers invisible, encoded, enigmatic directions to buried treasure in "The Gold-Bug." By the late nineteenth century, detective fiction had become an influential form, especially as adapted by Arthur Conan Doyle in *A Study in Scarlet* (1887) and other works about Sherlock Holmes. Although Doyle stresses dramatic action, vivid settings, memorable characters, and crisp storytelling rather than metaphysics, some of his tales raise interesting philosophical questions, as in "The

Man with the Twisted Lip" (1891), and all of them focus on Holmes's mental processes.

Modernist Formulas and Fabulations: 1890s to 1930s

As detective fiction grew more and more popular, largely due to the success of the Holmes stories, it also became increasingly repetitive. Readers delighted in tales featuring the same detective, even as writers tried to find new gimmicks by devising ever more bizarre ways to murder someone or ever more distinctive traits for an investigating protagonist. Such repetitiveness betrayed the genre's artifice and lay the groundwork for later metaphysical detective stories that parodied its formulaic structure. A fundamental aspect of that formula, of course, was the sleuth's ability to solve any mystery, no matter how farfetched. It seems inevitable that authors would eventually conceive of a hero who, for one reason or another, fails to solve the crime. By the early twentieth century, indeed, two writers had done just that in narratives mocking the genre's assumptions about the infallibility of rational logic.

The first was G. K. Chesterton, who came up with a new variation on the amateur detective in Father Brown, a Roman Catholic priest. In "The Blue Cross" (1911) and some fifty additional stories, collected in *The Innocence of Father Brown* and other volumes, Chesterton's hero uses his ability to understand the criminal mind—thanks to his experience in the confessional—to solve various bizarre crimes. As Jorge Luis Borges later pointed out in "Modes of G. K. Chesterton," however, the crime in a Father Brown story always has two aspects: an earthly riddle, which the detective ingeniously solves, and a divine mystery, which by its nature defies human understanding. The plot thus invites readers to contemplate more profound mysteries that cannot be explained away. Indeed, the term "metaphysical detective story" was first coined by Howard Haycraft, in 1941 to describe this aspect of Chesterton's tales.

Two years after the arrival of Father Brown, E. C. Bentley published his novel *Trent's Last Case* (1913), which he dedicated to

Chesterton, a close friend. Ironically, *Trent's Last Case* was the first work in which its hero, Philip Trent, appears; it was also the first detective story to undermine the figure of the great detective. At the end of the novel, after Trent has solved the murder of business tycoon Sigsbee Manderson, he discovers (in a reversal of the usual scene in which the detective explains the mystery) who actually killed Manderson, how it came about, and where he himself went astray. Abashed, Trent announces that he "will never touch a crime-mystery again" (166). Bentley's engaging novel led the way for later metaphysical detective stories by describing the failure of the detective's apparently flawless reasoning.

After World War I, other writers continued to test the limits of the detective story's relationship to reality. By this point, two major subgenres had emerged: golden age and hard-boiled detective fiction. Novels of the primarily British golden age by Agatha Christie, Dorothy Sayers, and others resembled puzzles in narrative form and were placed in an isolated location (typically, a country house in an English village), peopled by stock characters, and augmented with ingenious murder weapons, complicated timetables, and ornate settings. (Ironically, just as Poe's "The Man of the Crowd" actually preceded his first detective story, so *Trent's Last Case*, the first spoof of the golden age, was also the first novel of that period set in a country house.) Raymond Chandler complains, in "The Simple Art of Murder," that the golden age detective novel never changes and always offers

the same careful grouping of suspects, the same utterly incomprehensible trick of how somebody stabbed Mrs. Pottington Postlethwaite III with the solid platinum poignard just as she flatted on the top note of the Bell Song from *Lakmé* in the presence of fifteen ill-assorted guests; the same ingénue in fur-trimmed pajamas screaming in the night to make the company pop in and out of doors and ball up the timetable; the same moody silence next day as they sit around sipping Singapore slings and sneering at each other. (230)

In response to such absurdity, Chandler adds, American authors developed "hard-boiled" fiction, giving "murder back to the kind of people that commit it for reasons, not just to provide a corpse; and with the means at hand, not with hand-wrought duelling pistols, curare, and tropical fish" (234). Accordingly, Dashiell Hammett and several other writers—including Chandler himself—began producing more realistic crime stories that take place in a gritty urban setting, usually Los Angeles, and feature bootleggers, blackmailers, confidence men, and dangerous dames. The investigator is no longer an amateur or dilettante, but a tough private eye. Although he completes the job he was hired to do, his investigation leads to further crimes and an awareness of widespread corruption and "nastiness," as Chandler puts it (*Big Sleep* 216), quite unlike the sense of tidy resolution in earlier detective stories. Even so, the hard-boiled crime novel—especially as perfected by Chandler, with first-person narration in the private eye's own wisecracking voice—soon became as familiar a formula as the country-house mystery.

Golden age and hard-boiled novels did more than just provide later metaphysical detective stories with material for parody, however. In different ways, they exposed both the genre's artifice and its reliance on positivist approaches to knowledge. In addition, at least one work in each subgenre—Christie's *The Murder of Roger Ackroyd* (1926) and Hammett's *The Maltese Falcon* (1930), respectively—explored the kind of self-reflexive storytelling that became characteristic of metaphysical detective stories. *The Murder of Roger Ackroyd*, Christie's most important contribution, is a tour de force that defies readers' expectations and transcends generic formulas at the level of discourse as well as plot. More precisely, the novel's first-person narration—in the form of a document meant to subvert previous accounts of Hercule Poirot's successes—relates to the crime. Christie's novel thus exploits the literary nature of detective fiction as a genre consisting of texts written and read according to established rules. *The Maltese Falcon* is much less showy, but Hammett also engages in storytelling that reflects the very text the reader is reading. Midway through the novel and for no apparent reason, Hammett's private eye, Sam Spade, tells his client, beautiful Brigid O'Shaughnessy, a tale about his search for a missing person. Spade's account of the Flitcraft case seems, in fact, like a metaphysical detective story framed within a realistic crime novel. As such, it mocks the positivist thinking of traditional detective fiction and points, instead, to a world of absurd coincidences, unconscious repetition, and narrative constructions rather than truth.

Postmodernist Parodies: 1930s to 1950s

By the late 1930s, approximately one hundred years after Poe invented detective fiction, the genre had become ripe for appropriation and revision by other writers. Two high modernist or early postmodernist authors—Jorge Luis Borges, in Argentina, and Vladimir Nabokov, a Russian émigré in Europe—produced the first true metaphysical detective stories around this time. Coincidentally, both writers were born in 1899, grew up in Anglophile families (in Buenos Aires and St. Petersburg, respectively), and learned to read English early. As children, both were fascinated by the tales of Poe, Stevenson, and Doyle, which may explain the similar bent of their fiction. At any rate, their transformations of the detective genre—along with other revisions by Felipe Alfau in *Locos* (1936), and Flann O'Brien, in *The Third Policeman* (written in 1939, but not published until 1967)—demonstrate its philosophical and literary significance.

The richly suggestive stories in Borges's *Ficciones* (1944; English translation, 1956) revise several aspects of detective fiction, including the search for a missing person in "El acercamiento a Almotásim" (1936; "The Approach to Al-Mu'tasim"); the quest for a meaningful pattern in "La bibliotheca de Babel" (1941; "The Library of Babel"); the discovery of a staged assassination in "Téma del traidor y del héroe" (1944; "Theme of the Traitor and Hero"); and the backward structure of narratives composed by a fictitious author in "Examen de la obra de Herbert Quain" (1941; "An Examination of the Works of

Herbert Quain"). Borges's stories are highly self-reflexive, too. They emphasize reading books (indeed, they usually take the form of reviews or outlines of imaginary texts) as well as the search for a divine Word that might explain earthly mysteries.

One of Borges's most striking revisions of the detective genre is "El jardin de senderos que se bifurcan" (1941; "The Garden of Forking Paths"). The tale is actually narrated by the murderer, but not until the final sentences can readers apprehend his crime, grasp its motivation, and understand "the infinite penitence and sickness of the heart" with which he executes it (101). As this design suggests, Borges's tales explore the psychological and philosophical implications of narrative structure at multiple levels, a trait they share with Poe's fiction; John Irwin even argues in his magisterial study *The Mystery to a Solution* that three of Borges's metaphysical detective stories, including "The Garden of Forking Paths," deliberately repeat and extend the structure of Poe's Dupin tales, which were published in the same order a century before. Indeed, if Poe created themes and plot devices that continue to dominate detective fiction, Borges explored other concepts that still haunt the metaphysical detective story—especially the labyrinth, one of his favorite subjects. "The Garden of Forking Paths," for example, bears out its title in a series of spatial, temporal, textual, and logical labyrinths that echo the maze-like structure of every mystery plot.

"La muerte y la brújula" (1942; "Death and the Compass") is Borges's most famous metaphysical detective story. It introduces the protagonist, Lönnrot, as the kind of brilliant, arrogant sleuth familiar to readers of detective fiction for the preceding century and then recounts his strangest case, which concerns a murdered rabbi. The police inspector assumes that the victim died during a burglary attempt, but Lönnrot, proclaiming that he "would prefer a purely rabbinical explanation," and inspired by a single sentence on a page left in the rabbi's typewriter—"The first letter of the Name has been spoken"—hypothesizes that his death was the first in a series of sacrifices meant to spell out the secret name of God (130, 131). Two subsequent crimes, elsewhere in the city, suggest a temporal, spatial, geometrical, and verbal pattern confirming Lönnrot's theory. Deducing when and where the fourth murder will occur, he goes there to prevent it and is chagrined at having spent so much time on such a simple problem. He discovers, however, that he himself is the intended victim: The pattern he discovered was devised by the criminal to lure him to his doom. Lönnrot not only fails to solve the crime (as it turns out, the murder did result from a bungled burglary) but this failure leads to his own death. Meanwhile, the philosophical questions generated by the mystery remain unresolved, just as in those stories by Chesterton that Borges admired. Readers are left to ponder the implications of what Lönnrot conjectured, including the possibility that the detective and the criminal are part of a larger pattern neither understands.

During this same period, Vladimir Nabokov was composing elegant novels about tawdry crimes in *Korol', Dama, Valet* (1928; *King, Queen, Knave*, 1990) and *Kamera Obskura* (1932; translated as *Laughter in the Dark*, 1990), and about the surreal experience of being sentenced to death for thinking thoughts others cannot understand in *Priglashenie na kazn'* (1936; *Invitation to a Beheading*, 1990). In addition to such tales of crime and punishment, Nabokov produced several metaphysical detective novels: *Sogliadatai* (1930; *The Eye*, 1965), in which the first-person narrator seeks the true identity of a man who turns out to be himself; *Otchaianie* (1934; *Despair*, 1965), in which another narrator tries to commit the perfect murder by staging his suicide; *The Real Life of Sebastian Knight* (1941), discussed below; *Lolita* (1955), an inverted detective story in which readers know the identity of the murderer (again, the first-person narrator) but not his victim; and *Pale Fire* (1962), a novel masquerading as an unfinished poem by one man, with commentary on it by another, in which readers know who was murdered but encounter contradictory explanations as to the murderer's identity and exactly whom he meant to kill.

Clearly, if Borges's major contribution to the metaphysical detective story is the labyrinth in all its forms (the maze, the library, the riddle), then Nabokov is chiefly responsible for the theme of mistaken identity. Like Christie in *The Murder of Roger Ackroyd*, moreover, he skillfully extends the enigma of each novel's plot to its discourse. In other words, the confusion regarding characters' identities recurs in the narration, so that readers face the problem of figuring out who tells the story and why. The narrator may deceive the reader just as he deceives other characters, even constructing a confession in the form of the novel's text that somehow repeats his crime. He himself may be equally deceived, however, because he senses that he is a character in someone else's book; the narrator of *Despair*, for example, forwards his manuscript to a certain Russian writer, a "well-known author of psychological novels" (80), despite his fear that the other—presumably "Vladimir Nabokov"—will publish it under his own name.

The Real Life of Sebastian Knight, the first novel Nabokov wrote in English, encapsulates all of these themes. It also establishes another key trope of metaphysical detective stories: the fictitious literary biography. On the first page, we learn that Sebastian Knight, the great English novelist, is dead; his Russian half brother, who is named only once in the text when Sebastian calls him "V." (71), has decided to write his biography. Unfortunately, V. and Sebastian were never close, although V. claims to understand him better than anyone else. Accordingly, V. tries to discover the real Sebastian by interviewing those who knew him—his governess, his secretary, an old school friend—while tracking down the mysterious woman who broke his heart. V.'s narrative shifts back and forth between Sebastian's life (recounted mostly in chronological order), his own bumbling quest to gather information, and extensive summaries of and quotations from Sebastian's works, which are mostly metaphysical detective stories about missing persons and mistaken identities. One novel, for example—which V. describes as a parody of traditional detective stories—begins with G. Abeson's mysterious death and ends when another character, "absentminded and harmless" old Nosebag, doffs his disguise and reveals himself to be Abeson: "one dislikes being murdered," he explains (94,

95). Meanwhile, V.'s experiences while conducting his research echo not only incidents in Sebastian's life but also, more oddly, episodes, images, and characters from his books. Does such repetition mean that V. has adopted his half brother's persona? Or that *The Real Life of Sebastian Knight* is Sebastian's latest novel, and V. merely its narrator? Or that both Sebastian and V. are transparent versions of Nabokov himself? The novel underscores the mystery of identity (and of identifying with another) by concluding with V.'s remark that "any soul may be yours, if you find and follow its undulations. Thus . . . I am Sebastian, or Sebastian is I, or perhaps we both are someone whom neither of us knows" (204–05). Readers are left, then, to contemplate their own reflections within the imaginary characters whose trail they have followed.

The metaphysical detective story continued to develop after World War II, thanks to Alain Robbe-Grillet, a leading exponent of the *nouveau roman* ("new novel") in France. Robbe-Grillet's early novels—especially *Le voyeur* (1955; *The Voyeur*, 1958) and *La jalousie* (1957; *Jealousy*, 1959)—are constructed around murders that do not appear in the text but which readers are led to infer by the narration's seemingly objective, yet increasingly obsessive, descriptions of the same objects, characters, and events. Later novels, such as *Project pour une revolution à New York* (1970; *Project for a Revolution in New York*, 1972), imply scenarios involving scientific experimentation, pornography, terrorism, and other social crimes that are also obliquely suggested by the narration. Robbe-Grillet altered metaphysical detective stories by making readers (not criminals, detectives, or even narrators) responsible for the crime—or rather, for imagining a crime that may not have occurred.

Robbe-Grillet's first novel, *Les gommes* (1953; *The Erasers*, 1964), explores another implicit pattern that the detective himself completes. After an attempt on his life, a political figure fakes his own death and goes into hiding only to be killed, accidentally, by a detective investigating the very murder that, until then, had not happened. This circular narrative structure in which the investigator himself is the murderer he seeks recalls the myth of Oedipus, a literary pretext that has haunted detective fiction, and especially metaphysical detective stories, from the beginning. *The Erasers* alludes to this pretext in a typically indirect way. Throughout the novel, the detective recalls vague childhood memories that suggest that, like Oedipus, he may be his victim's unacknowledged son. Descriptions of various objects—an embroidered curtain, a statue—refer to episodes in Sophocles' *Oedipus Rex* without explicitly naming the play. The detective even goes to one store after another, seeking a particular brand of eraser; he cannot recall the name stamped on its surface, which was partly obliterated by the act of erasing, but based on the two remaining middle letters—"di"—it might be "Oedipus" (126). *The Erasers* thus obscures not only the detective's connection to the crime, but also the literary pretext that would elucidate his situation.

Popular Paranoia: 1960s to 1970s

The limitation that Robbe-Grillet imposed upon himself in this novel—not mentioning Sophocles' play—led within the next decade to the *Ouvroir de Littérature Potentielle* (OULIPO; "workshop of potential literature"), a French movement that employed even more artificial textual constraints such as palindromes and numerical sequences to generate fiction. One remarkable result was Georges Perec's lipogrammatic novel *La Disparation* (1969; The disappearance), composed entirely without the letter *e* (and later ingeniously translated into English as *A Void*, 1994). Its plot involves a world in which something fundamental has disappeared, and any characters who try to articulate that missing shape or sound are killed. Despite such playfulness, it is one of several French novels—including Patrick Modiano's *Rue des boutiques obscures* (1978; translated as *Missing Person*, 1980) and some of Robbe-Grillet's later fictions—that use frustrated detective-story plots to evoke the unthinkable crime of the Holocaust.

Meanwhile, metaphysical detective stories were flourishing in other languages and cultures as well. In Switzerland, Friedrich Dürrenmatt's novella *Das Versprechen: Requiem auf den Kriminalroman* (1958; *The Pledge: Requiem for the Detective Novel*, 1959) explicitly criticized the tidy endings of traditional detective fiction; in his tale, a retired policeman's inability to confirm his solution to a cold case, a solution that is actually correct, eventually destroys him. In Italy, Leonardo Sciascia produced equally dark postmodernist mysteries about political corruption and the Mafia, especially *A ciascuno il suo* (1966; *To Each His Own*, 1968). The Latin American boom, a movement partly influenced by Borges, included surreal detective stories by fellow Argentinean Julio Cortázar—author of both "Continuity of Parks" and "Las babas del Diablo" (1959; translated as "Blow-Up," 1965), about a photographer who projects a crime narrative onto snapshots of strangers—as well as by Colombian novelist Gabriel García Márquez, whose magic realist fictions include *Crónica de una muerte anunciada* (1981; *Chronicle of a Death Foretold*,1982), in which everyone in a community knows a murder is being planned, but no one prevents it.

By this point, postmodernist themes and structures had also surfaced in American fiction, largely due to the belated translation of Borges's *Ficciones* into English, as John Barth notes in his essay "The Literature of Exhaustion." Detective fiction was a particularly "exhausted" genre, in Barth's sense, making it ideal for ironic revision. Because it focused on alienation, troubled social institutions, and the investigation of past wrongs, moreover, it was especially suited for addressing the political unrest of the period.

In the early 1960s, American writer Thomas Pynchon began combining Borges's indeterminate patterns, Nabokov's playfulness, and Robbe-Grillet's obsessive narration with a new emphasis on paranoia, which became another key trope in metaphysical detective stories. Pynchon's satirical novels about ominous forces shaping European and American history offer a mixture of styles, voices, genres, and allusions. However, he channels detective fiction, in particular, throughout his oeuvre—from his first novel, *V.* (1963), in which a man traces a mysterious woman's involvement in various international crises, to his most recent works, *Against the Day* (2006) and *Inherent Vice* (2009), which parody adventure novels, spy stories, and hard-boiled noir.

Pynchon's most significant metaphysical detective story is his second novel, *The Crying of Lot 49* (1966), which opens as a California housewife named Oedipa learns that a former lover has died, making her executor of his estate. In settling his estate—which includes, among other things, a collection of forged postal stamps—she finds traces of the Tristero, an underground postal system that has apparently existed for centuries and is now used by many alienated American citizens. Although she discovers more and more evidence of the Tristero's existence, Oedipa cannot tell whether she has stumbled onto an important secret, whether she is imagining it, or whether her former lover fabricated it as a conspiracy against her. Because the narration is limited to Oedipa's consciousness, readers share her paranoia. And because most evidence of the Tristero involves written communication—letters, graffiti, historical documents, even a Jacobean revenge tragedy—her anxiety reflects readers' own struggles to find definitive meaning in Pynchon's text. The novel ends abruptly, just as Oedipa is about to witness the auction of those forged stamps—that is, "the crying of lot 49"—which might reveal the truth. Since the text withholds such a revelation, the paranoia it evokes remains unresolved—with the effect, perhaps, of making its readers less likely to trust official histories and institutions.

Pynchon's emphasis on conspiracy theories and historical revisionism led to other novels during the next two decades, which expressed similar anxiety about American culture. Ishmael Reed's *Mumbo Jumbo* (1972) blends historical figures and events, photographs, and typographical experiments in its satirical account of a conspiracy to suppress African culture in the United States, particularly in the form of the Jes Grew virus that spreads dancing among black people. Instead of a traditional detective, Reed's novel features PaPa LaBas, a "conjure man" who uses intuition and voodoo to discover truth (39). Joyce Carol Oates's *Mysteries of Winterthurn* (1982)—an elegant mixture of horror, gothic romance, and detective fiction, set in nineteenth-century America—recounts an amateur sleuth's utter failure to solve a series of frightening, irrational, and violent crimes. *White Noise* (1985), by Don DeLillo, combines satire, science fiction, and noir to investigate an "airborne toxic event" that seems to embody a pervasive malaise in contemporary American society (117).

A Locked Room of One's Own: 1980s

Despite such mixed genres, by the early 1980s the metaphysical detective story itself had become a well-established literary category. Its ascendancy was due not only to the influence of various writers mentioned above—especially Borges, Nabokov, Robbe-Grillet, and Pynchon—but also to the international success of Umberto Eco's novel *Il nome della rosa* (1980; *The Name of the Rose*, 1980). Eco's book, along with another from this period—Paul Auster's *New York Trilogy* (1990)—encapsulates all of the themes, tropes, pretexts, and literary influences that shape the metaphysical detective story.

The Name of the Rose is a witty revision of golden age detective novels, in particular, although it also alludes to other authors, works, and subgenres. The setting is not a British country house, however, but a medieval abbey. William of Baskerville, a former inquisitor, and his assistant (the young novice who narrates the novel) investigate a series of bizarre murders with apocalyptic implications, not unlike those in Borges's "Death and the Compass." The murders are linked to a forbidden document hidden within the abbey's labyrinthine library, thus recalling Borges's story "The Library of Babel"; in fact, the criminal, a blind librarian named Jorge of Burgos, is clearly modeled on Borges, who suffered from progressive blindness and was director of the National Library of Argentina. The detective, like Dupin in "The Purloined Letter," manages to reconstruct this hidden text—a lost work of literary criticism extolling the practice of irony—without ever seeing it directly. However, William fails to solve the mystery in time to keep Jorge from obliterating the text, destroying the abbey, and killing himself (thus completing the apocalyptic pattern). *The Name of the Rose* marked a new advance in the metaphysical detective story's development: it was an immense popular and critical success, despite its difficulty, and incorporated allusions not only to traditional detective texts by Poe and Doyle, but also to metaphysical detective stories like those by Borges. At the same time that it referred to the entire history of detective fiction—including metaphysical tales—it also explored various modes of reading suggested by that history. Indeed, before writing this novel, Eco was an influential literary theorist who studied semiotics (how signs and symbols convey meaning); in particular, he claimed that texts are written with an ideal reader in mind and that readers learn to understand them by identifying with that ideal reader. *The Name of the Rose* thus demonstrates, in fictional form, Eco's analysis of how readers can actively complete meanings that are only implicit within a text.

A few years later, Paul Auster published, one by one, the three novellas comprising his 1990 *New York Trilogy*: *City of Glass* (1985), *Ghosts* (1986), and *The Locked Room* (1986). Remarkably, Auster's revision also addresses the entire history of detective fiction—including metaphysical tales by Borges and others—but results in a text that is the complement and very nearly the opposite of *The Name of the Rose*. Instead of Eco's sprawling, encyclopedic, historical detective novel, narrated by a traditional Watson figure, Auster offers three spare, enigmatic, and recursive tales. Instead of Eco's exuberant pastiche of the puzzle-like aspects of armchair detection, golden age novels, and Borges's recondite stories, Auster combines hard-boiled crime fiction with the dark introspection of allegorical romances by Poe, Hawthorne, and Melville, as well as Nabokov's chain of mistaken identities among readers, writers, narrators, and protagonists. At the same time, Auster's three-part series inevitably echoes earlier trilogies by Poe and Borges. The first novella, *City of Glass*, begins by introducing the protagonist:

Daniel Quinn, an isolated man perpetually grieving for his dead wife and son, who writes a series of popular novels under the pseudonym "William Wilson" (an allusion to Poe's 1839 story about doubles and the first of many references to Poe), featuring a fictional private eye named Max Work. Quinn keeps getting telephone calls intended for a real detective who happens to be named "Paul Auster"—until, eventually, he pretends to be Auster and meets the prospective client. The case, featuring a father and son with identical names, involves an apocalyptic scenario not unlike the apparent pattern linking the crimes in *The Name of the Rose*, but with additional echoes of Poe, Borges, and Pynchon. Quinn is unable to solve this mystery, of course; but he also becomes increasingly obsessed with it to the extent that he abandons his own identity altogether. The other two novellas describe detectives who lose themselves as well: Blue, in *Ghosts*, a private eye trapped in a case that asks him to do nothing but observe and record another man's existence; and the unnamed narrator of *The Locked Room*, a literary critic who foregoes his own identity—rather like V. in Nabokov's *The Real Life of Sebastian Knight*—when he tries to preserve, publish, and promote the writing of his best friend who is supposedly dead. The dizzying duplication of roles, relationships, and names continues throughout the trilogy. Characters from one novella show up in another, although they seem like entirely different people. The three novellas—all of which are recorded by narrators, at some point, in a red notebook—also seem to be variations of each other, to the extent that the narrator of *The Locked Room* claims to have written the first two novellas in the series. Indeed, if *The Name of the Rose*, in a sense, is all about reading, then Auster's *New York Trilogy* primarily concerns the difficulty of being a writer.

Border Crossings: 1990s and Beyond

The metaphysical detective story is not yet as familiar a formula as the country-house mystery or the hard-boiled crime novel. Even so, unresolved, ambiguous, ironic, and self-reflexive investigations featuring doomed detectives are now common, not only in fiction but also in popular narrative forms such as Hollywood films, television series, and electronic games. Meanwhile, metaphysical detective stories have responded to multicultural literature, to other subgenres (especially in science fiction), and to the changing nature of crime.

Several writers have extended earlier critiques of American society by Pynchon and others to more multicultural narratives. In Barbara Wilson's lesbian feminist detective novel *Gaudí Afternoon* (1990), a literary translator disentangles mistaken identities that reflect preconceptions about sex, gender, sexuality, and social roles. Chang-Rae Lee's *Native Speaker* (1996) revises espionage fiction and political thrillers to describe Asian Americans' alienation in the United States. Colson Whitehead's *The Intuitionist* (1998) uses a detective plot—about a female African American elevator inspector who advocates intuition, rather than empiricism, to solve cases—in an allegory of racial uplift. In *The Yiddish Policemen's Union* (2007), Michael Chabon blends alternate history and hard-boiled detection to explore the Jewish diaspora.

Other writers have combined detection with science fiction. For several decades, the themes, plots, and narration of hard-boiled crime novels have shaped cyberpunk, a sci-fi subgenre that investigates virtual reality in works like William Gibson's *Neuromancer* (1984). Recently, cyberpunk and its younger sibling, steampunk—science fiction set in an alternative early industrial era—have influenced metaphysical detective stories, in turn, in works like Jonathan Lethem's *Gun, with Occasional Music* (1995), China Miéville's *The City and the City* (2009), and Jedediah Berry's *The Manual of Detection* (2009).

Still other writers have addressed the increasingly anonymous, impersonal nature of contemporary crime. A sense of overwhelming paranoia returns in Gibson's *Pattern Recognition* (2003), which concerns conspiracy theories, international terrorism, and viral marketing. David Gordon's recent novel, *The Serialist* (2010), focuses on serial murder. Despite such grimness, however, *Pattern Recognition* partly functions as a send-up of Pynchon's *The Crying of Lot 49*, while *The Serialist* wittily associates its killer with the author of a detective series. Indeed, no matter how disturbing the questions asked by metaphysical detective stories may become, they still involve both crimes and texts that do not permit themselves to be read.

Works Cited

Alfau, Felipe. *Locos: A Comedy of Gestures*. 1936. New York: Vintage, 1988. Print.
Auster, Paul. *City of Glass*. Los Angeles: Sun & Moon, 1985. 1–158. Print.
___. *Ghosts*. Los Angeles: Sun & Moon, 1986. 159–232. Print.
___. *The Locked Room*. Los Angeles: Sun & Moon, 1986. 235–71. Print.
___. *The New York Trilogy*. 1987. New York: Penguin, 1990. Print.
Barth, John. "The Literature of Exhaustion." *Atlantic* Aug. 1967: 29–34. Print.
Bentley, E. C. *Trent's Last Case*. 1913. New York: Dover, 1997. Print.
Berry, Jedediah. *The Manual of Detection*. New York: Penguin, 2009. Print.
Borges, Jorge Luis. *Ficciones*. 1956. Ed. and introd. Anthony Kerrigan. New York: Grove, 1963. Print.
___. "Modes of G. K. Chesterton." 1936. Trans. Karen Stolley. *Borges: A Reader*. Ed. Emir Rodríguez Monegal and Alastair Reid. New York: Dutton, 1981. 87–91. Print.
Chabon, Michael. *The Yiddish Policemen's Union*. New York: HarperCollins, 2007. Print.
Chandler, Raymond. *The Big Sleep*. 1939. New York: Random, 1976. Print.
___. "The Simple Art of Murder." *The Art of the Mystery Story: A Collection of Critical Essays*. Ed. Howard Haycraft. New York: Simon, 1947. 222–37. Print.
Chesterton, G. K. "The Blue Cross." 1911. *The Complete Father Brown*. New York: Penguin, 1988. 3–23. Print.
Christie, Agatha. *The Murder of Roger Ackroyd*. New York: Grossett, 1926. Print.
Cortázar, Julio. *Blow-Up and Other Stories*. 1965. Trans. Paul Blackburn. New York: Pantheon, 1990. Print.
DeLillo, Don. *White Noise*. New York: Viking, 1985. Print.
Doyle, Arthur Conan. *The Complete Sherlock Holmes*. Introd. Christopher Morley. 2 vols. Garden City: Doubleday, 1930. Print.
Dürrenmatt, Friedrich. *The Pledge: Requiem for the Detective Novel*. 1958. Trans. James Agee. Chicago: Chicago UP, 2006. Print.
Eco, Umberto. *The Name of the Rose*. 1980. Trans. William Weaver. New York: Warner, 1983. Print.
García Márquez, Gabriel. *Chronicle of a Death Foretold*. Trans. Gregory Rabassa. New York: Vintage, 2003. Print.
Gibson, William. *Neuromancer*. New York: Ace, 1984. Print.
___. *Pattern Recognition*. New York: Berkley, 2003. Print.

Gordon, David. *The Serialist.* New York: Simon, 2010. Print.

Hammett, Dashiell. *The Maltese Falcon.* New York: Grossett, 1930. Print.

Hawthorne, Nathaniel. *The Scarlet Letter.* 1850. New York: Bantam, 1981. Print.

Haycraft, Howard. *Murder for Pleasure: The Life and Times of the Detective Story.* New York: Appleton-Century, 1941. Print.

Irwin, John T. *The Mystery to a Solution: Poe, Borges, and the Analytic Detective Story.* Baltimore: Johns Hopkins UP, 1994. Print.

Lee, Chang-Rae. *Native Speaker.* New York: Riverhead, 1996. Print.

Lethem, Jonathan. *Gun, with Occasional Music.* New York: Tor, 1995. Print.

Merivale, Patricia, and Susan Elizabeth Sweeney, eds. *Detecting Texts: The Metaphysical Detective Story from Poe to Postmodernism.* Philadelphia: U of Pennsylvania P, 1999. Print.

Miéville, China. *The City and the City.* New York: Del Rey, 2009. Print.

Modiano, Patrick. *Missing Person.* 1978. Trans. Daniel Weissbort. London: Cope, 1980. Print.

Nabokov, Vladimir. *Despair.* 1934. Rev. and trans. by Nabokov. 1965. New York: Vintage, 1990. Print.

___. *The Eye.* 1930. Trans. Dmitri Nabokov and Vladimir Nabokov. New York: Phaedra, 1965. Print.

___. *Invitation to a Beheading.* 1935–36. Trans. Dmitri Nabokov and Vladimir Nabokov. New York: Vintage, 1990. Print.

___. *King, Queen, Knave.* 1928. Trans. Dmitri Nabokov and Vladimir Nabokov. New York: Vintage, 1990. Print.

___. *Laughter in the Dark.* 1932. Rev. and trans. by Nabokov. 1938. New York: Vintage, 1990. Print.

___. *Lolita.* 1955. New York: Vintage, 1990. Print.

___. *Pale Fire.* 1963. New York: Vintage, 1990. Print.

___. *The Real Life of Sebastian Knight.* 1941. New York: New Directions, 1959. Print.

Oates, Joyce Carol. *Mysteries of Winterthurn.* New York: Dutton, 1984. Print.

O'Brien, Flann. *The Third Policeman.* 1967. New York: Plume, 1976. Print.

Perec, Georges. *A Void* 1969. Trans. Gilbert Adair. New York: HarperCollins, 1994. Print.

Poe, Edgar Allan. *Poetry, Tales, and Selected Essays.* Ed. Patrick F. Quinn and G. R. Thompson. New York: Lib. of Amer., 1996. Print.

Pynchon, Thomas. *Against the Day.* New York: Penguin, 2007. Print.

___. *The Crying of Lot 49.* Philadelphia: Lippincott, 1966. Print.

___. *Inherent Vice.* New York: Penguin, 2009. Print.

___. *V.* 1963. New York: Bantam, 1964. Print.

Reed, Ishmael. *Mumbo Jumbo.* 1972. New York: Bard, 1978. Print.

Robbe-Grillet, Alain. *The Erasers.* 1953. Trans. Richard Howard. New York: Grove, 1964. Print.

___. *Jealousy and In the Labyrinth: Two Novels.* Trans. Richard Howard. New York: Grove, 1965. Print.

___. *The Voyeur.* 1955. Trans. Richard Howard. New York: Grove, 1994. Print.

___. *Project for a Revolution in New York.* 1970. Trans. Richard Howard. New York: Grove, 1972. Print.

Sciascia, Leonardo. *To Each His Own*. 1966. Trans. Adrienne Foulke. New York: New York Review, 2000. Print.

Sophocles. *Oedipus Rex*. New York: Dover, 1991. Print.

Stevenson, Robert Louis. *The Strange Case of Dr Jekyll and Mr Hyde*. 1866. New York: Dover, 1991. Print.

Tani, Stefano. *The Doomed Detective: The Contribution of the Detective Novel to Postmodern American and Italian Fiction*. Carbondale: Southern Illinois UP, 1984. Print.

Whitehead, Colson. *The Intuitionist*. New York: Doubleday, 1998. Print

Wilson, Barbara. *Gaudí Afternoon*. Seattle: Seal, 1990. Print.

Native American Detective Fiction
Rhonda Harris Taylor

Finding Common Ground: Defining Boundaries

In addressing Native American detectives, the fundamental questions are what "Native American" is and what a "Native American" detective is. What is "Native American"? This term and other designations (American Indian, Native, Indian, Indigenous, and so on) are simply inadequate.[1] There is no universally acceptable collocation for the more than five hundred federally recognized sovereign Native American nations within the United States, which are part of more than seven hundred contemporary Native American nations.[2] Thus, the deficiencies of these terms are not offset by privileging one over another. However, in this chapter, "Native American" and "nation" are the primary designations.

What is a "Native American" detective? The US Office of Management and Budget has characterized "American Indian or Alaska Native" as an individual "having origins in any of the original peoples of North and South America (including Central America), and who maintains tribal affiliation or community attachment." This chapter applies these criteria in selecting its population of fictional detectives. The selection is also limited to monographic (book-length) series written by US authors, although not all of the series have continued to publish new volumes.

Regarding detective status, the selection omits series with Native American adjuncts for non-Native protagonists.[3] In choosing series, the standard used for the "detective" category was the Encyclopedia Britannica's succinct parameters for detective stories: "a crime is introduced and investigated and the culprit is revealed." Thus, these series have Native Americans as recurring detective protagonists who investigate the crimes and reveal the culprits.[4] These elements of detective, crime, and culprit are necessary for identifying Native

American detective books because some cross genres. For instance, two of Tony Hillerman's Native American mysteries earned Western Writers of America awards, and he received a lifetime achievement award ("Awards"). Furthermore, Louis Owens's mystery novels belong to the canon of contemporary Native American literature, while Rudolfo Anaya's works are placed in the canon of contemporary Chicano[5] literature.

Finally, these series are relevant to topics being discussed but do not definitively capture of all Native American detective mystery series.

The Detectives: First Appearances of Those Who Came Before

Credited as the first US Native American detective story is Manly Wade Wellman's "A Star for a Warrior" (Pronzini 26), which was first published in the April 1946 edition of *Ellery Queen Mystery Magazine* and received an Ellery Queen Mystery Magazine award that year (Lachman). The detective, David Return, belongs to a fictional tribe, the Tsichah (supposedly a derivation of the Cheyennes and the Pawnees), and is a tribal police officer (Pronzini 26).

However, a case for the first US Native American detective designation can be made for an earlier publication: that of pulp-magazine character, Jim Anthony, who is Irish and Comanche and whose maternal grandfather was a chief. His adventures, initially tending to the superheroic but evolving into hard-boiled detective action, were the focus of a periodical, *Super-Detective*, starting in 1940 (Bloom; McMahan).

Tony Hillerman is often credited with initiating the Native American detective novel, and his body of work is frequently used as the benchmark for reviews of other authors' books featuring Native American detectives. His Navajo (Diné) characters are tribal police lieutenant Joe Leaphorn (introduced in *The Blessing Way*, 1970) and sergeant Jim Chee (first appearing in *People of Darkness*, 1980). Beginning with *Skinwalkers* (1986), both characters appear in each novel. Hillerman's Leaphorn and Chee books received multiple awards. The Mystery Writers of America (MWA) granted an Edgar Award for Best Novel in 1974 to *Dance Hall of the Dead* and four Edgar nominations (Best First Novel for *The Blessing Way* in 1971; Best Novel for *The Fly on the Wall* in 1972, *Listening Woman* in 1979, and *A Thief of Time* in 1989). Hillerman also received a 1991 Grand Master from MWA for "important contributions to this genre, as well as a body of work that is both significant and of consistent high quality." The books also enjoyed broad popularity, including Anthony Award Best Novel nominations in 1989 and 1994 (*A Thief of Time* and *Sacred Clowns*) and a Best Novel award in 1988 (*Skinwalkers*) ("Anthony Award"). The novels have also appeared on best-seller lists, including those of the *New York Times*.

Film adaptations of Hillerman's books further indicate their popularity. A 1991 effort cast Lou Diamond Phillips as Chee in *Dark Wind*. It was panned by reviewers (Hollandsworth 130; Preston 16; Keezer 1). Three subsequent PBS productions (*Skinwalkers*, 2002; *Coyote Waits*, 2003; *A Thief of Time*, 2004) were very well received, with the first one bringing PBS its highest rated program in seven years ("Wes Studi") and providing cast members with American Indian Film Institute Best Supporting Actor and Actress awards (Thundercloud 8B). The films starred Native American actors, including Wes Studi (Cherokee) and Adam Beach (Salteaux) as Leaphorn and Chee, and Chris Eyre (Cheyenne and Arapaho) directed two of the productions.

With Hillerman's popularity and award successes, it is not surprising that other authors followed. The 1990s were a prolific era for inaugurating Native American detective series, and while some of those works followed Hillerman's model of tribal law enforcement protagonists, there are also private investigators and amateur detectives. They include men and women, contemporary and historical persons, and a diversity of Native American nation affiliations.

The Storytellers: Authorial Identity and Relationships

In contemplating the authors who write Native American detective fiction, one issue of potential significance is the author's identity—particularly, a Native American author writing a mystery series about a Native American detective, as compared to someone who is not Native American devising such a series or to an individual of a Native American nation creating a detective from another nation. Assuming that the lens of "insider" contributes more authenticity to the portrayal of the detective, the plot, and the context of the mystery, this issue has consequence and consequences. A sustained record of misrepresentation and stereotyping of Native Americans in media and creative interpretations has been well documented.[6] Such assumptions and presentations might be attributed to lack of knowledge and/or political, economic, and social agendas. Those agendas have been summarized by Louis Owens: "The indigenous inhabitants of North America can stand anywhere on the continent and look in every direction at a home usurped and colonized by strangers who, from the very beginning, laid claim not merely to the land and resources but to the very definition of the Natives" (14–15). Integral to discussions of literature that portrays Native Americans is Owens's emphasis on the "definition of the Natives." Numerous commentators note that representations of "Indians" are essential to the construction of "American," from Leslie A. Fiedler's 1968 premise that "everyone who thinks of himself as being in some sense an American feels the stirrings in him of a second soul, the soul of the Red Man" (12) to Philip J. Deloria's conclusion thirty years later that from pre-Revolutionary times, the "critical dilemma of American identity" was that there was "no way to conceive an American identity without Indians" (37). Thus, the possible morass for writers in creations of Native American detectives is that, on the one hand, there is the potential for Native American characters to provide merely exotic, possibly stereotypical, flavor to the story (Donaldson). If so, and given devastating historical interactions with Native American peoples and a self-constructed American identity, it is possible that the popularity of fictional detectives who are Native American is an indicator that they are not dispelling preconceived ideas but reinforcing them. In a 1990 documentary on Native American storytelling, Gerald Vizenor, an Anishinaabe poet, novelist, and critic, suggested that popularity of Native Americans portrayals by non-Native writers, in contrast to often less popular writing by Native Americans, reflects a comfort level with inauthentic representations of Native Americans (*Distant Voices*).

However, there is a more positive view that the Native American detective genre provides readership with "individual, fully human representatives of the numerous and diverse Native American cultures" (Donaldson). For at least some of these authors, that goal is an articulated one. For example, Louis Owens, a fiction and nonfiction writer who created an amateur detective, said that his writings were targeted to audiences encompassing readers who were not Native Americans and his own Choctaw and Cherokee relations ("In Memoriam"). Peter Bowen, whose detective is Métis (mixed-blood), says on his website that one reason for writing the series is because "the Métis are a great people, a wonderful people, and not many Americans know anything about them." Robert J. Conley (United Keetoowah Band of Cherokee Indians) has noted that his agenda when writing fiction about Native Americans is educational and that fiction reaches more readers (Birchfield, "Teaches" 4B). Mardi Oakley Medawar (Eastern Band of Cherokee Indians of North Carolina) has said that her Tay-bodal mystery series counters old stereotypes about Native Americans in history (Adare 13B).

There is a third view. Michael Dorris, whose own identity as a Native American writer became a controversy within Native American literary circles, suggested that there could be "good writing tied to Indian culture, be it by Indians or non-Indians" and that one should not "make too much of it sociologically" ("Native American Writing" 1). Similarly, poet Heid E. Erdrich (Turtle Mountain Band of Chippewa and German American) was asked about her opinion of writers who are not Native American, such as Tony Hillerman, including Native American cultures and characters in their works. She replied that in regards to Hillerman, his work is popular and commented, "I've known some Navajos who think he's just great. . . . It's a world of ideas. You can't control what people think" ("Café Literati").

These three views about this genre are not necessarily exclusive. Beyond what these approaches might reveal about the construction of Native American detectives, there are insights to be gleaned by also utilizing an anthropological concept that has been applied to Native American literature: the "lived experience" (Shanley 119). If the lens of lived experience is applied to the authors of these series (most of whom are not Native American), what is conspicuous are relationships with their own individual and family histories, with the landscapes in their lives, with their communities, with communities of Native Americans, with their fans, with the literary profession, and with their own literary creations. It is a truism that writers should write about what they know—what do these writers' lived experiences suggest about their Native American detective creations?

Because all authors work in an environment of legacy from writers who precede them, this coverage of authors uses the chronological order in which their detectives made their first print appearances.

March 1, 1970

Tony Hillerman (1925–2008) is viewed as the father of this mystery subgenre. In interviews with Lise Balk King and Deborah Stead and in his memoir, Hillerman recounted his Oklahoma childhood in a community of Potawatomis, Seminoles, and Blackfeet (his father had a general store). Wounded and highly decorated in World War II, he returned to Oklahoma to attend college and begin a career in journalism, which moved him to New Mexico. A master's degree from the University of New Mexico launched him into writing and a journalism faculty position.

Viewing a Navajo (Diné) healing ceremony for veterans spurred an interest in the culture. His travels throughout the Southwest, his interaction with members of local Native American communities and his research about the Navajo, Zuni, and Hopi cultures informed his mysteries. It is easy to draw parallels between Hillerman and his first Navajo detective, Leaphorn, who is an older skeptic with an anthropology degree and links to the University of New Mexico. His second Navajo detective, Chee, is younger, more traditional, and deeply invested in his spirituality, which Hillerman viewed as an important aspect of his own worldview (Colby; Graham).

Two recognitions Hillerman received, besides those from mystery and western writing associations, include being named a Special Friend to the Dineh from the Navajo Nation in 1987 (Starr 1) and honored as 1992 Red Earth Ambassador of the Year, an Oklahoma award for an individual making significant contributions to fostering positive images of Native Americans ("Chief" 3).

March 2, 1989

Jean Hager is an Oklahoma author who was educated in Oklahoma. A former high school English teacher whose first book was a 1970 children's mystery, Hager discussed being one-sixteenth Cherokee and her family's connections with the area around Tahlequah, the capital of the Cherokee Nation of Oklahoma ("Interview"). In 2000, Hager received a Medal of Honor from the Cherokee Nation of Oklahoma, honoring Cherokee descendants with lifetime achievements of excellence (Snell 30). Her two detectives are contemporary Cherokee characters who live in the Tahlequah area: Mitch Bushyhead, a half-Cherokee police chief introduced in 1989 (*The Grandfather Medicine*), and Molly Bearpaw, Cherokee investigator for the Cherokee Nation, appearing in 1992 (*Ravenmocker*).

March 3, 1990

Robert J. Conley (b.1940), of the United Keetoowah Band of Cherokee Indians, is another author born in Oklahoma. He has had a career in higher education and a stint in the Cherokee Nation of Oklahoma's

Programs Office. He publishes prolifically as a poet, novelist, short story writer, historian, and playwright (Birchfield, "Extraordinary" 19), and his fiction includes a short story and several western novels honored by the Western Writers of America ("Awards"). Like Hager, Conley received a Medal of Honor Award from the Cherokee Nation in 2000 (Snell 30), and he has also earned the 2009 American Indian Festival of Words award for major contributions to literature from the American Indian Resource Center of the Tulsa City-County Library as well as the only public library award for Native American authors ("Seqyouyah Professor" 17). Conley was inducted into the Oklahoma Writers Hall of Fame in 1995, which recognizes authors living and writing in Oklahoma and making significant contributions to American literature. Conley's western writings, interests in Cherokee history and culture, and academic links are reflected in the characters of his Native American detectives: a nineteenth-century district sheriff of the Chero- kee Nation, Go-Ahead Rider, and his deputy, a mixed-blood Cherokee and graduate of Harvard, George Tanner. The series, which began with Go-Ahead Rider, uses Tahlequah, Oklahoma, as its location.

March 4, 1992

Dana Stabenow (b. 1952), a native Alaskan, spent her childhood on a fishing boat where she was also home-schooled by her mother (Drew). She earned her bachelor's degree in journalism and master's degree in fine arts from the University of Alaska. Her diverse work experi- ences in Alaska include her employment with pipeline and petroleum companies before returning to college for her master's degree.[7] She has written three science fiction books in addition to her series about Kate Shugak, with the first book (*A Cold Day for Murder*) receiving an Edgar Award for Best Paperback Original in 1993 ("Edgar Awards"). Stabenow's varied life and work experiences in Alaska are mirrored in Shugak, a self-sufficient Aleut woman who has left her job as an investigator with the district attorney to support herself with gold pan- ning, trapping, rafting tourists, guiding hunting parties, and freelance private investigation. Shugak lives with her dog, Mutt, in a log cabin in a fictional Alaskan national park.

March 5, 1994

Peter Bowen (b. 1945) resides in Montana, north of Yellowstone Park, but has spent time in Colorado, Indiana, and Michigan. His website provides a self-description of a "cowboy, hunting and fishing guide, folksinger, poet, essayist, and novelist." Bowen's detective character is Gabriel Du Pré, a Métis who resides in Toussaint, Montana, and is a fiddler. He makes his first appearance in *Coyote Wind* in 1994.

James Doss (b. 1939), a Kentuckian, is retired from Los Alamos National Laboratory in New Mexico and now lives in a cabin near Taos, according to HarperCollins Publishers. In an interview with Art Taylor, he notes that archaeology, a lifelong hobby, led to an interest in Native Americans. Visits to Utes on the reservation and books on the tribe provided background information for his plots and characters. Doss has contemplated his own Christian identity and the dual beliefs in Christianity and traditional practices among Utes, and he has concluded that the two belief systems are compatible. His series protagonist is Charlie Moon, a Ute who retired from the tribal police to ranch and do part-time investigation. He is assisted by his aunt, Daisy Perika, a shaman and practicing Catholic whose insights are essential to the plots. They live in Montana. Moon and Perika had minor roles in the first book in the series, *The Shaman Sings*, but later became its central characters.

March 6, 1995

Another New Mexican mystery series author, Rudolfo Anaya (b. 1937), is renowned for his 1972 book *Bless Me Ultima*, a classic of Latino literature. Besides novels, his works include poetry (for which he has received numerous awards), drama, and children's books. Anaya is a 2001 recipient of the National Medal of Arts in Literature from the National Endowment for the Arts and a 2001 Wallace Stegner Award from the Center of the American West, which is presented to individuals who make a sustained contribution to the cultural identity of the West. Anaya was born in New Mexico and resides in Albuquerque. He has two degrees from the University of New Mexico, taught in public schools, and is a University of New Mexico professor emeritus. Growing up in a small Spanish-speaking town, Anaya's first language is Spanish, and he has recounted the challenge of learning English upon starting school ("Anaya"). He has also addressed the indigenous aspect of his identity, saying, "As mestizos, we have to understand not only our European heritage, but also our Native American heritage" (Espinoza 65). Elements of Anaya's identity are mirrored in his mestizo private investigator, Sonny Baca, who is, like Anaya, a bilingual resident of Albuquerque. Baca, who describes himself as a descendant of "Indohispano" culture, made his first appearance in *Zia Summer*.

Another mystery writer from the western United States is Margaret Coel (b. 1937), a native of Colorado who lives in Boulder. She is a journalist who also taught writing at the University of Colorado. Coel is a self-described historian who wrote a book about the Arapaho chief Left Hand, as well as other nonfiction books. Coel has discussed being inspired by Hillerman's work to write her own mystery series (Jawort 9). She combines history and mystery in her series about Arapaho attorney Vicky Holden. Holden and a Jesuit priest, Father O'Malley, are a detective duo. Using a partnership with O'Malley as the outsider was Coel's device to allow readers to join O'Malley in learning about Arapahos and their culture (Daly 1). The setting is the Wind River Reservation in Wyoming, and Coel has found assistance with information for the series among its residents: as reported in the *Wind River News*, a 1995 give-away provided her appreciation for locals who had helped in the creation of the series' first book, *The Eagle Catcher* (Beckwith 1). Several books in the series have received Colorado Book Awards (which honors Colorado literary figures), including *Wife of Moon* in 2005, *The Shadow Dancer* in 2003, and *The Spirit Woman* in 2001. Coel received a 2010 High Plains Book Award Emeritus Award; these annual awards are presented by the public library in the Billings and Yellowstone counties in Montana and recognize regional authors and literature of the High Plains.

As with Anaya, Louis Owens (1948–2002) came to the mystery genre from the world of novels, scholarship, and higher education. He was a faculty member at the University of California, Davis, and his work received numerous awards, including a 1997 American Book Award for American literary excellence from the Before Columbus Foundation for his novel, *Nightland*. Owens, who was Choctaw, Cherokee, and Irish American, spent his childhood in rural Mississippi and in California, where his parents were migrant farm laborers. Of nine siblings, he was one of two who finished high school and was the only college graduate. His detective character, Cole McCurtain, is self-described as Choctaw, Cherokee, Irish, and Cajun. In the first book, *The Sharpest Sight* (1992), McCurtain returns to Mississippi to solve his brother's murder. In *Bone Game* (1994), McCurtain, like Owens, is a faculty member at the University of California, Santa Cruz, and once again, murder intrudes on McCurtain's life. *The Sharpest Sight* received a 1993 Josephine Miles Award from the PEN Oakland Awards, recognizing multicultural literature. It also received a 1995 French Roman Noir Award, given for mysteries, and *Bone Game* received the 1994 Julian J. Rothbaum Prize from the University of Oklahoma.

Thomas Perry (b. 1947) was raised in New York but lives in California. He has a PhD, served in the US Air Force, and has been employed in such fields as park maintenance, factory labor, commercial fishing, university-level administration and teaching, and writing and producing for television. Perry's mystery novels have been critically acclaimed and have garnered such prestigious awards as the 1983 Edgar Award for Best First Novel. His series features Jane Whitefield, who is of Seneca descent and uses her talents to help people in danger to disappear into new lives. The series is placed in the same upstate New York region from which Perry came.

Aimée and David Thurlo are a husband-and-wife writing team living in New Mexico. David Thurlo grew up on the Navajo reservation because his father worked for the US Bureau of Mines. He has a master's degree from the University of New Mexico and middle school teaching experience. Aimée Thurlo is from Cuba. The Thurlos have a sizeable output of romance and suspense books, besides their Native American detective series that features Navajo Ella Clah. Clah was formerly with the FBI but has become a special investigator for the Navajo Nation. She first appears in *Blackening Song* (1995).

March 7, 1996

Mardi Oakley Medawar (Eastern Band of Cherokee Indians of North Carolina) was born in Louisiana and lives on the Red Cliff Chippewa Reservation in Wisconsin. Medawar's protagonist is Tay-bodal, a nineteenth-century Kiowa healer. Medawar has attributed her interest in Kiowas to her father's remembrances of a World War II romance with a Kiowa woman in Oklahoma, but she describes her interests in Native Americans as "intertribalist" (Adare 13B). Medawar's research for the series included consultations with Kiowas, traveling to historic sites, and drawing on oral and written histories (13B). Her first Tay-bodal novel, *Death at Rainy Mountain*, netted her recognition as the Wordcraft Circle of Native Writers' 1998 Prose Fiction Writer of the Year.

March 8, 1998

William Kent Krueger was born in 1950 in Wyoming to a family that moved frequently. His freshman year at Stanford University was followed with jobs in timbering and construction. His own family's relocation to Minnesota was prompted by his wife's enrollment in law school. He resides in St. Paul, Minnesota, and his detective series is also set in the state. In an interview with David J. Montgomery, Krueger attributed his decision to write mysteries to the influence of Hillerman's books. His detective is Cork O'Connor (Ojibwe and Irish American), a former sheriff who first appears in *Iron Lake*. In the series, O'Connor has a wife who is a lawyer and two daughters; in real life, Krueger has a wife who is an attorney and two children. Krueger has been nominated for multiple awards and received the 1998 Bouchercon Anthony Award for Best First Novel for *Iron Lake*, the Best Novel award in 2005 for *Blood Hollow*, and the Best Mystery Novel award in 2006 for *Mercy Falls* (nominations included *Thunder Bay* in 2008 and *Red Knife* in 2009). The series has multiple nominations and wins from the Minnesota Book Awards, which recognize Minnesota book creators.

Another New Mexico series is penned by Robert Westbrook (b. 1945), who wrote his first book while in college. His subsequent writing includes a mystery series set in historical Los Angeles; a nonfiction book about his mother, Sheilah Graham, and her relationship with F. Scott Fitzgerald; ghost writing; and novels based on screenplays. He has also taught writing classes in the United States and English classes abroad. Westbrook began writing the Howard Moon series when he moved to Taos, New Mexico, and the series is named for its young private investigator, Howard Moon, who is Lakota Sioux and first appears in *Ghost Dancer* (1998). The books also feature a blind ex-policeman, Jack Wilder, who has a detective agency. Some of the reviews on Westbrook's website compare the series to Rex Stout's Archie Goodwin and Nero Wolfe books. The series is set in San Geronimo, New Mexico.

March 9, 1999

Book jackets for *Ancient Ones* (2001) and *Dance of the Thunder Dogs* (2004) report that Kirk Mitchell (b. 1950) has law enforcement experience as a deputy sheriff on Paiute-Shoshone reservations of Inyo County, California, and as a California SWAT officer and that he resides in California. The jacket for *Dance of the Thunder Dogs* says that Mitchell has "long been fascinated with American Indian cultures." Mitchell's books introduce a number of Native American cultures. His detective partnership consists of an investigator for the Bureau of Indian Affairs, Emmett Quanah Parker, and an FBI agent, Anna Turnipseed; Parker is a Comanche from Oklahoma and is now based in Phoenix, and Turnipseed is Modoc and Japanese, originally hails from

California, and is now based in Las Vegas. They first appear in *Cry Dance* (1999). Their cases take them to various states, including New York (*Sky Woman Falling*, 2003), Oklahoma (*Dance of the Thunder Dogs*), and Oregon (*Ancient Ones*), bringing the two into contact with the diversity of local Native American communities.

The Detectives: Identities

All stories, oral and written (including novels), are about collective and individual identities, whether affirming, seeking, or questioning them. In the mystery genre, the detective restores balance, in the form of justice, to a world in chaos because of the criminal's transgressions—the crime. If listing essentials for the Native American detective subgenre, they would include reflecting an identity authentic to a specific Native American culture or cultures, a contextualizing of that identity with relevant place, and viewing and addressing the crime/transgression with relevant ways of knowing that are indicative of that culture. Relevant knowledge should emanate from understandings of history and its often-turbulent encounters with spirituality, with language, and with family and community relationships and interactions. In addition, as in the mystery genre as a whole, the Native American detective can be dealing with self-identity, which can be complex in a Native American context. Native American identity is more nuanced than tribal identification, although all of the series include this information, a step beyond a too-common assumption of generic "Indian" identity. Incorporating one or all three of these essentials in a book requires great skill, because it is too easy to reduce them to a veneer devised by an outsider to the cultures—a mention does not necessarily indicate or convey an understanding of an object, an event, an interaction, or a place. At the same time, too much information can cross ethical boundaries of respect for the culture being represented. The books in this chapter incorporate these three attributes with varying degrees of success.

Self-Identity

Collectively, the series provide examples of Native American detectives with affirmed identities and identities yet to be affirmed. For instance, throughout the Hillerman mysteries, Chee tries to reconcile his identity as a *hatathali*, a traditional healer, with his role as police officer and with his choices in romance. In Owens's two Cole McCurtain books, McCurtain tries to reconcile his self-described mixed-blood identity with a meaningful location of place/home through an interweaving of his own ideas; the advice of his uncle who says that Native Americans must know their people's stories and each person must also make his own story (*The Sharpest Sight*); and observations of the stereotypical assumptions of his students and others at the university where he teaches (*Bone Game*). In Stabenow's *A Cold Day for Murder*, Kate Shugak and her *emaa* (grandmother), fiercely debate the wisdom of Shugak's young cousin relocating to Anchorage. Shugak envisions a future in the mainstream, while her grandmother sees the loss of culture and identity. However, Hager's two detectives and Conley's two protagonists seem at ease in their Cherokee identities and with their places in their communities, as does Perry's Seneca detective, Jane Whitefield.

Place

Land (homeland) equals Native American identity because land is physical sustenance, spiritual renewal, and memory (Kidwell and Velie).[8] If a "real" portrayal, representation of land and landscapes also engages readers who know the areas or want to know them. For instance, Barney Hillerman and Laurance D. Linford have both written books on Hillerman's landscapes in the Chee and Leaphorn mysteries, and Hillerman theme tours are offered in the Four Corners region (Arizona, Colorado, New Mexico, and Utah) that was the books' setting. Place is so necessary for identity that Dana Stabenow has repeatedly spoken of resistance to media adaptations of her series unless filmed on-site in Alaska. Medawar's historical series emphasizes the importance of places integral to Kiowa culture by using the site names in the book titles: *Death at Rainy Mountain*, *Witch of the Palo Duros*, *Murder at Medicine Lodge*, and *The Ft. Larned Incident*. In Perry's *Vanishing Act*, Whitefield's knowledge of the historical location of a Seneca village lends her the vision of the memory of its demise and the necessity of maintaining a ceremonial connection with it. She knows that mainstream inhabitants do not see this place or its history, but they also cannot see her role as a guide for the endangered. Presumably, the authors of series that have been recognized with regional awards created place accuracy that resonated with people in those areas. Perhaps one indicator of how accurately an author of a Native American detective book has represented place and identity is a response to the following questions: Could these protagonists be easily translated, in their current identities, to a different landscape? If the assigned signifiers of Native American identity, including landscape, were removed from these protagonists, would they still be viable characters?

Ways of Knowing

Ways of knowing emanate from an integration of self, place, community, and culture, and in detective stories, ways of knowing can be used to understand and solve the crime. For instance, in Hillerman's *Skinwalkers*, Chee and Leaphorn demonstrate knowledge of how interactions proceed in a Navajo context as they wait for their visits to homes to be acknowledged before going up to doors. In the same mystery, they use their understanding of Navajo protocol of literally not stepping over people to deduce that a murderer who has obviously avoided stepping over a body is probably Navajo.

Because of the long history of misappropriation, misuse, and misrepresentation of Native American cultures, objects, and knowledge by the mainstream, dealing with Native American cultures in fiction presents an ethical delicacy to the balancing act of accurate representation versus inappropriately crossing boundaries. For example, Hillerman recounted an incident where he was queried by Pueblo representatives after publication of *Dance Hall of the Dead*. They were concerned about sacred information of the Zunis being revealed. His response was that all information had been previously published in other sources, and their response was that they wanted a conversation with him before any more writings about Zuni culture were published (Coale 66). Similarly, Doss, in his interview with Art Taylor, has discussed incidents in which Utes told him that information about some ceremonies should not be published, and his response was to modify the information so that it was inaccurate but believable. This technique has also been utilized by the Thurlos: an author's note prefacing *Blackening Song* says that, out of respect, rituals in the novel have been "abbreviated and altered slightly." Is inaccurate but authentic portrayal oxymoronic? Where does artistic license clash with misrepresentation?

Part of knowing is understanding history and current issues, with the latter especially important because of a persistent tendency to relegate representations of Native Americans to a vanished past. These authors demonstrate their Native American protagonists' knowledge of their peoples by using the plots to introduce histories and issues that are often unfamiliar to mainstream audiences. Medawar's *Murder at Medicine Lodge* focuses on the 1867 treaty signed between the Kiowas, Comanches, Apaches, Cheyennes, and Arapahos and the US government. The book's final pages trace the treaty's devastating consequences, name the government representatives, and end with excerpts from White Bear's speech of resistance. In Coel's series, she frequently uses actual historical events to spin off the plots of the contemporary novels, depicting, for example, the ramifications of the federal allotment acts that distributed tribal lands to individuals (*Wife of Moon*) and the loss of generations of Native American children to disease, war, federal boarding schools, and adoptions (*The Lost Bird*). Hager also traced the history of the federal boarding schools that attempted to eradicate Native American children's own languages (*The Fire Carrier*).

Twentieth- and twenty-first-century issues important to Native Americans are also addressed in these series. For instance, Stabenow incorporates discussion of the 1971 Alaska Claims Act in *A Cold Day for Murder*, exploring its ramifications for Alaskan communities. In 1989's *Talking God*, Hillerman wove the plot around issues that drove the enactment of the Native American Graves Protection and Repatriation Act (NAGPRA) of 1990. In 2004's *Dance of the Thunder Dogs*, Mitchell incorporated the contemporary federal trust debacle of millions of dollars of royalties that never went to the individual Native Americans to whom they were owed and that would result in the long-running lawsuit of *Cobell v. Salazar*. Stabenow's *The Singing of the Dead* raises the issue of contemporary mainstream and Native American mythologizing of traditional lifestyles. In the Thurlos' *Bad Medicine*, the rise of youth gang involvement and drug use on the reservation is discussed.

Knowledge also includes understanding beliefs and practices of spirituality, possibly the most difficult topic for outsiders to accurately (if that is the intent) and effectively represent in fiction. However, spiritual beliefs appear regularly in these series. In the Doss series, Charlie Moon is assisted by his elderly aunt, who is a shaman and who communicates with a *pitukupf* (mischievous spirit). Perry's Jane Whitefield receives guidance through dreams. As a hatathali, Hillerman's Chee performs sacred ceremonies. Magic and shamanism is also an integral part of Anaya's Baca series, as the protagonist investigator moves toward what Anaya has described as "a journey into enlightenment" (Ponce 50).

Another, often-overlooked aspect of knowing is understanding humor. Native American humor has been described as "tribal comic wisdom" with "powers to heal and to hurt, to bond and to exorcise, to renew and to purge" (Lincoln 5). Several strategies are employed to incorporate Native American humor into these series. Hager's *The Redbird's Cry* includes a joke about a Cherokee, a white man, and rain, as well as a trickster story, which are recounted in social settings. In Owens's *Bone Game*, there is a lengthy and hilarious episode in which the protagonist interacts with a young Native American faculty member who is field-dressing a deer on campus to the chagrin of university authorities.

It is the ways of knowing that can lend the most "authenticity" to the portrayal of Native American detectives, since a deft treatment means that multiple aspects of knowing are seamlessly folded into the representation of the character and her or his interactions.

Notes

1. For well-articulated information in the long-running examination of the etymology, usage, and implications of these descriptors, see the articles below by Prins, Retzlaff, and Yellow Bird, as well as "What's in a Label?" and "The Use of 'Native-American.'"

2. Native American nations in the United States include multiple language groups, cultures, and histories, and their homelands circumvent current political boundaries (national, state, county, city). There is no totally satisfactory collective term for Native American nations, tribes, bands, reservations, rancherias, tribal towns, colonies, pueblos, communities, and villages.

3. An example is Mary Anna Evans's Faye Longchamp mysteries: the detective is an archaeologist with a Native American assistant who is also her romantic interest.

4. These criteria eliminate mystery series that simply weave Native American characters and topics into the story line (either throughout the series or in one title), including John Straley's Cecil Younger series and James Lee Burke's Dave Robicheaux series (specifically, the novel *Black Cherry Blues*). The restriction to series also ignores one-time appearances of Native American detectives, such as Mercedes Lackey's 1995 book *Sacred Ground*, featuring Jennifer Talldeer, an Osage and Cherokee private investigator and "shamanic apprentice," and D. L. Birchfield's 2006 novel, *Black Silk Handkerchief*, with Choctaw lawyer Hom-Astubby.

5. As with "Native American," there is no universally accepted collective term for people and literature designated "Hispanic," "Latina/o," "Chicano/a," and so forth. In this context, "Chicano" is used because it is often applied to Rudolfo Anaya's works.

6. See, for example, Bataille and Silet, Bergland, Berkhofer, Deloria, Fiedler, Mihesuah, Marubbio, Prats, and Stedman.

7. For additional biographical information on Stabenow, see Stabenow or White.

8. Historical forced relocations are a crucial factor in the diaspora of Native Americans from traditional homelands, but place, both original and more recent locations, is a fundamental part of Native American identity. Place, the totality of a natural environment, is "a source of tribal memory" (Kidwell 22). As such, it is often integrated into Native American detective stories, serving such roles as empowering the protagonist or connecting that person with a tribal community.

Works Cited

Adare, Sierra. "Murder at Medicine Lodge." *News from Indian Country* 15 Apr. 1999: 13B. Print.

Aimée and David Thurlo: Mystery, Intrigue, and Family Values. Aimée and David Thurlo, n.d. Web. 6 Nov. 2012.

"American Book Awards/Before Columbus Foundation." *American Booksellers Association.* American Booksellers Association, n.d. Web. 6 Nov. 2012.

"Anaya, Rudolfo." *Ninth Book of Junior Authors & Illustrators.* Ed. Connie C. Rockman. New York: Wilson, 2004. Print.

"Anthony Award Nominees and Winners." *Bouchercon World Mystery Convention.* Bouchercon World Mystery Convention, 2012. Web. 6 Nov. 2012.

"Awards." *Western Writers of America.* Western Writers of America, 2012. Web. 6 Nov. 2012.

Bataille, Gretchen M., and Charles L. P. Silet. *The Pretend Indians: Images of Native Americans in the Movies.* Ames: Iowa State UP, 1980. Print.

Beckwith, Cynthia. "Author Offers Thanks for Help with Novel." *Wind River News* 11 July 1995: 1. Print.

Bergland, Renée L. *The National Uncanny: Indian Ghosts and American Subjects.* Hanover: UP of New England, 2000. Print.

Berkhofer, Robert F., Jr. *The White Man's Indian: Images of the American Indian from Columbus to the Present.* New York: Vintage, 1978. Print.

"Best Sellers." *New York Times.* New York Times, n.d. Web. 6 Nov. 2012.

Birchfield, D. L. "Robert J. Conley: Extraordinary Cherokee Author." *Appalachian Heritage* 37.4 (2009): 19. Print.

___. "Robert J. Conley Teaches through Fiction." *News from Indian Country* 31 Oct. 1999: 4B. Print.

Bloom, Harold, ed. *Classic Mystery Writers.* New York: Chelsea, 1995. Print.

Bowen, Peter. *Peter Bowen.* N.p., 2012. Web. 6 Nov. 2012.

"Cafe Literati." *The Circle: News from an American Indian Perspective* 30 Apr. 1997: 10. Print.

"Celebrated Chicano Author Receives Wallace Stegner Award." *La Voz* 24 Oct. 2001: 13. Print.

"Chief Named Red Earth Ambassador of the Year." *Native American Times* 29 May 2009: 3. Print.

Coale, Samuel. *The Mystery of Mysteries: Cultural Differences and Designs.* Bowling Green: Bowling Green State UP, 2000. Print.

Colby, Vineta, ed. "Tony Hillerman." *World Authors, 1985–1990.* New York: Wilson, 1995. Print.

"Colorado Book Awards History." *Colorado Humanities.* Colorado Humanities, n.d. Web. 6 Nov. 2012.

Daly, Coralina. "Author Visits Reservation to Discuss Latest Book." *Wind River News* 19 May 2005: 1. Print.

Deloria, Philip J. *Playing Indian.* New Haven: Yale UP, 1998. Print.

"Detective Story." *Encyclopedia Britannica.* Encyclopedia Britannica, 2012. Web. 6 Nov. 2012.

Distant Voices, Thunder Words. Dir. Luis Peon Casanova. NAPBC, 1990. Film.

Donaldson, John K. "Native American Sleuths: Following in the Footsteps of the Indian Guides?" *Telling the Stories: Essays on American Indian Literatures and Cultures*. Ed. Elizabeth DeLaney Hoffman and Malcolm A. Nelson. New York: Lang, 2001. 109–29. Print.

Doss, James D. "An Interview: James D. Doss, Author of the Charlie Moon Mysteries." By Art Taylor. *Twilight Lane at Mystery Net*. Newfront Productions, n.d. Web. 6 Nov. 2012.

Drew, Bernard A. *100 Most Popular Contemporary Mystery Authors: Biographical Sketches and Bibliographies*. Santa Barbara: Libraries Unlimited, 2011. Print.

"The Edgar Awards." *TheEdgars.com*. Mystery Writers of America, 2012. Web. 6 Nov. 2012.

Espinoza, Martha. "A Passion for History." *Hispanic* 1999: 64–65. Print.

"Events: Stegner Award." *Center of the American West*. U of Colorado, 2012. Web. 6 Nov. 2012.

Fiedler, Leslie A. *The Return of the Vanishing American*. New York: Stein, 1968. Print.

Graham, Judith, ed. "Tony Hillerman." *Current Biography Yearbook*. New York: Wilson, 1992. 258–61. Print.

Hager, Jean. "Interview with Jean Hager: This Author Writes B&B-Themed Mysteries." By Elizabeth Arneson. *About.com*. IAC/InterActiveCorp, 2012. Web. 6 Nov. 2012.

Hillerman, Barney. *Hillerman Country: A Journey through the Southwest with Tony Hillerman*. New York: HarperCollins, 1991. Print.

Hillerman, Tony. *Seldom Disappointed: A Memoir*. New York: HarperCollins, 2001. Print.

___. "Tony Hillerman's Cross-Cultural Mystery Novels." Interview by Deborah Stead. *New York Times*. New York Times, 16 Aug. 1988. Web. 6 Nov. 2012.

___. "The Tony Hillerman Interview: On the Set of *A Thief of Time*." By Lise Balk King. *Native Voice* 16 May 2003: 2. Print.

Hollandsworth, Skip. "Lou Diamond Phillips." *Texas Monthly* Sept. 1996: 130. Print.

"In Memoriam: Louis Owens." *Currents Online*. University of California, Santa Cruz, 5 Aug. 2002. Web. 6 Nov. 2012.

"James D. Doss." *HarperCollins Publishers*. HarperCollins Publishers, 2012. Web. 6 Nov. 2012.

Jawort, Adrian. "Wind River Mystery Book Series Honored." *Indian Country Today* 27 Oct. 2010: 9. Print.

Keezer, Everette. "Review of Tony Hillerman's *The Dark Wind*: Lou Diamond Phillips Blamed and Victimized." *Ojibwe News* 4 Feb. 1994: 1. Print.

Kidwell, Clara Sue, and Alan Velie. *Native American Studies*. Lincoln: U of Nebraska P, 2005. Print.

Krueger, William Kent. *William Kent Krueger*. N.p., n.d. Web. 6 Nov. 2012.

___. "Interview with William Kent Krueger." By David J. Montgomery. *Mystery Ink*. Mystery Ink Online, Mar. 2004. Web. 6 Nov. 2012.

Lachman, Marvin, comp. "Prizes, Awards, and Nominations Given for Material Originally Published in EQMM." *Ellery Queen Mystery Magazine*. Penny Publications, 2012. Web. 6 Nov. 2012.

"Lifetime Honors: National Medal of Arts." *National Endowment for the Arts*. National Endowment for the Arts, 2011. Web. 6 Nov. 2012.

Lincoln, Kenneth. *Indi'n Humor: Bicultural Play in Native America*. New York: Oxford UP, 1993. Print.

Lindsay, Elizabeth Blakesley. "Margaret Coel." Great Women Mystery Writers. 2nd ed. Westport: Greenwood, 2007. 48–50. Print.

Linford, Laurance D. *Tony Hillerman's Navajoland*. Salt Lake City: U of Utah, 2001. Print.

Marubbio, M. Elise. *Killing the Indian Maiden: Images of Native Women in Film*. Lexington: UP of Kentucky, 2009. Print.

McMahan, John. Introduction. *Super-Detective: Flip Book!* Castroville: Off-Trail, 2008. Print.

Mihesuah, Devon A. *American Indians: Stereotypes & Realities*. Atlanta: Clarity, 1996. Print.

"Minnesota Book Awards." *Friends of the Saint Paul Public Library*. Friends of the Saint Paul Public Library, n.d. Web. 6 Nov. 2012.

Mitchell, Kirk. *Ancient Ones*. New York: Bantam, 2001. Print.

Mitchell, Kirk. *Dance of the Thunder Dogs*. New York: Berkley, 2004. Print.

"Native American Authors: Mardi Oakley Medawar." *Internet Public Library2*. Drexel U, n.d. Web. 6 Nov. 2012.

"Native American Writing Increasing." *Wind River News* 27 Jul 1993: 1. Print.

"Oklahoma Writers Hall of Fame." *Oklahoma Center for Poets & Writers*. Oklahoma State U, 2012. Web. 6 Nov. 2012.

Owens, Louis. "If an Indian Were Really an Indian: Native American Voices and Postcolonial Theory." *Native American Representations: First Encounters, Distorted Images, and Literary Appropriations*. Ed. Gretchen M. Bataille. Lincoln: U of Nebraska P, 2001. 11–24. Print.

"PEN Oakland Award Winners: Josephine Miles Award." *PEN Oakland*. PEN Oakland, n.d. Web. 6 Nov. 2012.

Perry, Thomas. *Thomas Perry*. N.p., n.d. Web. 6 Nov. 2012.

Ponce, Mary Helen. "Latino Sleuths." *Hispanic* 1998: 44–52. Print.

Prats, Armando José. *Invisible Natives: Myth & Identity in the American Western*. Ithaca: Cornell UP, 2002. Print.

Preston, Sheldon. "Preview of Movie *Dark Wind*." *Navajo Nation Today* 15 Oct 1991: 16. Print.

"Previous Winners." *Parmly Billings Library*. City of Billings, n.d. Web. 6 Nov. 2012.

Prins, Harals E. L. "Indian, Red Man, or Native American: What's in a Name?" *Pequot Times* 2002: 4. Print.

Pronzini, Bill, and Martin H. Greenberg, eds. *The Ethnic Detectives: Masterpieces of Mystery Fiction*. New York: Dodd, 1985. Print.

Retzlaff, Steffi. "What's in a Name? The Politics of Labeling and Native Identity Constructions." *The Canadian Journal of Native Studies* 25.2 (2005): 609–26. Print.

"Seqyouyah Professor Robert Conley to Receive Indian Author Award." *News from Indian Country* 13 Oct. 2008: 17. Print.

Shanley, Kathryn. "Literature: The Lived Experience; American Indian Literature after Alcatraz." *Native Americas* 31 Dec. 1994: 119. Print.

Snell, Travis. "Honor Society Recognizes Cherokee Citizens: Tribal Descendants from all Walks of Life Receive 2000 Medal of Honor." *Cherokee Phoenix and Indian Advocate* 31 Jan. 2001: 30. Print.

Stabenow, Dana. *Dana Stabenow: The* Official *Dana Stabenow Web Site*. N.p., 5 Nov. 2012. Web. 6 Nov. 2012.

Starr, Arigon. "Murder, Mayhem, and Mystery! How the PBS Television Series Will Transform into an American Series by Featuring Native Americans." *Native Voice* 16 Aug. 2002: 1. Print.

Stedman, Raymond William. *Shadows of the Indian: Stereotypes in American Culture*. Norman: U of Oklahoma P, 1982. Print.

Strom, Karen. "Louis Owens." *Index of Native American Book Resources on the Internet*. Hanksville, 6 Nov. 2012. Web. 6 Nov. 2012.

"Thomas Perry." *World Authors, 1995–2000*. Ed. Mari Rich. New York: Wilson, 2003. Print.

Thundercloud, Anne. "2002 American Indian Motion Picture Awards." *News from Indian Country* 30 Nov. 2002: 8B. Print.

Tortorella, Erica. "Hispanic Americans You Want to Know." *Hispanic Outlook in Higher Education* 19 Oct 2009: 20–23. Print.

United States. Bureau of Indian Affairs, Department of the Interior. *Indian Entities Recognized and Eligible to Receive Services from the Bureau of Indian Affairs*. *Fed. Reg.* 10 Aug. 2012: 47868–73. PDF file.

___. Office of Management and Budget. "Revisions to the Standards for the Classification of Federal Data on Race and Ethnicity." *Fed. Reg.* Notice. Office of Management and Budget, 30 Oct. 1997. Web. 7 Nov. 2012.

"The Use of 'Native-American.'" *Akwesasne Notes* 9.30 (1977): 17. Print.

"Wes Studi on PBS." *Native American Times* 1 Oct. 2003: 7A. Print.

Westbrook, Robert. *Robert Westbrook*. N.p., n.d. Web. 6 Nov. 2012.

"What's in a Label? Depends on Who You Ask." *Sho-Ban News* 27 Oct. 1988: 6. Print.

White, Claire E. "A Conversation with Dana Stabenow." *Writers Write: The Internet Writing Journal*. Writers Write, Inc., Feb. 2000. Web. 6 Nov. 2002.

Yellow Bird, Michael. "What We Want to be Called." *American Indian Quarterly* 23.2 (1999): 1–21. Print.

American Crime Fiction Readers and the 3 Percent Problem_____

Malcah Effron

Despite the spectacular success of Stieg Larsson's Millennium trilogy and the very respectable sales of other European crime writers, conventional wisdom holds that American readers are reluctant to read translated work. This reluctance has been attributed to some sort of stubborn provincialism on the part of Americans, but other factors can be seen at work to account for the relative infrequency with which translations appear on the lists of US publishers. These other factors seem particularly important, as this reluctance is at odds with the origins of the detective genre because its nineteenth-century origins are heavily indebted to the translations of such proto–crime fiction authors as François Vidocq, Eugène Sue, and Émile Gaboriau. Their French narratives inspired the founding fathers of Anglophone crime fiction, including Edgar Allan Poe and Arthur Conan Doyle. However, the rise of writers like Doyle coincided with British and American expansionism in the nineteenth and twentieth centuries, so the proliferation of the detective genre arrived with the rise of English as the global *lingua franca*, or common language. These international distribution networks coupled with the high percentage of publications in English compared to those in other languages means Americans do not need to reach beyond texts written in English for quality detective fiction. Thus, a major consideration is a commercial one, as translated work involves additional costs, including the quality of translation and the difficulty of bringing a translation, especially from a minority language, to the attention of a US editor, US book reviewer, and US reader, all of whom most likely only read English. However, the tremendous success of international authors like Stieg Larsson has recently burst these commercial fears and has expanded the crime fiction market to receive translated crime fiction with enthusiasm.

We Used to Publish Translations

The so-called lack of translated crime fiction seems at odds with the origins of the genre, as crime fiction draws heavily from literary innovations brought to the Anglo-American market through translations, particularly from nineteenth-century French writings. As Sita Schütt suggests, "French contributions to the development of crime fiction, in particular the detective story, are significant in the sense that one cannot conceive of the developments in nineteenth-century English detective fiction without them" (59). The works of three French writers in particular serve as noticeable influences on Anglophone crime fiction writing throughout the nineteenth century: Eugène François Vidocq, Eugène Sue, and Émile Gaboriau. These writers' early pioneering in narrating and fictionalizing the investigation of crime in the modern urban environment influenced the pioneering detective fiction authors in the English language, notably Edgar Allan Poe, Wilkie Collins, and Arthur Conan Doyle.

Eugène François Vidocq's *Mémoires de Vidocq, chef de la police du Sureté* (Memories of Vidocq, head of the security forces, 1828), caught the attention of the French- and English-speaking world. Published as the true memoirs of a thief who eventually became the head of the French police force—although their accuracy has been called into question (Schütt 61)—these accounts of crimes and their investigations caught the attention of the nineteenth-century reading community. His *Mémoires*, "full of accounts of his criminal days, [are] followed by equally lurid adventures detailing his activities as a policeman, where detective methods are limited to various acts of provocation, disguise, and incitement to betrayal, were instant best-sellers in France and England" (60–61). These tales fit nicely into the true crime narrative tradition already made popular during the eighteenth century with publications like *The Newgate Calendar*, which Ian A. Bell describes as a collection of "ballads and 'true narratives' relating criminals' lives and (often fabricated) last confessions" (7). Vidocq's *Mémoires*, however, add the twist of conveying the process of investigation as well as the commission of the crime or the flight of the criminal, which is one of its main influences on the development of the detective genre as a genre in its own right.

Vidocq's popularity also extends to America, as can be seen Edgar Allan Poe's reference to him in "The Murders in the Rue Morgue" (1841). "The Murders of the Rue Morgue" is generally accepted as the first detective story that provides the general format for the genre, so Poe's acknowledgment of Vidocq in the story indicates the popularity and influence of the French translation on the American reading populous. Poe's newly crafted detective, C. Auguste Dupin, critiques the work of his predecessor, claiming, "Vidocq, for example, was a good guesser, and a persevering man. But, without educated thought, he erred continually by the very intensity of his investigations" (171). By highlighting the faults of his literary forerunner, Poe creates space for his new form of criminal investigation, which he names a tale of "ratiocination," or logical reasoning. Highlighting the difference between Vidocq, the guesser, and Dupin, the reasoner, Poe develops a new form of investigation that ultimately developed into the detective fiction genre. Nevertheless, as Vidocq serves as the literary foil for the rise of the detective fiction genre, literature in translation can be seen as paramount to the foundations of the modern crime genre.

While Vidocq's literary influence comes from autobiographical accounts of his experiences, and thus provided nonfiction or true crime contributions, Eugène Sue's *Les Mystères de Paris* (1842–43) provided fictional accounts of the criminality and general seediness underlying Paris. The sensational subject matter proved popular to the nineteenth-century reading public, and the popularity of the novel led to imitations. In England, for instance, G. W. M. Reynolds sought to cultivate British interest in French literature by translating French novels, including the works of Sue (Pearson 100). As Richard Pearson suggests, these translation projects influenced him to try his hand at "the darker side of English fiction with his reworking of Sue's epic, *The Mysteries of London*" (Pearson 118 n10). *The Mysteries of London* (1844–48) sold with what Stephen James Carver calls "prodigious popularity" (147). Similarly, the genre of city mysteries took hold of the American population. LeRoy Panek notes that "in America cheap pamphlet or serial fiction exposed the 'mysteries and miseries' of New York, Baltimore, Boston, San Francisco and, among other smaller towns, Lowell and Fitchburg, Massachusetts" (10). The nineteenth-century popularity of such forms, derived from a French novel, contributed to the sensation culture that spawned the Anglophone forerunners of the detective form, like the sensation fiction of Victorian novelist Wilkie Collins, whose novel *The Moonstone* (1868) dramatized a police investigation.

While Sue contributed to a popular form of nineteenth-century Anglophone crime fiction, namely the "mysteries and miseries" genre, later in the century, Émile Gaboriau pioneered novels that privileged the investigation over the criminal acts. Despite Pearson's sense of English resistance to French fiction at large in the nineteenth century (100), Gaboriau's works found a very receptive audience in the Anglo-American population. Schütt notes, "Gaboriau was quickly translated and widely read in England. The first official translation appeared in Boston in 1870 and in England in 1881, although pirated translations found their way across the Atlantic and thence to England before then" (63). While Schütt's phrasing suggests a British-focused bias, she implies the American popularity of Gaboriau's works, in that they were first officially translated for the American market. Furthermore, not only were the works published in English on both sides of the Atlantic, but also Gaboriau "was evidently extremely popular, judging by the number of editions issued" (Schütt 63). This popularity underscores the importance of literature in translation to the evolution of the dominant and dominating form of the detective novel written in English.

Gaboriau is important to the development of crime fiction in English not only because of the general popularity of his stories but also because of his influence on important nineteenth-century writers of detective fiction. Julian Symons reports, "[Wilkie] Collins admired and kept upon his shelves the crime stories of Emile Gaboriau" (54), and T. S. Eliot refers to Collins's *The Moonstone* as "the first and greatest of English detective novels" (412). Most importantly, however, Gaboriau influenced Arthur Conan Doyle, the author of the Sherlock Holmes stories. Schütt suggests that "many of Holmes's techniques and characteristics can also be traced directly to Gaboriau's detectives" (63). Just as Poe acknowledges his literary debt to Vidocq through contradiction, Doyle identifies a similar relationship with the works of Gaboriau. In the introduction of the first consulting detective Sherlock Holmes, Doyle places his detective in direct relation to Gaboriau's: "Lecoq was a miserable bungler . . . he had only one thing to recommend him, and that was his energy. That book made me positively ill. . . . It might be made a text-book for detectives to teach them what to avoid" (Doyle 18). As in Poe's case, the author writing in English creates his space in the literary marketplace by situating himself against his French influences. Also, Doyle's approach, like Poe's, indicates the popularity of crime fiction in translation in the nineteenth century.

After Gaboriau, however, the discussion of the development of crime fiction becomes English-language focused, to the point where Maxim Jakubowski writes, "Anglo-American mystery fiction is widely translated throughout the world, and there are frequent instances where it has cross-pollinated and provided a fresh impetus to local authors and themes . . . most current followers would argue this is a one-way traffic." This sense of "one-way traffic" appears in academic considerations, where the foundations for the development of the crime fiction genre acknowledge French precursors, but after these nineteenth-century origins, the history of the genre describes itself in terms of English dominance. For instance, Howard Haycraft's *Murder for Pleasure* (1941)—which is to detective fiction scholarship what Poe's Dupin stories are to the detective genre—includes Vidocq and Gaboriau. After these initial chapters, however, the main chapters of the work are subdivided into "America" and "England." Although twenty-first-century academic works on crime fiction acknowledge the international scope of the genre, key texts still remain English-focused, as Martin Priestman laments: "As with any book aiming to comprehend such a vast genre, some omissions have sadly been inevitable; doubtless of many well-loved individual works, as well as of any non-Anglophone fiction apart from the French or high-cultural" (Introduction 6). Gaboriau and the French influence can thus frequently be seen as the last stop before Anglophone dominance of the crime genre.

Reasons We No Longer Publish Translations

In this sense, then, Sherlock Holmes becomes the threshold for the mutual influence of foreign- and English-language publications on the development of crime fiction. As Schütt describes it, "Although an amalgam of Poe and Gaboriau provided Conan Doyle with the basic recipe for his new detective, Sherlock Holmes's success goes beyond the mere combination of these influences. Conan Doyle's stories were rapidly translated and Holmes became an international by-word for the act of detection" (68). Holmes's profile has become the icon to indicate mystery novels in libraries, and "Sherlock" is frequently used as slang for "detective." Holmes's popularity contributed to formalizing detective story conventions around the world, a process that creates the genre's "cross-pollination" yet "one-way traffic" from English to other languages.

While Sherlock Holmes's international popularity can generally be attributed to Doyle's successful manipulation and formulation of the character of the consulting detective, some of his success could be attributed to the changing position of English and the English in the global arena at the turn of the twentieth century. The early twentieth century saw the political dominance of the British Empire followed by the commercial dominance of the United States following World War II. Caroline Reitz suggests that "not only was detective fiction an important player in the arena of imperial literature, it both served and challenged the interests of Empire in a more direct way than either its status as fiction or the scholarship that declares it a minor genre wants to admit" (xiii). While Reitz speaks specifically about the British Empire in her analysis of how detective fiction supports the dominance of English culture, including the English language, the underlying mentality associated with these analyzed texts transmits itself to all the readers, not just the British ones. Thus, if, as Reitz argues, "the detective narrative helped change public perception of domestic criminal justice" (xiv), this changes the assessment of the English-speaking world from "poorly trained detectives whose failure to solve crime was much criticised by the press" (Schütt 59) to the global power that Britain, and then America, became. This sense of the supremacy of the Anglophone nations, particularly their ability to promote and to "reconcile liberty with authority" (Reitz xiv), can be seen underlying the historical turn from a multilingual trend in detective fiction publishing to a largely Anglophone one.

This colonial impact underlies Chad W. Post's sense of the English language's ability to control the literary marketplace and to keep down the percentage of texts translated into English, particularly in the American marketplace. He sees "English as an 'invasive language' that serves as a mediating language between 'smaller' tongues . . . [that influences] the number of literary translations being published in English" (Post 68). Post focuses on English's status as *lingua franca*, to the point where cultures, such as Chinese and Spanish, require their children to learn English, so they can later participate in the global economy, even though Chinese and Spanish are two of the most-spoken languages in the world (72). This trend of requiring English in non-Anglophone cultures means that "a book published in English truly reaches a global audience, not just an American or British one" (78–79). This means that books published in English reach a wider commercial audience, creating demands for books in English but without requiring a reciprocal demand for English translations of non-Anglophone publications.

The issue with understanding how these historical developments relate particularly to the evolutions in American readership of translated crime fiction stems from the difficulties in tracking the number of works in translation in each genre. As Post admits, "that 3% figure includes all books in translation—in terms of literary fiction and poetry, the number is actually closer to 0.7%" (5248–49). This suggests that popular fiction, which Post excludes from literary fiction, might have a larger share of the market than literary fiction. To understand the reception of crime fiction translated into English, we can consider the position of crime fiction in the publishing marketplace alongside the position of translation in the marketplace.

The detective and mystery book category is often a top-selling subcategory of literary fiction. For instance, in 2008, the *Book Publishing Report* reported that "fiction titles favored repeat buyers far more than nonfiction, with mystery taking first place in the subcategories of fiction" ("Business of Mystery" 12); and in 2011, it reported that "while some consumer book categories like travel and trade reference have been hollowed out by online content, the mystery & detective book category continues to attract readers with page turners and—for better or for worse—a small but influential pack of top tier authors" ("Mystery & Detective" 2). These reports indicate that mystery and detective novels traditionally top the American market, suggesting that Americans enjoy reading and, importantly, buying crime fiction.

While there are statistics to show that mystery and detective novels remain a very popular form of literature, we do not have similar statistics to identify the popularity of literature in translation. As Post notes, "Every year Bowker is able to report on the number of sports books published, but not translations" (103–4). Similarly, magazines of the publishing industry that rely on Nielson ratings, like *Publishers Weekly*, do not distinguish works in translation from works in English printed in the same genre. Titles listed in the top-ten columns do not identify the original language of the publication. Furthermore, while the book reviews identify the translator and original language of publication when relevant, there is otherwise no callout or special indication to highlight that a book is a translation. While this lack of distinction makes it difficult to track and to identify translations' share of the American publishing marketplace accurately, it seemingly should eliminate readers' prejudices against translations by blinding them to the translated status.

This complication suggests that the issues with translations do not exclusively arise from a stubbornly provincial reading public, but also from the publishing houses. What reasons do publishers have for assuming translations will not prove a marketable commodity? There are two standard reasons given for why publishing translations is not a profitable enterprise. The first centers on the presumed ethnocentrism—a more politic description of stubborn provincialism—of the Anglophone reader, and particularly the American reader. The second deals with the added expense of publishing translations. The combination of both elements indicates the decreased profitability of publishing works in translation when compared to the profitability of publishing works written in English.

Possibly stemming from what Post characterizes as English's nature as an invasive language, there is a similar presumption that Anglophones are ethnocentric. This is frequently commented upon in relation to comparatively few languages that Anglophones, and particularly Americans, speak in comparison to members of other language groups. This leads to what Esther Allen, a reputable scholar and spokesperson in the area of translation publishing, describes as "a very entrenched attitude on the part of mainstream commercial houses that the U.S. consumer of books does not want to read translations" (qtd. in Rohter C1). These prejudices—whether presumed or accurate—influence the translation publishing process, including decisions as to whether or not the texts should be "as 'Englished' as possible so that every 'Midwesterner' gets every reference . . . [or should retain] some of the so-called 'foreignness' and forc[e] the readers to realize they're reading a book from another country" ("Publishing Literary Translations"). These issues, as will be discussed later, highlight the translators' and publishers' assumptions that Americans will not readily gravitate to international literature, emphasizing their presumption of American ethnocentrism.

Different publishing houses answer these questions relating to translation publishing in different ways. Harvill Press in the United Kingdom opts for the "as 'Englished' as possible" approach, distinguishing even between American and English: "We made it a rule to put all translations into 'English English', even those undertaken by American translators" (MacLehose). On the one hand, this approach creates a normalized reading experience that justifies the lack of differentiation between literature in English and literature in translation, such as is found in the *Publishers Weekly* reviews. However, as Margaret Schwartz proposes, "To some degree, doing that effaces the fact of the text's translation and thereby contributes to the ongoing xenophobia of American literary culture" ("Publishing Literary Translations"). The dominant attitude that accepts the xenophobia of American literary culture, from the outset, prevents the perception of literature in translation as a profitable commodity.

This ethnocentrism or cultural xenophobia would seem to be the biggest factor in understanding why translations are not a profitable enterprise, particularly considering certain financial incentives publishers receive for works in translation. First, there is a comparatively low cost of acquiring works in translation. The rights to non-English novels tend to be cheaper than those to works written by Americans, as "foreign rights rarely exceed four or five figures" (Alter), and, as Post has deplored extensively, translators make low salaries for their work as translators (2290–91). Furthermore, in the contemporary literary market, Anglophone publishing houses do not necessarily have to translate the texts after acquiring them, as "instead of sample chapters, a handful of LSL [lesser-spoken language] publishers are commissioning their own high-quality English translations of an entire book" (Watson). In addition to American publishers receiving already translated texts, "from Romania to Catalonia to Iceland, cultural institutes and agencies are subsidizing publication of books in English" (Rohter C1). The governments of non-Anglophone countries offer subsidies to Anglophone publishers, offsetting the costs of publishing translations.

For example, the first translation of Swedish detective novelist Henning Mankell's Kurt Wallander books "was published by the non-profit New Press and some support for the publication had been provided by a cultural arm of the Swedish government" (Fister). While the prospect of English-speaking accolade and revenue clearly appeals to non-Anglophone publishers, American publishers do not seem to find the incentives compelling enough to enlarge significantly the percentage of books published in translation.

The subsidies and free translations provided do not seem to eliminate the added expense of publishing translations in the American market. As Alexandra Alter suggests, "translating a book can add tens of thousands to production costs. Marketing a book by an unknown author poses challenges, particularly if the writer doesn't speak English." These marketing expenses go to making the author a familiar quantity and thus a desired product, and the challenges come in the ability of the author to break through in a publishing environment now characterized as "a marketplace where (thanks to chains, WalMart, etc.) at any point in time, twelve to twenty books are selling spectacularly well and are everywhere (a la *Shadow of the Wind* or *The Da Vinci Code*) while most everything else is puttering along" (Post 530–34). This is particularly the case "in a category like mystery & detective fiction, where there are so many prolific authors, it is difficult to break above the familiar names" ("Mystery & Detective" 4–5), even for authors writing in English. Publishing houses need to make sure that these works are heavily marketed to make the significant return desired on their investment, and the costs are much higher when financing the author's book tour includes international airfare.

Furthermore, translations have a harder time finding reviewers than texts produced in English. As Mark Athitakis claims, "When a book review editor receives a work in translation, it's probably from an author they've never heard of before. Even worse, when it's an author from a country whose literary tradition is unknown to you . . . it can be hard to decide where an author fits into a particular tradition." These issues complicate the work of the reviewer and thus prevent the texts from becoming a priority for the reviewer. Athitakis also argues that "the vast majority of translations (about 85%) are coming from small, independent, and university presses. Presses that aren't necessary in the position to know a lot of book reviewers personally or capable of throwing a lot of money at a book, etc." These issues prevent the publishing houses from successfully marketing the books and drawing the attention of the reviewers and the public. As Victoria Adams states, "New titles by celebrity and front-list authors are more or less guaranteed review space, as are titles which have for one reason or another excited public curiosity" (30–31). In particular, the ability to excite public curiosity most often leads to unknown authors breaking through on the best-sellers' list—which, as will be discussed later, might be the case of Stieg Larsson. With reviewers' inability to qualify their readings of unknown authors from unknown cultures, publishers have a higher financial burden to market texts in translation successfully.

It becomes increasingly clear how heavy this burden is when we remember that the translations are competing against the wide selection of manuscripts originally written in English. The vastness of the English publishing market can be understood when comparing the number of new books published in different countries in the European Union. According to the Federation of European Publishers (FEP), in 2010:

European publishers held a total of close to 7.5 million different titles in stock, the countries reporting the largest being the UK (3.4 million), Germany (around 1.2 million), Italy (almost 700,000), France (around 600,000) and Spain (around 400,000). The countries reporting the largest new titles output were in the UK (151,969), Germany (84,351), Spain (42,300), France (40,021), and Italy (36,856). ("FEP Statistics")

These statistics show that the United Kingdom is responsible for half the books published in Europe and nearly twice as many new titles as its nearest competitor, Germany; the United Kingdom is also responsible for over 40 percent of the new works published in Europe, over one-third of the new book market. The statistic becomes even more disproportionate if publishing statistics from the United States are included. When competing against so many texts in English, the financial challenges of marketing unknown authors from unknown (literary) cultures become even more daunting.

The competition is even more daunting in the mystery and detective genre because of the high number of volumes originally published in English that are set in international locales. Natasha Cooper proposes that "ideally, any translated novel would take the reader into new worlds, present new ideas and ways of living, new perceptions on the human condition even. . . . In order to understand an unknown society you will usually need explanations." Cooper also suggests that works in an original language rarely provide these explanations because a domestic reading population does not need such clarifications and would find them condescending and boring. However, English-language works published in America but set outside the United States frequently provide such explanations, allowing for literary tourism complete with a tour guide. Eva Erdmann identifies this phenomenon in the Venetian detective series of Donna Leon: "In much the same way as travel guides give foreigners basic linguistic help, Leon's insertion of Italian sentence and word fragments and her explanation of these is part and parcel of the repeated thematization of national idiosyncrasies" (22–23). One could make similar claims about the use of French in Cara Black's Aimée Leduc series set in Paris. Qiu Xiaolong's Inspector Chen series has been mistaken as translated from Chinese, rather than correctly identified as originally written in English and translated into Chinese (Lara). When faced with English novels that provide the touristic appeal associated with literature in translation—"the attraction of the unfamiliar location, the unfamiliar politics" (MacLehose)—the added expense of publishing literature in translation can be perceived as an excessive obstacle.

Ethnocentric readership and thus economic antitranslation biases are criticisms generally leveled against American readers to indicate a lack of erudition. For instance, Harvill senior editor Alison Hennessey notes, "Before the real explosion of translated crime fiction, a lot of the readers of authors like Mankell were more literary readers, who preferred to read European translated crime fiction over US or UK crime fiction as they felt it was of a better quality" (qtd. in Wood). However, there are intellectual and academic discourses that create an undervaluing of literature in translation, as well. Much of this centers around the idea that a text in translation is a unique text from the original, which is supported by translation studies theories that argue "the translated text is criticized without reference to the source text" (House 7) and therefore implies that the translated text need not be tied to the original. Cooper emphatically argues that her distaste for reading translations stems from this position. She claims, "I dislike the interposition of the translator between the author and me" and "even when a translation is produced by a skilled and sensitive writer, it is going to be different from—and probably less than—the original" (Cooper). While Post would object to the categorization of the translated form as "less than the original," even he acknowledges that the translated text is not identical to the original text, stating, "The words you read in translation are the translator's as much as they are the author's" (Post 2204–5). This basic tenet is what led the British Crime Writers Association (CWA) to change their awards policy and create separate competitions for books originally published in English and books originally published other languages: "yet one reason for the ban was given by a CWA committee member as being (so friends of his had told him) that much was lost in the translation of foreign crime novels" (MacLehose). This sense of loss can alienate readers who are otherwise willing to and interested in reading non-Anglophone literature.

Proponents of literature in translation might argue that whatever potential loss is associated with the translation is negligible compared to the loss of not reading the work at all. However, this sense of loss, of not actually reading the text, creates a barrier for certain readers and reduces the market for literature in translation. While the merits of each side can be debated, the translator, the English-language publisher, or both can make decisions that alter the reading experience of the text in a significant way. Consider, for instance, the different reading experiences of Swedish and American audiences with the first novel in Larsson's trilogy, as the Swedes read *Män som hatar kvinnor* (Men who hate women) and the Americans read *The Girl with the Dragon Tattoo*. Such cases make readers feel that they can never truly experience the original text through the translation, so they prefer not to read in translation, and this sentiment cannot wholly be tied to the elitism implicitly associated with American ethnocentrism.

Why We Have Restarted Publishing Translations

Despite this sentiment that underscores Post's claim that "typically translations are greatly undervalued in the academy" (93), the publishing trends indicate "for better or worse (and in my opinion, it's definitely for better), the majority of books published in translation are works of so-called 'high literature'" (Post 2181–218). This category tends to distinguish texts from so-called mainstream or popular novels and thus from novels with higher sales rates in the United States. For this reason, Post relates that one of his friends suggested, "What we need is a great translated beach book. Something that will appeal to tons of people and convince them that it's safe to come in the water" (1293–94). In this sense, crime fiction in translation seems to meet the needs identified by Post's unidentified friend.

Crime fiction provides a useful medium for introducing translations into American culture for multiple reasons, some of which have to do with the nature of the genre and its international popularity. As mentioned when discussing the rise of English as the dominant language of crime fiction, the conventions of crime fiction have been widely translated and adopted, and thus are widely recognized across the globe: "the global influence of American and British crime writing has also led to the widespread adoption of familiar tropes and plot conventions" (Alter). Even accounting for the differences in criminal justice systems, the generic conventions create a medium that unifies the form, providing an international literary tradition that allows reviewers to understand the work's place in its field without needing to know other literary cultures. Furthermore, as Alter argues, "mystery novels translate well across cultures, because they usually prize plot over literary acrobatics." This eliminates certain complications in translation that occur with experimental forms that now characterize contemporary "high literature." In this sense, the familiarity and conventionality provide a safe space in which to explore what Kristi Chadwick describes as the principle appeal of translated crime fiction: "interesting people and places, plus puzzles to uncover." (24).

Stieg Larsson's Millennium trilogy fits perfectly into the space created by the notions above, and the colossal success of these three novels seems to validate the point. Selling over forty million copies around the globe (Alter), Larsson's success can be measured in terms of its impact on mystery and detective fiction and its impact on literature in translation. The *Book Publishing Report* indicates that 2009 had the highest sales since 2004 for the mystery and detective fiction subcategory "due in part to the phenomenal success of titles by Stieg Larsson" ("Mystery Led" 2). The success of this novel has helped maintain the sales of genre fiction at a time when other genres are losing readers ("Mystery & Detective" 2). With regard to translation, Larsson's success has, in some sense, broken open the international crime fiction market for English-language publishers. In one sense, it breaks translation out of the sole domain of the literary reader. According to Hennessey, "readers have woken up to the possibilities of what crime fiction has to offer, whereas beforehand there was perhaps a bit of snobbery about it" (qtd. in Wood). Similarly, David Varno argues, "libraries are able to expand the market for translated books because of novels like Stieg Larsson's. Apparently, now that more readers are becoming comfortable with reading in translation, librarians are able to turn their patrons onto books from other authors who write in the language from which a very successful book originated." Publishers are also responding to the popularity of Larsson's novels, "as those fans search for read-alikes, U.S. publishers are importing more mysteries from around the globe" (Chadwick 24). Furthermore, the sales figures have opened European agents' and publishers' eyes to the possibility of a positive reception in the American publishing market, "encouraging foreign publishers and agents to have their titles translated for consideration in the United States" (24). In Larsson, it seems as though Post's friend has found his translated beach novel, which opened the door to other beach novels in translation.

Larsson's success, however, should not solely be written off as part of the general appeal of crime fiction. Crime fiction has been published in translation, and Scandinavian authors such as Henning Mankell and writing duo Maj Sjöwall and Per Wahlöö have played an important role in particular, but these authors have not achieved the sales of Larsson's series. Larsson has achieved a status similar to Dan Brown after the publication of *The Da Vinci Code* (2003), which has sold over eighty million copies. These similarities are not just in the sales statistics. Both novels feature an investigative team of an older man and a *gamine*, or mischievous girl, if we consider the casting of actress Audrey Tautou as Brown's Sophie Neveu in the film adaptation. Furthermore, both involve a treasure hunt of sorts and involve unveiling long-buried secrets. Beyond these very broad plot similarities, both Brown's *The Da Vinci Code* and Larsson's trilogy have fascinating stories that surround their publication and "excit[e] public curiosity" as Adams argues is necessary for breakthrough authors like Larsson. *The Da Vinci Code* has the Vatican's response to its treatment of the Opus Dei and tenets of Catholic doctrine, and the Millennium trilogy has its status as a posthumous publication. With Larsson dead before the publication of the first novel, the trilogy necessarily stood from the moment of publication as a completed whole—barring a revitalization such as is occurring with Robert Ludlum's Jason Bourne series. Finally, both novels have been turned into major films, and those films have drawn a larger reading audience for the books. In fact, in Brown's case, it drew a larger readership for his whole oeuvre, and in Larsson's case, it spawned "a group of people who are now reading [Scandinavian] authors like Mankell, because they have come to him off of the back of the Stieg Larsson *films*" (Wood; emphasis added). Wood's suggestion indicates that the initial trend for crime fiction in translation is not necessarily a literary impulse. The success of the films thus apparently generates and supports the rest of the publicity that surrounds the novels themselves. Moreover, this publicity has been so successful, according to *Publishers Weekly*, that as of February 2012, the last novel in the trilogy was still a hardback best seller—three years after it was published. As of June 2012, it was still an e-book best seller. Thus, the Larsson books have in themselves and their surrounding materials generated enough public interest to float the translation market.

This floating has increased the amount of crime fiction available in translation because, as "spurred by the popularity of Swedish writer Stieg Larsson's trilogy . . . U.S. publishers are combing the globe for the next big foreign crime novel" (Alter). American production culture gravitates toward imitation, as can be seen in the number of *Scream* films (four to date) and the number of parodies mocking the excessive production of genre films like *Scream* (the original 1991 *Scary Movie* plus its parodies, four to date). Crime fiction publishing also caters to this impulse, as can be seen particularly in the series titles that are derived from a repeated formula, such as Sue Grafton's alphabet novels (with private investigator Kinsey Millhone), Janet Evanovich's number series (with bounty hunter Stephanie Plum), and James Patterson's nursery-rhyme novels (with special agent Alex Cross). For these reason, critics record the recent increased publishing interest in translated crime fiction, particularly of the Scandinavian variety, by referring to this imitation culture. For instance, Wood proposes that "Japan is one of the countries being touted as the Next Big Crime Thing," and Post asks, "What's the over/under on Scandinavian crime novels coming out next year that are the 'next Stieg Larsson'?" (1328–30). This shows that the improvement in publishing publicity for international crime fiction is based on the clear demonstration that crime fiction in translation can be profitable.

Post worries, however, about this publishing trend because he fears that "this sort of pigeonholing, this looking to replicate what 'worked' leads to the publication of a lot of pale imitations that are generally uninteresting and create the viewpoint that all fiction from country X is all the same" (625–30). This is a legitimate concern and one that applies to the sense of uniformity tied into the crime genre. While generic conventions might provide a basis for international understanding of a novel, it risks standardizing literature. In fact, with regard to Scandinavian literature, some, like David McDuff, have worried that "Scandinavian crime has made it impossible for more serious literature to be translated" (Fister). As librarian and blogger Barbara Fister suggests sarcastically in response to this critique, "so the problem is that social issues are the stuff [of] crude entertainment; if people will just get over it, we can get on with the more vital concerns of new writing." As this response shows, the original comment implies that crime fiction is an inferior conduit for literary transmission. Post takes exception to people who object to differentiating between literary and popular writing: "And it always seems that whenever someone pushes for a greater appreciation of quality literature, a genre writer jumps up screaming about how that's elitist" (1459–60). On some level, such concerns are elitist, as, except for a brief reflection on Stieg Larsson, Post's statistics do not discuss the place of popular fiction in translation when bemoaning the state of "literature" in translation: "Mysteries and anything 'genre' related was excluded from these numbers, which is another reason it would be nice to have the list of books" (122–23). This suggests that we cannot have a full picture of the market for literature in translation because of the subcategories defined and failure to analyze the data to understand these situations.

There are two ways to look at the failure to differentiate literature in translation from the larger body of book-buying statistics. On the one hand, we can see this as an attempt to incorporate works in translation into the general category of new literature and thus deny those readers skeptical about reading translations the opportunity to filter out this literature beforehand. On the other, we can see this lack of data as a means of keeping us blind to the problem—having accepted that a 3 percent translation rate is a problem—and thus not allowing us to improve the volume and availability of works in translation. The interest and enthusiasm that Larsson's crime novels have garnered suggest, for those interested in increasing the market share of works in translation publishing in the United States, that there is a readership and thus a market for such works—perhaps even in proportion with the market for homegrown crime novels. And for critics who are worried that the influx of genre fiction in translation means inferior literary quality, crime fiction has proven itself of popular and scholarly interest, as indicated in "the dominance of the CWA awards by non-Anglophone writers [which] reflects the quality of writing but also challenges Anglophone writers to offer readers more socially and politically critical narratives" (Neale 307). While more open, as Christopher MacLehose of Harvill Press indicates, "the very few books that survive the filtering by English-language editors are, almost by definition, the best of the best." Furthermore, as Alter claims, "Much of the crime fiction being imported blurs the line between genre and literary fiction." In this sense, the blurred boundary between the literary form associated with translation and the popular form associated with crime narrative might be the right combination to open the American market to literature in translation—even if it only turns the 3 percent problem into a 5 percent problem. This seems reasonable, however, when we remember that Sherlock Holmes, the man who, even before the Girl with the Dragon Tattoo, made crime fiction an international favorite, only used a 7 percent solution.

Notes

1. I thank Sandy Marinaro at Stevenson University for her research assistance, Yvonne Klein for sharing her research, and John Woods at Stevenson University for his services as a reader.

Works Cited

Adams, Victoria. "Doing It by the Book: The Uses of Paratext in Creating Expectation and Determining Structural Genre in Contemporary British Fiction." Diss. Newcastle U, 2011. Print.

Alter, Alexandra. "Fiction's Global Crime Wave." *Wall Street Journal*. Dow Jones, 1 July 2010. Web. 2 Nov. 2012.

Athitakis, Mark. "Conversations with Literary Websites: Three Percent." *Critical Mass*. National Book Critics Circle, 20 July 2010. Web. 2 Nov. 2012.

Bell, Ian A. "Eighteenth-Century Crime Writing." Priestman, *Cambridge Companion* 7–18. Print.

"The Business of Mystery, the Mystery of Business." *Book Publishing Report* May 2008: 12. Print.

Carver, Stephen James. "The Wrongs and Crimes of the Poor: The Urban Underworld of *The Mysteries of London* in Context." *G. W. M. Reynolds: Nineteenth-Century Fiction, Politics, and the Press*. Ed. Anne Humpherys and Louis James. Aldershot: Ashgate, 2008. 147–60. Print.

Chadwick, Kristi. "Crime Travels." *Library Journal* 15 Apr. 2012: 24–30. Print.

Collins, Wilkie. *The Moonstone*. 1868. Oxford: Oxford UP, 1999. Print.

Cooper, Natasha. "Writing Crime in Translation." *Crime Time*. Crimetime.co.uk, n.d. Web. 2 Nov. 2012.

Doyle, Arthur Conan. "A Study in Scarlet." 1887. *The Complete Sherlock Holmes Long Stories*. London: Book Club Assoc., 1978. Print.

Eliot, T. S. "Wilkie Collins and Dickens." *Selected Essays, 1917–1932*. London: Faber, 1932. Print.

Erdmann, Eva. "Nationality International: Detective Fiction in the Late Twentieth Century." Trans. Fiona Fincannon. *Investigating Identities: Questions of Identity in Contemporary International Crime Fiction*. Ed. Marieke Krajenbrink and Kate M. Quinn. Amsterdam: Rodopi, 2009. 11–26. Print.

"FEP Statistics for the Year 2010." *Federation of European Publishers*. FEP-FEE.be, 2012. Web. 2 Nov. 2012.

Fister, Barbara. "The Popularity Perplex." *Scandinavian Crime Fiction*. Barbara Fister, 31 July 2009. Web. 2 Nov. 2012.

Haycraft, Howard. *Murder for Pleasure: The Life and Times of the Detective Story*. 1941. New York: Biblio, 1974. Print.

House, Juliane. *Translation Quality Assessment: A Model Revisited*. Tübingen: Narr, 1997. Print.

Jakubowski, Maxim. "Crime without Frontiers." *Literature Matters* (Spring 2006): N. pag. *British Council*. Web. 2 Nov. 2012.

Lara. "Detective Novels of Qiu Xiaolong." *Tales across the Sea*. Tales across the Sea, 29 Aug. 2009. Web. 2 Nov. 2012.

MacLehose, Christopher. "Other Worlds." *Literature Matters* (Spring 2006): N. pag. *British Council*. Web. 2 Nov. 2012.

"Mystery & Detective Shows Why It's No. 1." *Book Publishing Report* Aug. 2011: 2–5. Print.

"Mysteries Led by Reprints and Larsson's *Girl*." *Book Publishing Report* Aug. 2010: 2–5. Print.

Neale, Sue. "Crime Writing in Other Languages." *A Companion to Crime Fiction.* Ed. Charles Rzepka and Lee Horsley. Oxford: Wiley, 2010. 296–307. Print.

Panek, LeRoy Lad. *Probable Cause: Crime Fiction in America.* Bowling Green: Bowling Green State U Popular P, 1990. Print.

Pearson, Richard. *W. M. Thackeray and the Mediated Text: Writing for Periodicals in the Mid-Nineteenth Century.* Aldershot: Ashgate, 2000. Print.

Poe, Edgar Allan. "The Murders in the Rue Morgue." *Graham's Magazine* 18 Apr. 1841: 166–79. *Edgar Allan Poe Society of Baltimore.* Web. 2 Nov. 2012.

Post, Chad W. *The Three Percent Problem: Rants and Responses in Publishing, Translation, and the Future of Reading.* Rochester: Open Letter, 2011. E-book.

Priestman, Martin, ed. *The Cambridge Companion to Crime Fiction.* Cambridge: Cambridge UP, 2003. 1–6. Print.

___. Introduction. Priestman, *Cambridge Companion.* 1–6. Print.

"Publishing Literary Translations CLMP Roundtable." *ALTalk.* American Literary Translators Association, 13 Dec. 2010. Web. 2 Nov. 2012.

Reitz, Caroline. *Detecting the Nation: Fictions of Detection and the Imperial Venture.* Columbus: Ohio State U, 2004. Print.

Rohter, Larry. "Translation as Literary Ambassador." *New York Times* 8 Dec. 2010: C1. Print.

Schütt, Sita A. "French Crime Fiction." Priestman, *Cambridge Companion* 59–76. Print.

Symons, Julian. *Bloody Murder: From the Detective Story to the Crime Novel, A History.* Harmondsworth: Penguin, 1985. Print.

Varno, David. "Book Reviews: Who Should Write about Literature in Translation?" *Words without Borders.* David Varno, 24 Jan. 2011. Web. 2 Nov. 2012.

Watson, Elisabeth. "Anglophone, Anyone?" *Publishing Trends.* Publishing Trends/ Market Partners International, 1 June 2011. Web. 2 Nov. 2012.

Wood, Felicity. "Crime Scene." *Bookseller* 16 Mar. 2012: 20–23. *Literary Reference Center.* Web. 2 Nov. 2012.

RESOURCES

Additional Works on Crime and Detective Fiction _____

Long Fiction
Farewell, My Lovely by Raymond Chandler, 1940
In a Lonely Place by Dorothy B. Hughes, 1947
The Killer Inside Me by Jim Thompson, 1952
Les gommes by Alain Robbe-Grillet, 1953 (*The Erasers*, 1964)
The Talented Mr. Ripley by Patricia Highsmith, 1955
A Rage in Harlem by Chester Himes, 1957
Den skrattande polisen by Maj Sjöwall and Per Wahlöö, 1968 (*The Laughing Policeman*, 1970)
The Continental Op by Dashiell Hammett, 1974
Skinwalkers by Tony Hillerman, 1986
Black Dahlia by James Ellroy, 1987
LA Confidential by James Ellroy, 1990
Faceless Killers by Henning Mankell, 1991
Frøken Smillas fornemmelse for sne by Peter Høeg, 1992 (*Smilla's Sense of Snow*, 1993)
A Little Yellow Dog by Walter Mosley, 1996
Death of a Red Heroine by Qiu Xiaolong, 2000
Motherless Brooklyn by Jonathan Lethem, 2000
Yogisha X no Kenshin by Keigo Higashino, 2005 (*The Devotion of Suspect X*, 2011)
Abril rojo by Santiago Roncagliolo, 2006 (*Red April*, 2009)
Calling Out for You by Karin Fossum, 2007
The Eye of Jade: A Mei Wang Mystery by Diane Wei Liang, 2008
21 Immortals by Rozlan Mohd Noor, 2010

Nonfiction
Murder in Little Egypt by Darcy O'Brian, 1989
Midnight in Peking: How the Murder of a Young Englishwoman Haunted the Last Days of Old China by Paul French, 2012
A Wilderness of Error: The Trials of Jeffrey Macdonald by Errol Morris, 2012

Short Fiction
The Complete Sherlock Holmes by Arthur Conan Doyle, 1960
New Orleans Noir edited by Julie Smith, 2007
LA Noire: The Collected Stories edited by Jonathan Santlofer, 2011

Bibliography

Abbott, Megan E. *The Street Was Mine: White Masculinity in Hardboiled Fiction and Film Noir.* New York: Palgrave Macmillan, 2002. Print.

Anderson, Jean, Carolina Miranda, and Barbara Pezzotti, eds. *The Foreign in International Crime Fiction: Transcultural Representations.* New York: Continuum, 2012. Print.

Armchair Detective 1.1–30.3 (1967–1997). Print.

Ascari, Maurizio. *A Counter-History of Crime Fiction: Supernatural, Gothic, Sensational.* New York: Palgrave, 2007. Print.

Bailey, Frankie Y. *Out of the Woodpile: Black Characters in Crime and Detective Fiction.* Westport: Greenwood, 1991. Print.

Biressi, Anita. *Crime, Fear and the Law in True Crime Stories.* New York: Palgrave, 2001. Print.

Browne, Ray B. *Murder on the Reservation: American Indian Crime Fiction.* Madison: U of Wisconsin P, 2004. Print.

Cassuto, Leonard. *Hard-Boiled Sentimentality: The Secret History of American Crime Stories.* New York: Columbia UP, 2009. Print.

Cawelti, John G. *Mystery, Violence, and Popular Culture.* Madison: U of Wisconsin P, 2004. Print.

Christian, Ed, ed. *The Post-Colonial Detective.* New York: Palgrave, 2001. Print.

Close, Glen S. *Contemporary Hispanic Crime Fiction: A Transatlantic Discourse on Urban Violence.* New York: Palgrave, 2008. Print.

Clues: A Journal of Detection 1.1– (1989–). Print.

Craig-Odders, Renée W., Jacky Collins, and Glen S. Close, eds. *Hispanic and Luso-brazilian Detective Fiction: Essays on the Género Negro Tradition.* Jefferson: McFarland, 2006. Print.

Flanders, Judith. *The Invention of Murder: How the Victorians Revelled in Death and Detection and Created Modern Crime.* London: Harper, 2011. Print.

Geherin, David. *The Dragon Tattoo and Its Long Tail: The New Wave of European Crime Fiction in America.* Jefferson: McFarland, 2012. Print.

Gosselin, Adrienne Johnson, ed. *Multicultural Detective Fiction: Murder from the "Other" Side.* New York: Garland, 1999. Print.

Halttunen, Karen. *Murder Most Foul: The Killer and the American Gothic Imagination.* Cambridge: Harvard UP, 1998. Print.

Haycraft, Howard. *Murder for Pleasure: The Life and Times of the Detective Story.* London: Davies, 1942. Print.

Horsley, Lee. *Twentieth-Century Crime Fiction.* New York: Oxford UP, 2005. Print.

Irwin, John T. *The Mystery to a Solution: Poe, Borges, and the Analytic Detective Story.* Baltimore: Johns Hopkins UP, 1994. Print.

___. *Unless the Threat of Death Is Behind Them: Hard-Boiled Fiction and Film Noir*. Baltimore: Johns Hopkins, 2006. Print.

Knight, Stephen Thomas. *Continent of Mystery: A Thematic History of Australian Crime Fiction*. Victoria: Melbourne UP, 1997. Print.

___. *Form and Ideology in Crime Fiction*. Bloomington: Indiana UP, 1980. Print.

Lehman, David. *The Perfect Murder: A Study in Detection*. 1989. Rev. ed. Ann Arbor: U of Michigan P, 2000. Print.

Kawana, Sari. *Murder Most Modern: Detective Fiction and Japanese Culture*. Minneapolis: U of Minnesota P, 2008. Print.

Kenney, Catherine McGehee. *The Remarkable Case of Dorothy L. Sayers*. Kent: Kent State UP, 1990. Print.

King, Donna, and Carrie Lee Smith, eds. *Men Who Hate Women and Women Who Kick Their Asses: Stieg Larsson's Millennium Trilogy in Feminist Perspective*. Nashville: Vanderbilt UP, 2012. Print.

Kinkley, Jeffrey C. *Chinese Justice, the Fiction: Law and Literature in Modern China*. Stanford: Stanford UP, 2000. Print.

Klein, Kathleen Gregory. *Diversity and Detective Fiction*. Bowling Green: Bowling Green State U Popular P, 1999. Print.

Macdonald, Ross. *On Crime Writing*. Santa Barbara: Capra, 1973. Print.

Malmgren, Carl D. *Anatomy of Murder: Mystery, Detective and Crime Fiction*. Bowling Green: Bowling Green State U Popular P, 2001. Print.

Matzke, Christine, and Suzanne Mühleisen, eds. *Postcolonial Postmortems: Crime Fiction from a Transcultural Perspective*. Amsterdam: Rodopi, 2006. Print.

Most, Glenn W., and William W. Stowe, eds. *The Poetics of Murder: Detective Fiction and Literary Theory*. New York: Harcourt, 1983. Print.

Murley, Jean. *The Rise of True Crime: 20th-Century Murder and American Popular Culture*. Westport: Praeger, 2008. Print.

Nestingen, Andrew, and Paula Arvas, eds. *Scandinavian Crime Fiction*. Cardiff: U of Wales P, 2011. Print.

Nickerson, Catherine Ross, ed. *The Cambridge Companion to American Crime Fiction*. Cambridge: Cambridge UP, 2010. Print.

___. *The Web of Iniquity: Early Detective Fiction by American Women*. Durham: Duke UP, 1998. Print.

Ousby, Ian. *Bloodhounds of Heaven: The Detective in English Fiction from Godwin to Doyle*. Cambridge: Harvard UP, 1976. Print.

Panek, LeRoy Lad. *Origins of the American Detective Story*. Jefferson: McFarland, 2006. Print.

___. *Probable Cause: Crime Fiction in America*. Bowling Green: Bowling Green State U Popular P, 1990. Print.

Pearson, Nels, and Marc Singer, eds. *Detective Fiction in a Postcolonial and Transnational World*. Surrey: Ashgate, 2009. Print.

Porter, Dennis. *Pursuit of Crime: Art and Ideology in Detective Fiction*. New Haven: Yale UP, 1981. Print.

Pyrhönen, Heta. *Mayhem and Murder: Narrative and Moral Problems in the Detective Story*. Toronto: U of Toronto P, 1999. Print.

Reddy, Maureen T. *Traces, Codes, and Clues: Reading Race in Crime Fiction*. New Brunswick: Rutgers UP, 2003. Print.

Rzepka, Charles J. *Detective Fiction*. Malden: Polity, 2005. Print.

Rzepka, Charles J., and Lee Horsley, eds. *A Companion to Crime Fiction*. Chichester: Wiley-Blackwell, 2010. Print.

Saito, Saturo. *Detective Fiction and the Rise of the Japanese Novel, 1880-1930*. Cambridge: Harvard U Asia Center, 2012. Print. Harvard East Asian Monograph 346.

Sallis, James. *Chester Himes: A Life*. New York: Walker, 2001. Print.

Soitos, Stephen F. *The Blues Detective: A Study of African American Detective Fiction*. Amherst: U of Massachusetts P, 1996. Print.

Symons, Julian. *Bloody Murder: From the Detective Story to the Crime Novel*. Rev. ed. New York: Mysterious, 1993. Print.

Thompson, Jon. *Fiction, Crime, and Empire: Clues to Modernity and Postmodernism*. Urbana: U of Illinois P, 1993. Print.

Walton, Priscilla L., and Manina Jones. *Detective Agency: Women Rewriting the Hard-Boiled Tradition*. Berkeley: U of California P, 1999. Print.

About the Editor ─────────────────────────

Rebecca Martin comes to her interest in detective fiction through her early infatuation with Nancy Drew and a more mature engagement with the eighteenth-century English gothic novel. She completed degrees in English at the University of Oklahoma (BA), University of Iowa (MA), and City University of New York Graduate Center (PhD), where she wrote a dissertation on the early gothic novel, employing insights from modern film theory to examine the interaction of spectacle, repetition, closure, and the reading experience. In her academic career, she has published articles on Marcia Muller (creator of Sharon McCone, one of the earliest female private eyes) and mystery novelist Victoria Holt, as well as numerous essays on the gothic novel and film theory. She is a professor of English at Pace University in New York, where she teaches literature of crime and criminality, detective fiction, and film studies, including film history and American melodrama. She is working on a project on the detective novels and films of American director Oscar Micheaux and is cultivating an interest in contemporary Chinese crime writing. She is very happy to have a career in which she reads books and watches movies.

Contributors

Rebecca Martin, PhD, has published essays and articles on the eighteenth-century English gothic novel, Marcia Muller (creator of one of the first female private investigators, Sharon McCone) and mystery novelist Victoria Holt. Her work in the early gothic novel, on which she wrote her dissertation, has drawn her to a close study of modern American detective fiction and an interest in Victorian sensation fiction. She has recently begun a project on African American director, writer, and producer Oscar Micheaux and his detective novels and films, and has been pursuing an interest in contemporary Chinese writing about crime. She is professor of English at Pace University, where she teaches courses on literature and film.

Ruth Anne Thompson, PhD, is professor emerita at Pace University. Her field is the nineteenth-century novel, with a specialty in American periodical publishing, about which she has written extensively. Her particular area of interest is historical mystery fiction. She has served as an academic administrator at both Pace University and Fordham University, where she received her doctorate. She has taught online as well as in the classroom for several years. She is past president of the Children's Literature Association and former vice president of a nonprofit educational organization, Education and Community Opportunity for Stewardship, which collaborated with the federal National Diffusion Network.

Jean Fitzgerald, MA, has been teaching in higher education for over twenty years at Pace University, Quinnipiac University, and Southern Connecticut State University. Her postgraduate studies were in online education with a focus on composition; these were at the forefront of increased use of technology in the traditional classroom as well as in online courses. Her interest in detective fiction began at a very young age with Nancy Drew and *The Secret of the Old Clock*. This early feminism led to more mature tastes in such tough female detectives as V. I. Warshawski and others who populate the mystery novels of the late twentieth century.

Elizabeth Foxwell is coauthor of *The Robert B. Parker Companion* (2005); managing editor of *Clues: A Journal of Detection*, the only US scholarly journal on mystery and detective fiction; editor of the McFarland Companions to Mystery Fiction series; and cofounder of the mystery convention Malice Domestic. She received the George N. Dove Award from the Detective/Mystery Caucus of the Popular Culture Association for her contributions to the serious study of mystery and crime fiction. She regularly blogs about mystery history.

Kerstin Bergman, PhD, is a senior research fellow of comparative literature at the Centre for Languages and Literature, Lund University, Sweden. She is the coauthor of the crime fiction textbook *Kriminallitteratur: Utveckling, Genrer, Perspektiv* (Crime fiction: Development, genres, perspective, 2011) with Sara Kärrholm, and has published extensively on Swedish and international crime fiction. Her recent essays include "Fictional Death and Scientific Truth: The Truth-Value of Science in Contemporary Forensic Crime Fiction" in *Clues* (2012), "Beyond Stieg Larsson: Contemporary Trends and Traditions in Swedish Crime Fiction" in *Forum for World Literature Studies* (2012), "Lisbeth Salander and her Swedish Crime Fiction 'Sisters': Stieg Larsson's Hero in a Genre Context" in *Men Who Hate Women and Women Who Kick Their Asses* (2012), and "The Well-Adjusted Cops of the New Millennium: Neo-Romantic Tendencies in the Swedish Police Procedural" in *Scandinavian Crime Fiction* (2011).

Norlisha F. Crawford, associate professor of English and director of African American studies at the University of Wisconsin Oshkosh, teaches African American literature and crime fiction and an interdisciplinary survey of African American studies. A native of Washington, DC, she completed graduate studies at the University of Maryland, College Park. Her recent scholarly projects included completing a book-length critical examination of Chester Himes's Harlem hard-boiled police detective series.

Jeffrey C. Kinkley is a professor of history at St. John's University in New York City. He specializes in the modern intellectual history and literary history of China and is a translator of contemporary Chinese fiction. He has published monographs and articles on modern Chinese crime fiction and "anticorruption novels," and interviews with Chinese crime authors such as Qiu Xiaolong.

Amanda Seaman is an associate professor of Japanese language and literature at the University of Massachusetts Amherst. Her book *Bodies of Evidence: Women, Gender, and Detective Fiction in 1990s Japan* was published in 2004. She has written other articles on women and detective fiction in Japan for other publications, including the *Japan Forum* and *Japanese Language and Literature*. She is completing a book on representations of pregnancy and childbirth in modern Japanese literature.

Natalia Jacovkis, PhD, is assistant professor of Spanish and Latin American literature at Xavier University in Ohio. She has published articles on contemporary films and on crime fiction from Argentina, Brazil, and Mexico. Her research focuses on how urban spaces are articulated in contemporary Latin American cultural productions. She is working on a book manuscript that explores the representation of neoliberal Buenos Aires in books and films.

Sara Kärrholm teaches at the School of Arts and Communication at Malmö University and the Center for Languages and Literature at Lund University. She spent the spring of 2012 at Harvard University as a visiting Fulbright Hildeman Scholar, teaching a course titled Crime, Power and Politics in Contemporary Scandinavian Culture. She also gave several public and academic lectures on topics related to Scandinavian crime fiction. Her dissertation, *Konsten att lägga pussel* (The art of puzzles, 2005), is about Swedish crime fiction from the 1940s and 1950s. She recently coauthored a textbook on crime fiction *Kriminallitteratur: utveckling, genrer, perspektiv* (Crime fiction: Development, genres, perspective, 2011) with Kerstin Bergman. She has also contributed chapters to several recent books, including *Scandinavian Crime Fiction* (2011), *Men Who Hate Women and Women Who Kick Their Asses: Stieg Larsson's Millennium Trilogy in Feminist Perspective* (2012), and *Interdisciplinary Approaches to* Twilight: *Studies in Fiction, Media, and a Contemporary Cultural Experience* (2011).

Joseph Paul Moser, PhD, is assistant professor of English and film studies at Fitchburg State University in Massachusetts. His research interests include representations of gender, violence, and politics in film, as well as film genre studies. His first book, on film representations of Irish masculinity, is forthcoming.

Susan Elizabeth Sweeney, PhD, teaches American literature and creative writing at the College of the Holy Cross. She coedited *Detecting Texts: The Metaphysical Detective Story from Poe to Postmodernism* (1999) and has published several essays on the detective genre, including most recently "The Magnifying Glass: Spectacular Distance in Poe's 'The Man of the Crowd' and Beyond," in *Poe Studies* (2003) and "Crime in Postmodernist Fiction" in the *Cambridge Companion to American Crime Fiction* (2010). She is exploring both the influence of early photography on Poe's detective stories and the rise of "neuro-noir," or tales that feature detectives with neurological disorders. She also studies other popular narrative forms—such as the ghost story, the fairy tale, and the gothic romance—and other American writers, especially Vladimir Nabokov. She is past president of both the Poe Studies Association and the International Vladimir Nabokov Society.

Rhonda Harris Taylor is an associate professor in the School of Library and Information Studies (SLIS) at the University of Oklahoma (OU). She teaches graduate courses in the management of information and knowledge organizations, multicultural librarianship, popular culture and libraries, and the organization of information and knowledge resources, and her publications reflect these interests. She is the 2011 recipient of the OU College of Arts and Sciences Longmire Prize for Teaching. She has been an avid reader of detective fiction since the age of eleven. She is an enrolled member of the Choctaw Nation of Oklahoma.

Malcah Effron, PhD, is a lecturer in the English department at Case Western Reserve University. She edited *The Millennial Detective* (2011), contributed chapters to *A Companion to Crime Fiction* (2010) and *Constructing Crime: Discourses and Cultural Representations of Crime and 'Deviance'* (2012), and published articles in the *Journal of Narrative Theory* and *Narrative*. She is also the cofounder of the international Crime Studies Network (CSN).

Index

deduction. *See* ratiocination
Dee, Judge, 77
Department Q, 148
De Pré, Gabriel, 205
detection, tools of, 9
Detective Conan franchise, 111
Díaz Eterovic, Ramón, 119
disguise, xxvii
dokufu narratives, 99
Doss, James, 205
Double Indemnity (Cain), 26–27,
  161–63
Double Indemnity (film), 26–28,
  165–67
Doyle, Arthur Conan, 178, 224
drug cartels, 122
Dupin, C. Auguste, 178, 222
Easy Money (Lapidus), 148
Eco, Umberto, 190
Edgar Award, 16
Ekman, Kerstin, 140
endings
  Fisher vs. Himes, 65
  readers' experience of, xxiii
  thriller vs. whodunit, 50
English crime writing, xv–xvii, 22
Erasers, The (Robbe-Grillet), 186
ero-guro-nonsense movement, 104
escape fantasy, xx
ethics, code of
  detective's vs. law, 46, 65, 157
  professional vs. personal, 43, 155–56
ethnocentrism, translation and, 228
fallen man, 160
femikrimi subgenre, 142–43
feminism, 14, 142
femme fatale, 162, 164
Ficciones (Borges), 182
film noir, 16, 152–74
Finnish crime fiction. *See* Scandinavian
  crime fiction

Fisher, Rudolph, 55
Flitcraft (*Maltese Falcon*), xxvi, 155,
  182
Fonseca, Rubem, 124, 125
formula
  Chinese socialist, 84–85
  literary merit and, xxi
  metaphysical crime fiction as, 192
  noir, 168
  parody of, 179
  series publication, 237
Fossum, Karin, 141
French crime writing, 7, 221–225
Frimbo (*Conjure Man Dies*), 58
Gaboriau, Émile, 223–24
games, crime fiction in, xxv, 17
Gao Luopei. *See* Van Gulik, Robert
  Hans
"Garden of Forking Paths, The"
  (Borges), 183
Garfield, John, 169–70
Gaviria, Pablo Escobar, 122
genre shifts, 51
Ghosts (Auster), 191
Gillette, William, 9
Girl with the Dragon Tattoo, The (film),
  236
Girl with the Dragon Tattoo, The (Lars-
  son), 38–54, 132, 234
golden age, 10–12. *See also* whodunit
  genre
Gong an hun (Liu Zong Dai), 87
gongan narratives, 74, 85
gothic fiction, 4–6
gothic romance, xvi, xxvii
government, criminality of, 118. *See
  also* anticorruption literature
Grave Digger (*Blind Man with a Pistol*),
  65
Green, Anna Katharine, 23–25
"Guilty Vicarage, The" (Auden), xix

Hager, Jean, 203
Halvorsen, Anne-Kin, 140
Ham, General (*Blind Man with a Pistol*), 66
Hammett, Dashiell, 12, 153, 154–56
Hanshichi, Inspector, 103–4
hard-boiled detective
    femme fatale, resistence to, 157
    masculinity and, 153
    qualities of, 44, 181
    thriller investigator vs., 51
hard-boiled genre
    American, establishment of, 12, 181
    Latin American, 117–22
Harlem Renaissance, 56
Hawthorne, Nathaniel, 178
Hays Office, 28
Hedeby Island, 41, 48
Hedström, Ingrid, 149
hegemonic narrative, alternatives to, 119
He Jiahong, 90
Helú, Antonio, 116
Heredia, 119, 130
Higashino Keigo, 106
High Art (Fonseca), 124
highbrow literature, translation of, 234
Hillerman, Tony, 198–99, 202–3
Himes, Chester, 55
history
    appropriation of, 119
    Native American, knowledge of, 213–14
    revisionism, 189
Høeg, Peter, 143
Holden, Vicky, 206
Holmes, Sherlock
    Asia, influence in, 78, 103
    canon of, 31
    inspiration for, 224
    parody of, 30

popularization of, 225
ratiocination and, 9
Holt, Anne, 141
homme fatal, 164
hostage, 50
Huff, Walter (*Double Indemnity*), 161
humor, 42, 214
hunches, 45
Huo Sang, 78, 81
Icelandic crime fiction, 145. *See also* Scandinavian crime fiction
identity
    authors', 200
    characters', 210–15
    mistaken, 185
imitation, 237
immigration, Scandinavian concerns with, 146
imperialism
    British and American, 220, 225
    Japan, 105
Indriðason, Arnaldur, 145
Industrial Revolution, social effects of, 3
ingenuity, 75
In Search of Klingsor (Volpi), 128
instincts, 45
intertextuality, 41–42
intuition, 45
investigation, modes of, 44–47
investigative journalist, 42
Isakesen, Cato, 141
Japan , modernization of, 97–100, 102
Japanese crime literature, 89, 95–108
Jar City (Indriðason), 145
Jaspersen, Smilla, 143
Jenkins, Jinx (*Conjure Man Dies*), 59–60
Jes Grew, 67, 189
Kepler, Lars, 148
Killing, The (television series), 149
Kirino Natsuo, 108

Matsumoto Seichō, 106
McCurtain, Cole, 207
Medawar, Mardi Oakley, 208
media, critique of, 47
melancholic policeman, 138–39
Melo, Patrícia, 125, 127
Mémoires de Vidocq (Vidocq), 221–22
Men Who Hate Women (Larsson).
    See Girl with the Dragon Tattoo
    (Larsson); *Män som hatar kvinnor*
    (Larsson)
Mermaids Singing, The (McDermid), 41
metaphysical detective fiction, 176–94
Mexican crime fiction, 116, 118–19, 126
Meyer, Nicholas, 30–32
Millar, Kenneth. *See* Macdonald, Ross
Millenium trilogy, 52, 235–237
minorities
    literature by, 14, 193
    representation, issues regarding, 212
    Scandinavian depiction of, 146
misogyny, noir genre and, 162
mistaken identity, 185
Mitchell, Kirk, 209
Mitchum, Robert, 170–71
Miyabe Miyuki, 107
Montero, Mayra, 127
mood, weather indicating, 49
Moon, Charlie, 205
Moon, Howard, 209
morality
    architechure indicating, 48
    conflicts in, 43
    crime literature and, xiv, xvi
    detective's vs. law, 46
Móran, María Elena, 126
Morck, Carl, 148
Morgan, Harry (*Breaking Point*), 169
"Mousha fasheng zai Zingqiliu yewan "
    (Wang Hejun), 84
Mumbo Jumbo (Reed), 66–68, 189

Murder of Roger Ackroyd, The (Chris-
    tie), 181
"Murders in the Rue Morgue, The"
    (Poe), 7, 176, 222
Mysteries of London, The (Reynolds), 222
"Mystery of the Fire Bell, The" (Oka-
    moto), 103
Mystery Readers International, 16
Mystery Writers of America, 16
mythology, influence of, xxii
Nabokov, Vladimir, 182, 184–86
Name of the Rose, The (Eco), 190
narration
    circularity, 186
    deception in, 185
    structure, necessity of, xxii
Native American detective fiction, 197–215
Natsuki Shizuko, 107
Nattdykk (Småge), 140
neoliberalism, critique of, 127
neopolicial genre, 118
New Culture movement, 77, 79
Newgate Calendar, The, 5
Newgate novels, 4–7
New York Trilogy (Auster), 191
Nirdlinger, Phyllis (*Double Indemnity*),
    28, 161
Ni wei shui bianhu (Wang Xiaoying), 88
noir fiction, 152–63
Nonami Asa, 108
Norwegian crime fiction, 140–41. *See
    also* Scandivanian crime fiction
novela del sicariato genre, 122–23
O'Connor, Cork, 208
Oedipa (*Crying of Lot 49*), 189
Oedipus Rex (Sophocles), 187
Okamoto Kidō, 103–4
O'Malley, Father, 206
Operación masacre (Walsh), 116
O'Shaughnessy, Brigid (*Maltese Fal-
    con*), 155

Roldán, Máximo, 116
Roman Hat Mystery, The (Dannay, Lee), 11
Salander, Lisbeth (*Dragon Tattoo*), 38, 143
Sampson, Catherine, 90
Sandinista Revolution, 130
Santis, Pablo de, 129
Sayers, Dorothy L., xix–xxi, 10
Scandinavian crime fiction, 132–51
Schrader, Paul, 165
science fiction and detective fiction, 23, 193
See, Lisa, 90
Sejer, Konrad, 141
semiotics, metaphysical detective fiction and, 191
sensation fiction, xvii, 6–7
Séptimo Circulo, El (Borges), 115
Serialist, The (Gordon), 193
Serrano, Marcela, 126
setting
   Brazilian cities, 124
   China, 90
   exotic, 232
   Harlem, 63
   natural, 49
   Nordic landscape, 145
   small town vs. city, 145
Seven-Per-Cent Solution, The (Meyer), 30–32
Shanghai, cosmopolitanism of, 79
Sherlock in Shanghai (Wong), 79
Shinseinen (magazine), 102
Shi Yukun, 76
Shugak, Kate, 204
Simenon, Georges, 8
Sjöwall, Maj, 135–37
Småge, Kim, 140
Smilla's Sense of Snow (Høeg), 143
social class. *See* class
social disorder

detective fiction and, 97
failed politics and, 116
film noir and, 163
solvability, 176, 179
South Korea crime fiction, 109. *See also* Korean crime fiction
Spade, Sam (*Maltese Falcon*), xxvi, 155–56
Spillane, Mikey, 13
spirituality, representation of, 66–68, 214
Stabenow, Dana, 204
"Star for a Warrior, A" (Wellman), 198
state, corruption of, 118
steampunk, 193
Sternwood, Carmen (*Big Sleep*), 158
"Stieg Larsson effect", 148
Story of a Crime, The (Sjöwall and Wahlöö), 135–37
strange occurrences, 75
Sue, Eugène, 222
Sun Liaohong, 79
survival, 51
suspense, alternating perspectives for, 50
Swedish crime fiction, 39, 135–37. *See also* Scandinavian crime fiction
sympathy, noir fiction and, 168
Taibo, Paco Ignacio, II, 118
Taiwanese crime fiction, 110–11
Takamura Kaoru, 107
Tanizaki Jun'ichirō, 102
Tanner, George, 204
Tay-bodal, 208
television, crime fiction on, 17
testimonio genre, 123
thriller motifs, 50–51
Thurlo, Aimée and David, 207
Tiger in the Smoke, The (Allingham), 28–30
Tiger in the Smoke, The (film), 30
time pressure, 50